LOOSE CHANGE

"What happened to us in the sixties?" I asked my friend Rob in 1973. "How could so many bright, committed people have miscalculated so badly? We thought the center wasn't going to hold but it has, and now we're in pieces. We're all loose change."

"Are we?" Rob said.

Loose Change
THREE WOMEN OF THE SIXTIES

SARA DAVIDSON

DOUBLEDAY & COMPANY, INC., GARDEN CITY, NEW YORK

Grateful acknowledgment is made for permission to quote from the following material:

"My Generation," first published in *Esquire*, October 1968. © by Jacob Brackman. Used by permission.

"spring! may—" by E. E. Cummings, from *Complete Poems 1913–1962*. Reprinted by permission of Harcourt Brace Jovanovich, Inc.

"Sunday Morning," copyright 1923 and renewed 1951 by Wallace Stevens. Reprinted from *The Collected Poems of Wallace Stevens*, by permission of Alfred A. Knopf, Inc.

"The Idea of Order at Key West," copyright 1936 by Wallace Stevens and renewed 1964 by Holly Stevens. Reprinted from *The Collected Poems of Wallace Stevens*, by permission of Alfred A. Knopf, Inc.

"Cutting Loose," by Sally Kempton. First published in *Esquire*, July 1970. Used by permission.

"Cactus Tree," by Joni Mitchell. © 1968 by Siquomb Publishing Corp. Used by permission. All rights reserved.

"American Pie," words and music by Don McLean. © 1971 by Mayday Music and Yahweh Tunes, Inc. Used by permission.

Combat in the Erogenous Zone, by Ingrid Bengis. Copyright © 1972 by Ingrid Bengis. Reprinted by permission of Alfred A. Knopf, Inc.

The photographs in this book do not portray any of the principal characters, but reflect the events in which they were involved, the times in which they lived.

To my parents

CONTENTS

LIST OF ILLUSTRATIONS

ACKNOWLEDGMENTS

For their comments, ideas and time given generously at various stages of this book, I would like to thank Joan Didion and John Gregory Dunne, Jacob Brackman, Nora Ephron, Barry Farrell, Tom Pollock, Emmy Jacobson and Rudolph Wurlitzer.

For their love and encouragement, I'm grateful to Jonathan, my sister Terry and Gary.

I especially want to thank Jon Carroll for his invaluable contribution, and my editor at Doubleday, Kate Medina, for her wisdom, humor and constant support.

Some great wind was brewing as we breathed; not a new generation, but a new notion of generation with new notions of its imperatives. We would not default, succumb to the certainties of age . . . compromise maturely . . . We would not be normal. For normality was now disease.

Jacob Brackman, "My Generation," 1968

"Oh Ashley," said Scarlett. "Nothing's turned out the way I expected."

LOOSE CHANGE

PROLOGUE

On a rainy Saturday in 1972, I hurried into the lobby of the Prince George Hotel in lower Manhattan on my way to a seminar on Eastern meditation. A small woman walked ahead of me to the desk. She asked for the same seminar and was directed to a dark corridor. I followed her into an elevator. She turned. I dropped my eyes.

"Sara," she said.

I looked up and started. It was Natasha Taylor, whom I had not seen in eight years.

We had lived together at the University of California at Berkeley in the early sixties, and Tasha had been the most beautiful creature I had known or seen. At a time when most girls had short, pixie cuts, Tasha had white-blond hair that fell in a sensuous swirl to her waist. Her hair was longer, richer and blonder than anyone thought hair could be. She seemed the image of the California girl pushed to its extreme of perfection: sun-washed limbs, turquoise eyes, a tiny, supple frame and a laugh like wind in glass chimes.

I had loved her and hated her, envied her and always felt proud to be seen with her, but at the end of our senior year, we fought about who owned a rickety table in our apartment. I had given the table to a friend. "Thanks for asking me," Tasha said, hurt and imperious. We packed our belongings in silence. I left for New York and although I knew Tasha was planning to move there also, I was afraid to call her because she would be angry about the table. So I never called and never ran into her, but each year when the new phone book arrived, I checked to see if she was listed.

When I married, at twenty-four, I took pleasure in noting that Tasha apparently was still single. A year or so later, I dialed her number late at night and when a frightened voice said "Hello?" I hung up. Gradually I forgot about her and had long since dropped the phone book ritual when the doors slid shut on us in the elevator of the Prince George Hotel.

What I saw this morning in 1972 was not the vision of perfection I remembered. Tasha's hair was not white-blond and long; it was light brown and cut to shoulder length. She looked pale, had gained weight, and there were lines by her turquoise eyes that gave them a sad, defeated look.

"Tasha, you look beautiful."

She studied me as if making a sincere evaluation. Then she said, "You look the same."

Hours later, we sat fingering the silverware on the table of a coffee shop. Where to begin? How did you ever get interested in meditation? At Berkeley we were atheists. Do you remember . . .

Tasha said, "I remember you used to cook flank steak. Marinate the flank steak. Do you still do that?"

"No. I don't remember eating flank steak."

"When I read your article about the communes, I wanted to call you."

"Why didn't you?" I asked.

"I thought we'd have nothing to say." Awkward pause. "Do you ever hear from Susie Berman?"

"Not in years. But I saw a picture of her in a book about revolutionaries. She looked truly terrifying."

Tasha clicked her tongue and laughed. "She'd probably shoot me on sight!"

Tasha showed me a photograph of the man she was living

with. He was an artist I had not heard of. "He's older. I don't want you to be shocked when you meet him." She asked what my husband's name was. She had not heard of him, "but I don't listen to the radio," she said.

Whenever I am asked how I came to write this book, I return to that moment when I came upon Tasha in the elevator of the Prince George Hotel. It was a moment in which life freezes. One notices details. A door opens; a curtain flutters in the wind. In the weeks that followed our meeting, my mind returned to the time when Tasha and I had been in Berkeley and had been young.

In that time, that decade which belonged to the young, we had thought life was free and would never run out. There were good people and bad people and we could tell them apart by a look or by words spoken in code. We were certain we belonged to a generation that was special. We did not need or care about history because we had sprung from nowhere. We said what we thought and demanded what was right and there was no opposition. Tear gas and bullets, but no authentic moral opposition because what could that be? *"When you're older you'll see things differently?"* We had glimpsed a new world where nothing would be the same and we had packed our bags.

Change, change! I had been breathless for more. Yet by the rainy spring of 1972, I was beginning to be tired. My marriage was foundering, I was approaching thirty and my assumptions about the future were crumbling. I strained to see the visions of the sixties. Had they been a mirage? Nothing felt certain anymore.

It was at this time that I came upon Tasha in the elevator. The memories unloosed by that meeting gave rise to a curiosity. What had happened to the other young women I had known? Casually, and with gathering momentum, I began to track them down, for I was developing a notion that by tracing our journeys, I might piece together a social history of the sixties.

I flew to many cities, dropping into the lives of people with whom I had not been intimate in years. I slept in their guest beds and played with their babies and felt the tremors in their marriages and asked questions and took notes. They greeted me, at first, with nervous excitement. They were eager to hear about the others and compare memories, and apprehensive about being judged.

The three whose stories I've chosen to relate are Susie Hersh, who was to become Susie Berman; Natasha Taylor; and myself. I chose the other two because they were willing to collaborate and because they had a vantage point different from mine. I was a reporter through the sixties. Susie was immersed in the radical Left. Tasha moved in the world of art and Beautiful People.

For six months I interviewed Tasha in New York. To find Susie, I had to place phone calls to Santa Fe, Djakarta and Saigon before I caught up with her where I had last seen her—in Berkeley. We met once a week to relive the years. We read old letters and leaflets, looked at pictures of love-ins, happenings and street fighting and listened to rock records.

It was agreed, very early, that I would change names and details to respect the privacy of the women and people close to them. I have changed the names of all the principal characters except my sister and myself. There was a fourth woman I had wanted to interview and follow through the years, Candy Berenson, but she felt that changing names would not be enough. She appears in the book only as seen through others' eyes.

It has been my intention, in Tasha's and Susie's chapters, to recount each woman's life from her point of view. I have quoted from our interviews and have let each woman's style and idiom spill into the exposition. Susie tends to use blunt phrases; Tasha speaks in hyperbole and fairy tale images.

I doubt that any of us, when we began this project, suspected what was ahead: how draining and endless it would be; how entangled we would become with each other. There were moments when we would laugh helplessly. "What a life!" Susie said at the end of a monologue about her marriage. "Who gives a fuck about orgasms anyway."

But there were periods when the burden of memory was so painful for me and the others that, alone in my house, I would writhe on the floor. Why had I begun this and why was I continuing? What right did I have subjecting my friends' lives to mi-

croscopic examination? What compulsion made me risk the ex-
posure of myself? The grand notion of composing a social history
could not sustain me, although that history was beginning to
take form. The instinct to which I kept returning was that I
would have to face the past if I were to break the power by
which the images of the sixties held me.

Finally, the more I learned about the disparity between the
way things had seemed in that decade and the way they were,
the more I sensed that I did not have a choice. This was a story I
had to tell.

I. CALIFORNIA GIRLS

1943–1963

1. SARA

In September of my sophomore year, I stood outside a palace built of redwood, brick and dusky rose cement. Gold letters on the door said "Alpha Epsilon Phi." There were more than forty sororities at Berkeley in 1961, but only three accepted Jewish girls and of the three, A. E. Phi was best.

Inside the palace the light was rich and warm. Young girls walked softly on plush carpets and twittered with bright smiles that were impossible to read. They took me by the arm and ushered me through the house, asking questions designed to uncover secrets, then closed the tall doors and voted: yes or no.

What could they want? What would turn their minds? While they voted, I sat out the vigil with Susie Hersh. We picked at hamburgers and baked potatoes at Larry Blake's, then walked to a movie theater on Shattuck to watch *The Return of the Fly*.

"Somebody will blackball me," I said ruefully to Susie.

"Oh, Sara, don't worry. You've got great recommendations, and you're a big shot on the *Daily Cal*. They'd be crazy not to take you."

I had doubts. It was easy for Susie not to worry, she was a legacy, a daughter of a former member, and legacies were almost always accepted.

I had known Susie since the start of my freshman year, when we had been assigned to share a room in one of the tall "new dorms." My first memory of her has to do with clothes. She was sitting on the floor unpacking a trunk full of cashmere sweaters and matching skirts, Jax blouses, capri sets and monogrammed underwear. At once she jumped to her feet and called "Hi!" Her arms flew out and she talked very fast in a high voice that carried a puppylike insistence that we were going to be close and have a wonderful time.

Susie had gone to Beverly Hills High School where she had been part of the most popular crowd. She had glossy dark hair that was cut in a bouffant. She had two spit curls which she set by Scotch-taping them to her cheeks before she went to sleep. Her face was delicate, almost Oriental, and in most lights, enchantingly pretty, but in another mood her face could look bruised. Her eyes would recede as if she were peering, grudgingly, from the back of her skull. But I was not to see that bruised look often.

Susie loved adventure and was sexually advanced. She knew things I didn't. Like how big a penis was. One night as we were lolling on our beds, listening to the Kingston Trio, she held up a thick bottle of Jergens lotion.

"That big?" I said.

"Sure. When it's excited."

Even before we had decided to rush a sorority, Susie knew half the girls in A. E. Phi. She went through Rush Week cracking jokes. She had actually been absorbed in *The Return of the Fly*. As we walked out of the movie I asked her, "Do you really believe I'll get in?"

"Yes."

Her voice was so confident that I told myself to stop worrying. The next morning, however, Susie was as nervous as I was. With shaking hands we opened parchment envelopes. I screamed and jumped. Susie laughed and flung her head back. By noon we had moved into the palace.

As difficult as it is for me to believe this in retrospect, I remember feeling on that afternoon that I had arrived at a state of grace. "A. E. Phi," I whispered to myself. I was given a suite that was painted sky blue with redwood windows looking out on

Piedmont Circle, but I was not entirely happy about the pledges who had been assigned to share the suite with me. The first was a small girl who had the most astounding blond hair, it cascaded to her waist. Her name was Natasha and when she appeared in the doorway and poised, fawnlike, as if testing the air, I thought, she's too beautiful. She must be conceited.

The second girl called herself Candy—short for Candida— Berenson. I had noticed her during rushing and assumed she would not be pledged. On the day we had been asked to dress discreetly for tea, Candy had worn a kelly-green suit, purple lipstick and a white angora hat with a fake emerald dangling over her forehead. "A hussy," I had whispered to Susie, who had agreed. "She looks cheap."

Candy's eyes were brown and set close together. The iris in one eye was nearer the center of her face than was the iris in the other eye, which created a disturbing asymmetry and gave me the sense, looking at her, that something was not right. I assumed I had little in common with Candy or Tasha, but that was not important.

What was important was this: there was an order now to everything. The sorority gave us specific lists of proper and improper, *bien élevé* and *mal élevé*. As pledges we were protected, groomed and fussed over. We were told how to dress, when to study and when to sleep. We learned we must not smoke while walking or eat on the street. We must substitute the word "interesting" for Jewish, as: "Is he 'interesting'? He doesn't look it." Before going to a dinner dance we were to be fed, like Scarlett O'Hara before the barbecue, because ladies are supposed to eat like birds in public.

Each of us was required to spend two hours a week on phone duty. There were three phone lines in the house, pay phones that rang simultaneously in the lobby and on every floor. On my first tour, I answered phone number one and a male voice asked for Tasha Taylor. I pressed the intercom and called, "Tasha, phone on one." When Tasha didn't pick up, I asked the caller, "Would you like to leave a message?"

"No, I'll call back."

I wrote in the ledger: "Tasha. BCWCB." This meant: boy

called will call back. Boys rarely left their names because they knew that once they did, it would become public record.

When a boy arrived to pick up his date, I would call over the intercom, "Candy, you have a visitor." If it was a girl visiting, I would say, "Candy, you have a guest." Ten minutes later Candy would appear at the second-floor landing wearing loafers and a khaki trench coat, and, with her slightly cross-eyed, expectant look, descend the grand staircase.

I remember that I loved wearing my gold lavalier with Greek letters. It gave me a sense of place, and at a university with 27,000 undergraduates, the importance of place cannot be overstated. Most of my classes were held in auditoriums. Registration was accomplished with IBM cards, and papers frequently were returned bearing a grade and no comments, as if they had been read by a machine.

There were many nights during my freshman year when I had sat in my dorm room eating bags of cookies and potato chips to kill the depression and the sense of missing out. But there were also moments when the size of the university made me giddy with anticipation. There was something to discover around every corner. The History of Ideas! El Greco! Erik Erikson! When I lived at A. E. Phi it was not uncommon for me to rush home to dinner waving a book. One week it was Freud's *Future of an Illusion*. I told Tasha, "You've got to read it. Freud proves what Marx said, that religion is the opiate of the people." My next burst of enthusiasm was for Nikolai Leskov, an obscure Russian writer whose story, "The Enchanted Wanderer," I dreamed of turning into an epic film.

Candy began to call me the "enchanted wanderer." As the year progressed, I became attached to Candy and felt she was more attuned to me than any friend I had had. I was no longer disturbed by the asymmetry of her eyes. I thought she had a Reubenesque loveliness. Her father was a psychoanalyst who had been a leftist in the thirties, and Candy was the person that girls would seek out with sad eyes when they wanted to "talk." She had a gift for clowning and conducted her life at a pitch of dramatic exaggeration. "The greatest movie ever made!" "The worst teacher in the world!" That was how she spoke. She once called the president of A. E. Phi a fascist, and snuck out of the

house to attend meetings of SLATE, the liberal students' political party. She made me laugh, and she made me feel loved.

Tasha spent most of her time with Jim Lieberson, who was a
legend around campus: brilliant, seductive, hilarious, outrageously foul-mouthed and untamable. As a senior, he was Mark
Schorer's teaching assistant, a job usually awarded to graduate
students. Jim was 6'4", with black wavy hair and nicotine-
stained teeth. He was "interesting." He belonged to Z.B.T. and
liked to tell pledges, "The shittier you are to girls, the more desirable you are." Tasha was the only one of us who was not
afraid of him.

At a ferryboat party given by Z.B.T., Jim climbed up a mast
and dropped his pants. "Woo woo! B.A.!" the boys yelled. Tasha
left with another couple. Jim sent her funny notes but she refused to speak to him. I urged her to relent, "There's nobody
who compares to Jim," but she held out until one night at two in
the morning, a Z.B.T. pledge opened our window, climbed
through and dumped a basket of roses onto Tasha in her bed.
The next morning, Tasha met Jim for coffee in the Bear's Lair.
He offered to drive her home, but instead, headed the car down
Highway 1 to Big Sur.

It was a dramatic day, Tasha told us later, one of those days
following a rainstorm, when the earth looks greener, the bay
looks bluer and the clouds are like cutouts hanging in the air.
Tasha and Jim sat in a booth at Nepenthe, a restaurant perched
above the Big Sur breakers. They drank red wine and Jim read
poetry while Vivaldi played from speakers. Two days later when
Tasha came home from classes, she found a card in her mailbox
with the postmark Big Sur. Jim must have mailed it from
Nepenthe. On the card was a poem which she read to us, her
chin up.

> "brave! brave
> (the earth and the sky
> are one today) my very so gay
> young love."

>   —alas and alack,
>   e.e. and i are back. Jim.

As the months passed I saw less of Tasha. She liked to get up at dawn to study and was uneasy in the evening, particularly at six, when the bells in the Campanile, the tower in the center of campus, would chime out crude versions of assorted melodies: "Hail to California," then "Yes, We Are Collegiate," followed by the aria from *Carmen*. Every piece sounded as if it were being played on an amplified xylophone. For most of us the bells were background noise, but for Tasha they were an ordeal. She said the bells reminded her of students who kill themselves by jumping off the Campanile. "You know the story," she said, "a guy places his math book on the ledge and jumps. He leaves a note behind saying he was worried about grades."

One night when Tasha was in our room at six, she turned on the radio to the loudest rock 'n' roll station. An oldie came on, Frankie Lymon singing "Why Do Fools Fall in Love?" and spontaneously, everyone began to dance. We danced fast with partners, holding hands, the way we used to dance in high school and the way we never would again. The twist had changed everything, and even when the twist would be eclipsed by the frug or the boogaloo, the idea would be the same: to dance separately, not touching.

When Frankie Lymon finished, we fell back on our beds. Tasha was flushed, far removed from the bells. Susie had forgotten that she was failing Russian and I had forgotten the internecine battles raging at the *Daily Cal.*

"Are you and Jim back together?" Susie asked.

"Yeah."

"Did you see what he did to me at the ferryboat?"

"No."

"He grabbed me in front of a whole group of guys and said, 'Susie Hersh has the world's greatest ass.'"

Tasha rolled up her eyes. "When we're alone he's not like that. Did you die!"

"No," Susie said.

I told Susie, "Show them what you do at the beach."

Susie rolled onto her stomach and pretended she was lying on the sand. She was slender and delicate above the waist but had a voluptuous rear end which, by arching her back, she could raise to an inviting tilt.

"My God," said Tasha.

Candy jumped up and imitated Susie walking along with her rear end protruding. Susie threw a pillow at her.

I told Tasha that Jim was encouraging me to study English. But Tasha wasn't listening. She was checking the reflection of her backside in the mirror. "What?" she said suddenly. "What about Jim? What about English?"

I was about to change my major from Communication and Public Policy to English because I found I preferred reading Homer, Jane Austen, Faulkner—any piece of literature—to analyzing Hitler's or Billy Graham's power of persuasion. I was inspired by Schorer, who taught modern British literature, and by Jim. When Schorer had to fly to New York for a week, Jim planned a lecture on D. H. Lawrence. Word passed: Lieberson was up to something. On the day of the lecture the auditorium was packed. People taking the course brought friends, and members of Z.B.T. brought dates. I sat in the back row next to Tasha, who had not been able to eat lunch because of nervousness.

Jim arrived late, loping down the stairs with a cocky grin and a cigarette caught in his teeth. He was wearing a suit and tie and carrying his dress shoes, which he laced after vaulting on the stage. He unzipped a brief case and in that second, dropped all traces of frivolity.

"I want to talk about naturalism," Jim said. "I want to parse a passage from *Women in Love,* an extraordinary piece of naturalism where the symbol works, you don't even have to call it a symbol, it's just there and you should be able to breathe it in." He read aloud the passage where Gudrun watches while her lover, Gerald, tries to force a horse across railroad tracks in the face of an approaching train. "Horses do rear back from trains and noises," Jim said. "But the horse is also Gudrun, who of course is afraid of Gerald, afraid of him sexually. He's mounting the horse, controlling the horse, the train is coming, he pulls on the horse's bit, it splits the lip and blood runs. Now when you listen to a train, what sound does it make?" Jim panted and moaned like a locomotive approaching. "Gerald is struggling with the horse—with Gudrun—forcing her to abandon fear and give way to passion. Think about how much is going on and how it works naturally, without having to build artificial symbols. The rhythms of the train are the rhythms of . . . fucking!"

I was stunned. No one had said "fuck" before on the stage of Dwinelle Hall. Slowly, people began to applaud. Tasha lowered her head, burning with embarrassment and pride. That night in our room after lights out, Tasha, Candy and I talked in whispers about the lecture. We decided we were going to be like Lawrence's women. We would not marry for security or be hampered by convention. As Tasha would remember it ten years later, "It's almost as if we took vows then: we were going to make life as interesting a journey as possible and were willing to suffer pain if necessary."

Noon on Telegraph Avenue. People swirled up and down the sidewalk and into the street, greeting each other, laughing, coasting on skate boards, passing out leaflets and ducking into hamburger shops. On a cold bright day as I was walking with Susie, we approached a huddle of fraternity boys who liked to shout out comments. I stiffened. One boy said loudly, "There's a cute little . . ." Susie flipped him the bird. "Screw you."

I laughed and bumped Susie in the shoulder. "I don't believe you did that." We stopped to buy doughnuts and in violation of sorority rules, ate them as we walked down the street.

"You know," Susie said, "if you had any inclination to become a beatnik, this place would do it to you." I looked at her with disbelief. "Who would want to be a beatnik and wear ugly sandals and carry a dirty baby on your back?" Susie's voice, without warning, became shrill. "You shouldn't close your mind to people just because of the way they dress."

At the time of this conversation, in 1961, there were two visible groups in Berkeley: the Greeks and the beatniks. Many did not fit in either group, of course, but those were the stereotypes, and during my first year, I had flip-flopped from one camp to the other in two weeks. I had applied to be a reporter at the *Daily*

Californian and unwittingly stumbled into a war between the
paper and the student Executive Committee, called Ex Com.
The paper represented the liberal-beatnik point of view; Ex Com
represented the Greeks.

I went to a weekend training program at which the editors
presented their case. They described Ex Com as rah-rah kids
who spent their time arranging dances and charter flights to
Europe. The *Daily Cal* editors believed the student government
should take stands on "off-campus issues," such as hearings held
in San Francisco the previous spring by the House Un-American
Activities Committee. They showed us a film called *Operation
Abolition,* which showed protestors being hosed down the steps
of the Court House during the HUAC hearings. I didn't understand who was hosing whom, but by the end of the weekend I
had been convinced: Ex Com was a Mickey Mouse government
that should be replaced by liberals who would make it a true
voice of the students.

In the following week, I stopped by the *Daily Cal* every day,
eager to attack Ex Com, but no one spoke to me or gave me assignments. The staff regulars were pimpled and shabbily
dressed, and a stale cloud of body odor hung over the office. I
quickly lost interest and focused my attention on trying to make
myself look like a Tri Delt. Delta Delta Delta was a sorority of
gentile girls whose median height was 5'1". I was 5'10", but I
bought Peter Pan blouses and took to wearing a daisy behind
one ear. I was getting dressed for a mixer Thursday night when
the phone rang. An agitated boy told me the entire staff of the
Daily Cal was resigning in protest against Ex Com. Would I sign
the resignation petition?

No, I was not about to join that crowd of bohemian, pseudo-in-
tellectuals now. Besides, my father's last words when he had
dropped me at the dormitory had been, "Don't sign anything—it
could ruin your life." The following day, Ex Com sent out a call
for volunteers to put out a new *Daily Cal.* I went to the meeting
out of curiosity and found it packed with boys from the best fra-
ternities. I stayed to help write stories and by Thanksgiving, I
had been appointed a night editor. I was now a scab, a defender
of the Mickey Mouse government I had denounced a month be-

fore, but I had dates every weekend and was hopelessly infatuated with the new editor, Randy O'Neill.

Randy was a team player. He had a deep, sexy laugh and an air of cool assurance as he sat on top of his desk at meetings, holding a cigarette between his thumb and first finger. When he walked past my desk he would smile and call breezily, "Hi, beautiful!" I cut his picture out of the paper and taped it by my mirror. On Thursday nights, when it was my job to put the paper to bed, I would keep glancing at Randy's office, hoping he would offer to drive me home. When he did, we would park near the dorm, squirm into the back seat and make out. Because the making out could not progress to its natural conclusion, it would often lead to wrestling, grabbing, tickling, hammer locks. For months, Randy refused to take me out on regular dates. He was Catholic and wanted his wife to be Catholic. "Why can't we just go out and not think about marriage? You haven't married any of the other girls you've dated." Randy weakened, and in May he invited me to his fraternity's Daffodil Ball.

The following September when I moved into the A. E. Phi house, the old staff of the *Daily Cal* returned to the newspaper to depose Randy O'Neill. They called him "a conservative square peg trying to fit in a liberal round hole." I stayed on the paper as a feature editor but my heart was not there. I would finish work quickly and hurry to the sorority to talk about Big Game Week.

Spring came unusually early that year. In February of 1962, I packed away my woolen clothes. The warm nights encouraged mischief: panty raids; kidnapings; and contests where boys would climb into the dryers at Laundromats and see who could spin the longest. Susie played records by the new folk singer Joan Baez. Candy and I went to see *La Dolce Vita*. Squads of students set out on fifty-mile hikes, inspired by President Kennedy's talk about physical fitness.

At the height of this delicious early spring, on March 23, President Kennedy came to Berkeley to speak at Charter Day, the university's birthday. The two camps mobilized. An Ad Hoc Committee arose to picket the President in protest against nuclear testing. The Greeks drew up "Welcome Kennedy" petitions.

In our room at the sorority, a week before Charter Day, we

looked at pictures in *Life* magazine of Kennedy wading into the surf. We were in love with the President. How did he kiss? "Let's call him!" Candy said and marched right then to the pay phone. When she had been connected to the White House switchboard, she said, "I'd like to speak to President Kennedy, please. This is collect from . . ." She stopped and huddled over the phone. "Collect from Sara Davidson." I feigned grabbing the receiver. Candy twisted away. "Oh. Thank you anyway," she said and hung up. "They don't accept collect calls."

When Charter Day arrived, nobody went to class. I sat on the lawn in brilliant sunlight by Wheeler Hall, holding a pink balloon and watching the Straw Hat Band play "Chattanooga Choo-Choo." At noon, Susie and I began the trek to the football stadium. We passed a line of picketers demanding "Fair Play for Cuba." Susie laughed and clapped her hands. "Look at that!" she said. A dark-haired boy was marching by himself carrying a sign, "Fair Play for Penguins." Vendors were selling tiny American flags. Susie bought a flag and hooked it through a buttonhole. Inside the stadium students were running in every direction just to run, it seemed. Candy caught my arm from behind. She was wearing big round sunglasses, like Jackie. Then Tasha arrived with Jim Lieberson and as we were settling in our row there was an enormous roaring. We jumped to our feet. John F. Kennedy walked before us! He waved. We screamed. The stadium shook with noise and when at last we sat down, my throat was raw.

President Kennedy spoke about the tide of history that was carrying the world toward democracy. His accent—the strange broad *a*'s and the *r*'s tacked onto words like "Chiner" and "Cuber"—was exotic to my ears.

> "No one who examines the modern world can doubt that the great currents of history are carrying the world . . . away from Communism and towards national independence and freedom. . . . It would be foolish to say that this world will be won tomorrow. . . . The processes of history are fitful, uncertain and aggravating. There will be frustrations and setbacks. There will be times of anxiety and gloom."

I looked about the stadium and saw rapt faces. In the air, colored balloons were whipping on their strings.

> "Yet we can have a new confidence today in the direc-
> tion in which history is moving. . . . A world of knowl-
> edge—a world of cooperation—a just and lasting peace
> —may well be years away. But we have no time to lose.
> Let us plant our trees this very afternoon."

After Kennedy had left, I went down to the *Daily Cal* to help close a special edition. I sat in the printers' office, lulled by the smell of fresh ink and the clacking of the linotypes. At midnight, Randy came to pick me up carrying a bag of hamburgers which we ate under the fluorescent lights. Then we drove up winding roads to Grizzly Peak, parked and put the top down to let in the lush air scented with eucalyptus.

"Isn't this a wonderful school?" I said softly.

Before us were the winking yellow lights of the bridges and beyond them, the sea.

Randy tightened his grip around my shoulders. "It's the greatest university in the world."

2. SARA

In June we all went home to Los Angeles, bracing for the shock. We had gone to different high schools and not known each other before Berkeley, but the Los Angeles we had known was the same.

It was a city where the surf report was read with the morning news. A city where children tried to grow up quickly: at eight, girls started wearing training bras and at ten, boys taught themselves how to drive. I did not know, until I was seventeen, that the rest of the country was different. I was unaware that people in other regions do not eat their salad first or paint Christmas trees orange. I thought it was normal to see a restaurant built in the shape of a hot dog. I thought everyone grew up out of doors, with trampolines and Pogo sticks and bongos and surfboards. Sundays meant lying on the beach coated with cocoa butter. Cruising in cars. Lassitude in the air. I can hear it in the balmy harmonies of the Beach Boys, the promise that life would be like ice cream and we would spoon it down.

My grandfather had made the journey west to this land of dreams in 1913. He had come to New York from Debrecen, Hungary, but he didn't like New York, no sir. He bought a ticket for forty-five dollars to ride in a Pullman to San Francisco where he figured a working guy might find a job in the 1915 World's Fair.

When he reached San Francisco, jiminy Christmas! Dozens of young fellas had already gone broke waiting for World's Fair jobs. He had to buy them all a meal. There was nothing to do but go on down to Los Angeles, where he fell in love with what he saw. A city that had beautiful weather. Palm trees. Roses, gardenias, every kind of flower. Orange trees that bloomed in the winter. An ocean you could go and take a swim in, any time of year. There were only four business streets. The air was sweet and the birds sang all the night long. He found a job—boom like that!—as an upholsterer at Barker Brothers, rented a room in a pink bungalow and wrote to my grandmother in New York, "Sell everything you got over there and come to California."

My mother was born in Los Angeles the following year, which makes me something of a rarity: a second-generation native. While my mother was growing up, the city came to a stop at what is now Beverly Hills. It took my grandfather a full day to drive from his house to the beach at Ocean Park, a trip which today can be made on the freeway in twenty minutes.

My grandfather prospered and in 1940, opened an auction gallery in a building owned by Mary Pickford. He auctioned the estates of John Barrymore and Hedy Lamar. Family legend is that Hedy walked into the gallery and handed my grandfather her house key. "Sell it all," she told him. "I'm never going back." Her psychoanalyst had advised her to break with the past.

My mother brought home boxes of Hedy's clothes, and I wore the star's ice skates and hair ribbons with pride. But the city of Los Angeles was soon to transmute itself beyond my grandfather's vision. He let his money sit in banks instead of buying land, and by 1960, the rent on his store was so costly he was forced to abandon the auction gallery which was immediately razed to make way for a bank built of glass.

The Los Angeles of my childhood has disappeared as well. There are no more ponies to ride in Beverly Ponyland. The high school I attended collapsed in the last earthquake. Carolina's, the drive-in of my teen-age years, was sold and renamed Stat's, then Klix, then it became a car wash and now it is a McDonald's.

My grandfather will be ninety this year. He is 5'2", with blue eyes and white hair. He smokes Philip Morrises, eats a grapefruit every morning and has a jigger of Bourbon before dinner. Three days a week, he drives, at twenty miles per hour, never faster, to the Beverly Hills Health Club where he bends and stretches and rests plum naked in the sunroom.

He does not welcome interruption of routine, but recently, he agreed to move from the house on Orange Street where he had lived for thirty years to an apartment next door to my parents. When I visited him, I found him pacing the new living room in his slippers. He had sold his antiques and the room contained only a color television, a sofa and a Barcalounger. When I asked what was wrong, he said, "There's no place comfortable where I could sit and be in a straight line with the television."

"That's easy to fix, Grandpa. Let's move the chair and turn the TV around . . ."

"No, no, Sara dear," he said. "Leave it be. I can't take so much change."

My mother wanted to be an actress. She studied drama at UCLA, but when she graduated with honors in 1932, the country was in Depression. She had to work in a factory, later as a teacher, but she never lost her capacity to be inspired or her love of storytelling before friends.

It was in 1932 that my father came West from Syracuse, New York. He married the once-aspiring actress and opened a store called MarvAl Radio. He made a specialty of installing radios in cars. We were the first family on our block to own a television, and I would point out my house as "the one with the TV antenna."

In the fifties my mother started selling real estate, and was soon earning more than my father. She pressed him to sell the radio business. She didn't want him crawling under cars any longer. But he loved tinkering and when he did let go of the shop, he wandered, hat in hand, until he found a niche as a memorial counselor, selling plots in a Jewish cemetery.

My mother was the perfectionist in our house. If milk was spilled or a real estate deal fell through, blame had to be fixed. Somebody had failed. But the awarding of credit was more ambiguous. My mother insists that she was proud of my achievements and I believe her. But my memory is that any honor I received was tainted by a suspicion I saw in her eyes that the honor might not have been deserved.

When I was thirteen, I kept a diary in which I made entries like this: "I just can't seem to relax with my friends. I'm always worrying what they think of me." The words "perfect" and "control" recur on every page.

My Problems

Overcoming self consciousness with other kids.
Controlling my temper.
Keeping up my A average.
Perfecting my dancing.

But perfection and control were useless when applied to one area: the beanstalk-like growth of my body. In Los Angeles in the fifties, few people believed they looked as they should. My younger sister, Terry, became convinced she needed a nose job when her best friend underwent the operation. My mother to this day believes her right hand is too large and her neck too long, and when she saw me grow six inches in the eighth grade, shooting up from 5'2" to 5'8", she took me to a doctor who gave me painful hormone shots that were supposed to close my growth centers.

From the moment the doctor first stung my behind with a giant dose of hormones until perhaps six years later, there was not a day that I did not feel disadvantaged because of the misfortune of my height. Looking back, I can see that at sixteen I had a willowy, beautifully proportioned body, but at the time I was only aware of what I considered its unnatural elongation. When the shots failed to work and I grew to be 5'10", I calculated that 90 per cent of the men in the world were inaccessible to me because they were shorter. I daydreamed of going to

Sweden to have an operation on my legs that would diminish me by three inches. When friends offered to fix me up, my first question was always "Is he tall?" followed by "Is he cute?" (Later I would ask, "Is he bright?" and still later, "Is he sensitive?")

I devised ways of gauging whether a boy was as tall as I when we were seated in cars cruising Hollywood: I would scan the length of his forearm hanging out the car window and then scan my own. Sometimes I miscalculated. He would walk to my car, open the door, and as I stood up his head would swivel backward like the short clown watching the tall clown unfold from a midget car. "God, you're *tall*."

It was only in dance classes that I could forget about everything but perfecting my plié. I read books about Pavlova and imitated the queenly bearing of my ballet teacher, a severe-looking Spaniard named Carmelita. At a lesson one Saturday when I was fourteen, in the year I was growing six inches, Carmelita taught us a combination at the end of which we were to rise on our toes and look up, arm extended, to an imaginary partner. The piano tinkled as Carmelita walked, ducklike, among us making corrections. "On your toes and stay there!" My thighs began to tremble. I held my head high and despite the muscle spasms, tried to assume an expression of serenity as I gazed up into the yearning eyes of my imaginary partner. As Carmelita passed me she touched her cane to my neck. "You. Sara. Don't look up. Look straight ahead." With a throaty laugh, she added, "Let's be realistic."

It was not long afterward that I gave up dancing. But I was resilient in those days and soon had other plans: becoming a horse trainer; studying child psychology. As the time approached for me to graduate from high school, I had a sense of acceleration. College would be different. Smart girls would be appreciated. Boys would be mature. Height would not matter and I would, at last, come into my own.

3. TASHA

Her sixteenth birthday was a big big day. She took her savings and bought an old red Ford convertible that had a continental kit and a super-duper radio. The convertible top and the radio were important. In the morning before school, she would drive into the hills and watch the sunrise turn the sky all pink and orange. In the shapes of the clouds she saw elves, witches and prancing jungle beasts.

She switched on the radio. "Bye bye love." She knew all the words to the Everly Brothers songs but she also knew about the shapes of clouds. The world was full of fabulous creatures: monsters and demons, traps and enchanters, twigs that snapped and toads that leaped. She was the little girl with long gold braids, a basket in her hand, treading through the forest.

She knew about dark roads and secret journeys, but she talked about them only with her diary and her father. Tasha and her father took walks on Sunday morning. Ben Taylor was a lawyer who had worked with the IWW and had been forced to disappear for periods during the fifties to escape the House Un-American Activities Committee. He was tall, red-cheeked, dignified. On their walks he carried binoculars so that if he felt moved to tears of sentiment, as he often did, he could hold the field glasses to his eyes. Although he had two sons, it was with Tasha that he was closest.

Tasha was aware that her father was working too hard and that he had given up dreams of settling in Israel and helping to build a workers' state. By the time the Taylors had acquired a swimming pool and tennis court, Ben had had a serious coronary.

Because her parents were "liberal," Tasha, unlike her friends, did not have a curfew but was told to use her good judgment about when to come home from dates. She knew, though, that whenever she did, her father would be sitting in his study, smoking a pipe. Often they would talk and joke until four in the morning. Tasha's face would turn pink as she laughed, making a sound like the tinkling of glass chimes that was so infectious Ben would wipe his eyes and beg her to stop, "Please, no more, it hurts!"

When Tasha had problems, she turned to her mother. The problems had begun in the second grade, when the boys voted her an honorary member of their secret society and the girls refused to let her sit with them on the lunch bench. Then in junior high, all the boys in the best club, the Jesters, decided they were in love with Tasha. At parties they would scramble to cut in to dance with her, but she didn't like a one of them, she liked Bobby McBain, who went to a private Catholic school. When Tasha started wearing Bobby's I.D. bracelet, the Jesters decided to give her the freeze.

Tasha didn't care what those finky guys did. But one morning she came to school and found every locker, bulletin board and classroom plastered with little printed cards that said "Jesters" around the border and in the center: "Skag of the century—Tasha Taylor." She felt the ground rise up. Everywhere she walked there were more cards. Girls stood in little circles, laughing, and boys sang out to the tune of "Miss America," "There she goes, skag of the century."

How cruel the world was! Overnight Tasha had passed from being the most popular girl in school to the most hated. I'm in big trouble, she thought, I'm going to get out of it, help me. When she walked in the cafeteria, all the kids turned their backs except her best friend, Beth Warren. Tasha called up her mother and stayed home all week, during which her mother telephoned the principal and the parents of the Jesters. The result was that the president of the club came to visit Tasha and apologized.

"We're destroying the cards."

"You better," she said. "You're a lousy club anyway."

"Want to go to the show Saturday?"

"I shouldn't. Well, okay."

He took her to see *Rebel Without a Cause,* and they sat in the back row with all the Jesters and their dates.

"What a blast," Tasha wrote in her diary that night.

Some girls who are pretty know they are pretty, and some girls who aren't particularly pretty believe they are. But Tasha thought she was "just average." When she reminisces about growing up, she insists: "I couldn't understand why all the guys liked me and the girls were jealous when they had big breasts. I had no breasts, zippo. Objectively speaking, I had good hair, nice eyes and a lousy body. In every photograph of me I see a common-looking girl who seems from her expression to be very uncomfortable with herself."

What the others saw, though, was a girl with such uncommon beauty as to make them feel gray in her shadow. One male friend says, "Tasha didn't walk like someone who felt unattractive. She bounced along, and her hair was unreal. It was so long and luscious, it took your breath away. I used to tell people that if the tinkle in Daisy Buchanan's voice was money, the tinkle in Tasha's voice was sexual superiority."

What he didn't know was how many nights Tasha flung herself on her bed to cry about her breasts. They were the subject of endless teasing. Boys followed her home taunting, "Carpenter's dream, flat as a board." She tried stuffing Kleenex and socks in her bra, aware that she was fooling no one. "It made me feel ugly. I had no sex appeal. I'm thirty now and the hangup is still with me."

When several of Tasha's friends with overdeveloped breasts had surgery to reduce their size, Tasha gathered her courage and went to see the most famous plastic surgeon in Beverly Hills. "I have a real problem," she told the doctor. "It may not seem like a problem to you but it is to me and I want to know what can be done about it." The doctor took out a file and showed Tasha pictures of women who had three breasts, or a single breast at the navel. "Do you still feel you have a serious problem?"

The week before she was to start high school, Tasha went to a slumber party at which the girls sat about wearing Baby Doll nightgowns, speculating about who should cut her hair and who should try for which boys. When they landed on Tasha, a D-cup wearer named Rosie said, popping her gum, "I think you're in for a surprise. You're not gonna be popular. Guys in high school like big boobs." The girls laughed so hard they toppled over on the floor. Tasha pretended she thought it was funny but her heart was jumping like a trapped bird. She believed the girls were right.

But they weren't. The first week of school, Tasha was rushed by all the top top guys, but only one caught her interest: Kenny Livingston, who was quarterback on the football team and had a certain shy softness beneath the swaggering style of the time. Kenny had the best physique Tasha and her friend Beth had ever seen. He moved like a panther. He wore Brilliantine, and for Tasha, the aroma became so associated with Kenny and so arousing that she bought a bottle so she could dab it on her pillow before she went to sleep.

Tasha had concluded, by this time, that she herself must be giving off some kind of invisible perfume that was arousing to the opposite sex. How else could she explain Kenny's wanting to be her boy friend, when there were "a million girls who were crazy about him, all more beautiful than me?" She and Kenny studied together, played volleyball and spent hours making out parked on Mulholland Drive. When Tasha saw Paul Newman or Marlon Brando in movies, she thought, Kenny's so much better looking! He loved jelly beans so she brought bags of them to football games to cheer him up if the team lost. He called her Little Jelly Bean. She slipped notes in his locker: "I love you a heap."

The only discordant note was money. Kenny's father was a cleaner of swimming pools. The guys Kenny hung around with drove T-birds and Corvettes, but Kenny had to drive an old

Chevrolet. Tasha kept telling him she loved his car and she loved
the Apple Pan where they went after dates to eat hamburgers
with hickory sauce and homemade apple pie.

After a year had passed, and then another year, Tasha and
Kenny wanted to go all the way. Her parents had told her sex
was a beautiful experience to share with someone you loved, as
long as you were careful not to get pregnant. The problem was
finding a proper place. The answer seemed to come on New
Year's Eve of 1960, when Beth's parents flew to Mexico for the
holidays and Beth offered Tasha and Kenny their guest house.

On the afternoon of New Year's Eve, Tasha took a long bath
in Replique oil. She selected her sexiest outfit: a tight-fitting
black straight skirt, a black sweater and a string of turquoise
donkey beads to accentuate her eyes. Kenny borrowed money to
buy champagne and a rubber, but what he purchased, Tasha recalls, "was not a thin one that felt like skin but a thick one made
of material like dish-washing gloves." They drove to the guest
house in Benedict Canyon but found it was dingy and cold.
They took blankets from the back of Kenny's car, crawled under
them and, unable to stop shivering, opened the champagne.
Something was wrong; the champagne made them high and a
little sick. They kept stalling and when they did get down to pet-
ting, it was stiff. By the time Kenny got around to fussing with
the rubber, there was no possibility it would work.

"That thing feels like a bathing cap," Tasha said.

"I wanted to be extra safe," Kenny protested.

"There's no way that's going to fit in me."

"But you said . . ."

"Well you said . . ."

"It was your idea to come here!"

Oh Lord, it was so embarrassing and disappointing. They
blamed each other and reassured each other that it wasn't anyone's fault and they would have another chance. But they didn't
talk again about going all the way. In the summer, just after
Tasha's graduation, they were necking under a quilt in Tasha's
basement when Kenny, pressing against her, had an orgasm.
Tasha was wearing half her clothes and cotton underpants, so a
month later, when she woke up feeling nauseous and dizzy, she

didn't suspect anything. It was Kenny who wondered if, by some freak occurrence, Tasha might be pregnant.

"You're kidding! Is that possible?"

"I was very close to you that night. I've heard that people can get pregnant through their clothes." Kenny took her to see his doctor, who said it was highly unlikely but since Tasha was young and fertile, they ought to do a blood test. But first, he needed permission from one parent.

"Please, not my father," Tasha said. That night she told her mother she had been having fainting spells and didn't want to alarm her, so she'd gone to have a blood test to see if she was anemic. Betty Taylor called the doctor and asked, "Is it the pregnancy test?"

While they waited for the results, Tasha and Kenny wandered around the beach. Kenny said, with a strange look of zeal, "I'll work part-time and study hard and we'll make it, I promise you." Tasha couldn't believe she was pregnant. She spoke lines as if she were in a play. "I'll learn to cook and I'll knit baby sweaters."

As the time approached to call the laboratory, she grew jittery. She met her father for lunch at the Farmer's Market and when he asked what was wrong, she burst into tears. "I couldn't tell him," she recalled later. "It would have broken his heart." She and Kenny were trying to distract themselves, playing miniature golf, when Tasha went to a pay phone. "I'm sorry, Miss Taylor," the nurse said, "but I must tell you, you are pregnant."

When they walked in the door of Tasha's house, Betty Taylor looked at their faces and said, "Oh my God." Tasha was furious. It wasn't fair! She was a virgin, who would believe her? Was there a conspiracy in the heavens? Would she ever be able to travel or go to college? She had been planning to leave for Berkeley in six weeks.

Without asking questions, Betty Taylor took over. She told the two they could get married if they wanted but not to do it now just because Tasha was pregnant. Kenny sulked. Betty arranged for a doctor to come to the house. She instructed Tasha to tell no one, not her brothers, not even her father. Abortions were illegal and the risk was high. Tasha stood at the window in the early afternoon, watching for the doctor. Her teeth chattered. The operation was performed in her father's study on his oak desk covered with sheets. Although she was given a sleeping pill, she saw her father's dark legal books in their cases, saw the fetus with her eyes or her imagination.

Afterward, she couldn't bear to be with Kenny because whenever he touched her, she felt sick. She left for Berkeley, determined her life should go on. She was nominated for Frosh Doll and Sweetheart of Sigma Chi. She did not admit to herself that she had been through a trauma, that part of her was sorry she had given up the baby and that she was now effectively frigid. She pretended to enjoy necking as she always had, but her whole body reacted against it. When she started going out with Jim Lieberson, he sensed that Tasha had problems but assumed it was because she was a Jewish princess. Tasha thought the problem was with Jim, not her. He was too skinny and he smoked, there was a sour taste in his mouth. He had a super brilliant brain and he was funny like Lenny Bruce, but she wouldn't have wanted to crawl between his sheets. Jim took to calling her "the girl with the golden cunt."

Tasha never saw Kenny Livingston again after leaving Los Angeles for Berkeley, but she was to dream about him for the following twelve years. Every other month he appeared on a mountain or on the shore of an island, as young and sensual-looking as when they were in high school. In one dream she met him in Chamonix, France, where he was living in a cabin with a Scandinavian girl. Tasha told the girl, "You must understand. I was once pregnant by this man and that has made us permanently in each other's lives. I love Kenny so much that if he loves you, I love you too. But you'll have to accept my presence."

In 1970, ten years from the season of the abortion, Tasha dreamed of Kenny eight times in two weeks. She had undergone Jungian therapy by then and had learned to pay attention to her dreams. She became convinced that Kenny was trying to reach her, that he was in trouble or that she had to speak with him to work out something in her own psychic life. She made dozens of phone calls to locate him, then waited until it was 10:30 in New York, which was 7:30 A.M. in Los Angeles.

When Kenny answered the phone, Tasha recognized the voice she had heard every day of her life in high school.

"Hello," she said cautiously, "this is someone you may not remember . . ."

"Oh I remember," Kenny said.

"What are you up to?" she asked.

"Nothing much." There was silence, and Tasha said, "The reason I'm calling after all this time is that I've been dreaming about you for the last two weeks and I don't understand why."

"Tasha," Kenny said wearily, "if you could see me now, your dreams would be nightmares." He sighed. "I'm fat. I sell insurance. I've never gotten married."

"You mean you don't swim and play tennis like you used to?" Her voice was quivering.

"I never go to the beach. I never do any of those things."

She tried to joke: "Maybe you should go on a diet?"

There was a longer silence and Kenny said, "Now that you know what's happened, I'm sure you'll stop dreaming about me."

But Tasha didn't. Once or twice a year, Kenny continues to appear to her. He is always seventeen. They are always in love.

4. SUSIE

". . . and then, when I was ten, my parents died. Up until then everything had been pretty normal. After they died, nothing was normal. The world was never quite in balance."

After the plane crash, Susie, her two younger brothers and their collie were adopted by an aunt and uncle who had two sons of their own and a Dalmatian. They wanted her to call them "Mom" and "Dad." The words felt wrong.

She didn't fit in the new family. The boys had each other, even the dogs had company, but Susie was all by herself. Her new mother tried. Mrs. Hersh loved to take Susie shopping and told her she could have whatever her heart desired. She worried about Susie's eating habits: she was so thin and didn't seem to like any foods. At the dinner table Susie chewed mechanically. The two sets of brothers would quarrel and slam plates. "Dad" watched television and "Mom" cried quietly. After dinner, Susie went straight to her room to do her homework and wait for boys to call.

In her house she was a boarder but at school she was a star. She called a sunny "Hi!" to everyone. She walked with her back arched to show off her rear end. Her boy friends gave her presents: bracelets, pearl drops, a heart-shaped pendant inscribed, "Susie, you really are too wonderful to ever forget."

Girls vied to be her friend, she was so sparkly and sure of herself, but when Susie became angry she could get on her high horse. When she transferred schools, Susie says, "I would instantly spot the fast, popular kids and say, 'That's where I want to go.' In a short time I was in, and then I would move people around. I'd start rumors and set people against each other, saying things like, 'She's a jerk, she's got pimples, let's kick her out,' or 'She's cute, let's be friends with her.'"

Susie dressed beautifully and always looked harmonious. "Nobody ever had enough clothes," she recalls. On Saturdays, when her mother asked where she had been, she said, "Out." She couldn't tell the truth: that she had been at Saks shoplifting a cashmere sweater because she needed one to match a skirt and had spent her allowance. Some of the best-dressed girls at Beverly High shoplifted half their wardrobes.

Susie became bold and was caught by a store detective. When her mother brought her home, Susie folded her thin arms and stared at the floor. "Very well," her mother said, "you're grounded for the weekend." The door closed and Susie lay down to cry. She pulled at the venetian blinds. She thought about the party she would miss, the new blue princess dress she wouldn't be wearing, and then she thought about a girl at school who was so ugly she never went to parties, and how many poor children in Asia were starving? How many crippled kids had to live in iron lungs? She would cry for them all.

This connection between her sadness and the suffering in the world was so familiar that she could not say when it had begun. Even before the plane crash, she used to daydream about the Good Fairy appearing and offering her three wishes. She would make a bargain with the fairy. She didn't want three wishes, one was enough. Here it was: she wanted all her wishes in the future to come true.

What did Susie do with unlimited wishes? She didn't ask for cashmeres or a new boy friend. She imagined herself on a high-backed wicker throne, sitting on the grass in front of her yellow house on Beverwil while lines of needy people swirled around the block. Susie had two assistants, Negroes with palm fronds, who guided the pilgrims to her. With the power of her wishes, she could cause cripples to walk, provide food and restore lost love. When people asked how they could thank her, she said, "I need no reward because I have everything—I have the power to help."

Susie dreamed of being connected to those streams of people, connected in a way she never felt at home or at Beverly Hills High where it was all a big act. When she arrived at Berkeley and saw the rush of new faces on Telegraph, she thought, this is where I'll find my people.

Her roommate, Sara, was the first girl friend she had had who cared about studying and reading books. In fact, Sara studied like a crazy person. Susie would watch her at her desk scribbling notes and twirling her hair and wonder, what's she doing it for? Susie liked her a lot but kind of felt sorry for her because she was stuck on this jerk, Randy O'Neill, and when the phone rang in their room it was usually for Susie. Sara thought joining the sorority was a big deal, but to Susie it was high school all over again. Empty ritual. She was bored and that was what she hated: being shut off inside.

She decided she was going to make "new friends." She picked two girls in her political science seminar, Vicky and Renée, who wore black tights, carried green book bags and knew how to throw pots. Susie began having dinner with them and even slept at their apartment, but after a few nights she was back at the sorority worrying because there was only one BC for her in the ledger while Andrea Lustig had ten.

At the end of the year, Susie dropped out of the sorority. Her closest friends—Sara, Tasha, Candy—were leaving for Europe in the fall of '62, so Susie moved in with Vicky and Renée. A real adventure was starting! Susie bought white Levi's from the surplus store to wear around the house, but at school, she still had to dress conservatively because she had a job as a hostess in the Student Union.

The new Student Union was built on the edge of campus, directly facing Sproul Hall. From her desk, Susie could see the mall and the fountain where at noon, liberal students and religious fanatics would speak to small crowds.

In October of 1962, something changed. Susie watched as the crowds on the mall swelled to thousands. The Russians were sending a fleet of ships loaded with nuclear missiles to Castro in Cuba. Atomic weapons would be pointed at our cities. President Kennedy had ordered a naval blockade, but the Russian ships were forging ahead.

It was a deadly bluff game: one false move could launch World War III. Susie was too nervous to stay behind her desk. She walked outside. A dark-haired boy who was kind of cute in a ragged, beatnik way was shouting, "John F. Kennedy is insane. He's risking the future of the world to save his ego. I know people who have left the United States to work in Castro's revolution. They tell me the Cuban people are happy and well fed. Castro tried to have friendly relations with us but we refused. President Kennedy gave Castro no choice but to call on Russia for help!"

"Booo!" "Commie punk!" "Go back to Russia!" The air boiled with yelling. A straw poll was taken and the vote was seven to one in support of Kennedy's actions. Susie remembered the happy, handsome man who had stood in the stadium on Charter Day. How could such a man let a nuclear war begin? Around her kids were talking about buying canned food and building air-raid shelters. She closed her eyes and saw San Francisco in flames beneath a mushroom-shaped cloud. She went to a pay phone and called her mother to say good-bye. Mrs. Hersh ranted about Castro and Khrushchev and swore she would rather be dead than red. Susie repeated what she had heard on the mall, "It's President Kennedy who's risking everyone's life. We're the aggressors."

"Susie, you don't mean what you're saying! Why did I let you go so far away from home?"

The next morning, Susie woke up amazed to find herself alive. The crisis was over; the Russian ships had turned back. Weeks passed and one afternoon at the Union, the dark-haired boy who had attacked Kennedy at the rally came up and asked for *The*

New York Times. Susie handed him the desk copy and watched him sign for it:

Jeff Berman
(dangerous Commie punk)

An hour later, she walked into the lounge and spotted him dozing by the suspended metal fireplace. She tapped his shoulder.

"The paper is due back."

Jeff opened his eyes and saw an extraordinary girl smiling right down at him. Shit she was pretty. Spoiled-looking too.

"You don't want to go back to that desk," he said playfully. "Get a chair."

She sat smack on his lap, crushing *The New York Times*. "Who needs a chair?"

They walked home together and the next day, Susie waited to see if Jeff would come for *The New York Times*. He was not like anyone she had ever known. He was from Boston and had come to Berkeley after being kicked out of Amherst for political organizing. During the Bay of Pigs invasion, he had borrowed a hunting rifle and driven without stopping to Mexico City to volunteer to fight for Castro. The Cuban ambassador had looked at Jeff with his freckled baby face and said, in clipped English, "We have dealt with the Bay of Pigs. Go home and tell your American students the truth about our revolution."

Jeff had a funny happy way of walking bouncing high on the balls of his feet. He was tall and spindly, all elbows and knees. Susie thought he looked kind of like Beaver Cleaver. He wore jeans with holes in the knees, raggy sweaters and sneakers—black and white Chuck Taylor All-Stars. He had a junk bike that made a racket when he rode beside Susie on her blue Lady Schwinn three-speeder.

From the day they met, they traveled together. When Susie got off work Jeff was waiting at the fountain. He would run to meet her, grab her above the knees and lift her straight up. "Please! Don't dump me in the fountain." They would eat a fast dinner in the cafeteria—everything they did together, they did fast—and walk home as the lights were going on across the bay.

Susie looked forward to the walks home with Jeff. He would

talk about his friends who had visited the Soviet Union and about the newspaper he was starting called *Inch Worm*. Jeff was proud of his friends. Susie worried that she was too conservative-looking and not smart enough, but Jeff seemed to like explaining things to her.

Capitalism, he told her, was based on encouraging greed and fear rather than brotherhood and love. "We get rich by exploiting people all over the world. In our own country, thousands of children go hungry. Thousands of people can't afford medical care. It's a farce, but if we get enough people really committed, we can change everything."

Susie felt shivers. She confided in Jeff that she was thinking of joining the Peace Corps. He was suspicious of Kennedy's intentions for the program, but suggested she apply for Crossroads Africa. When Susie told her parents, they refused to pay for such a trip. Jeff wrote home and a week later loaned Susie a thousand dollars to go to Uganda.

Jeff lived in a redwood-shingled boardinghouse filled with beatniks and weird characters. When he brought Susie there she had to conceal her shock. His room was a yukky mess of leaflets, newspapers, dirty clothes and Coke bottles. On the ceiling over the bed, he had painted in red: "If God rules the universe, let's overthrow Him." Jeff asked Susie to stay.

"I can't."

"Why can't you?"

She was silent.

"All right, but I'm going to have to sleep with other girls. I can't live like a monk."

When they studied at the library, Jeff would slip his hand under her skirt and slowly work it up her thigh. Susie squirmed, afraid that people could see. She found it hard to concentrate on her books because she was worrying whether this was the night Jeff would go looking for someone else to sleep with.

"Let's take a break," she said. When they had settled on the cold marble floor outside, she turned to him with a flirtatious laugh. "I know it's silly but I can't help it, Jeff. I don't like to think of you with other girls."

"You know what that means, then," he said.

She nodded. No choice. Grit my teeth and get it over with. The next morning, she opened her eyes on the red words, "Let's overthrow Him." Jeff had bounded out of bed at six, talking a mile a minute, and she had turned back to sleep. As she began dressing, she noticed there were stains on the sheets. Oh yeah, she thought. Virgins bleed.

She pulled off the sheets and started scrubbing them under the cold water tap in the community bathroom, hurrying so no one would see. She had not felt anything the night before. She had not really been there. Now it was morning and she was washing up her blood, as if she were washing out food stains. "I was stuck in the dead place inside. The vacuum. The boring place where nothing's happening."

5. SARA

It was our junior year abroad. Candy went to Paris to study French. Tasha went to Perugia to study art. I was tired of studying, so I bluffed my way into a job in Milan, translating letters for a publisher, Arnoldo Mondadori.

At Thanksgiving, the three of us met in Paris. We rode in a cab to Les Halles at midnight and when a man offered to buy us onion soup, Candy shook her head vehemently and whispered, "Don't let a man pay for anything, not one sou, or he'll think you're going home with him."

We laughed so hard we could not get the soup down. We talked about the things we had discovered in Europe: garter belts; yogurt; François Truffaut; bidets; wine; bikinis (even in California few girls wore bikinis; the most daring wore two-piece suits); Lawrence Durrell; hitchhiking; Verdi; and eating with the fork in the left hand.

We went back to Candy's room near the Sorbonne and I fell asleep on her lumpy brass bed. I dreamed and started and then became aware of Candy whispering. I lay still, straining to hear, but could only catch breathy fragments: "clawing at him . . . this incredible hold on me . . . I'm scared I'd do anything he ever asked."

Tasha's voice hissed with alarm. "Candy, please be careful! You don't want to get knocked up."

I bolted upright. "Candy, what are you talking about? You told me . . . you said you were a virgin."

She took my hand and fixed on me her warm broody eyes set so close together. Sare, she called me, rhyming it with air. "I'm sorry, Sare, I couldn't tell you before but Chuck and I were making love in high school, when I was sixteen. I never told anybody. It was too risky."

Tasha gave a deep sigh. I spun around. "You mean . . ."

She shrugged and averted her eyes.

As I rode the Orient Express back to Milan, I could not sleep. I felt furious, amazed, foolish, frightened, and aroused to Gothic fantasy. The rhythm of the wheels was taunting, taunting. I had been holding back for nothing!

As December came on I felt a painful aching in my chest that I had come to call depression. To kill the ache I went out every night with groups from the office. At Christmas, Mondadori, a paternalistic company, took a busload of new employees to Verona. After eating an eight-course lunch with six kinds of wine on a terrace overlooking the city where Romeo and Juliet had been set, we wobbled obediently through the Mondadori printing plant. As we toured the factory I was stirred by sensations: the smell of fresh ink, the spinning of presses, the sound made by new books when they are opened for the first time. Everything was so soothingly familiar that on this gray afternoon, the pain in my chest lifted. I wanted to go home, and I wanted to write.

I returned to Berkeley in February of '63, to a cottage Susie had rented for the two of us. Before I had unpacked I called up Randy O'Neill, but I was surprised at how young he looked in bermuda shorts.

"You look so . . . sophisticated," Randy said.

I could not pretend interest in the Daffodil Ball. I was suffering from culture shock, I decided. I felt disconnected from everyone I had known. I missed drinking wine and riding on trains and hearing the exotic fall of European accents. The aching in my chest returned, only now it felt worse because the sun was shining and the breeze carried showers of pink and white petals from fruit trees.

I wandered by myself, reading Ezra Pound. I studied late at the library so I wouldn't have to see much of Susie and Jeff Berman, whom I disliked because he once joked that I had the political consciousness of a dinosaur. Jeff was at our cottage whenever Susie was, so I had no chance to find out if she believed what she was saying about capitalism being evil.

One afternoon while I was dawdling in Cody's Bookstore, I ran into a boy I had known from fraternity mixers. His name was Hank Smith and he had been nicknamed "Honcho" because even before it had been easy or fashionable, he had had a reputation for scoring. Hank was 6'5", beautifully built, with a mouth of bright white teeth which, when he smiled, gave his face a goofy cast.

I had thought he was dumb, sexy, childlike, racy, and now I learned he had intellectual aspirations. He had spent the previous year in Paris and had changed his major from business to comparative literature. Over coffee, he told me he had traveled through Morocco with a French girl. She had called him "Le Grand Américain."

"Let's walk over to my place," Hank said. "You can meet the guy I live with, Jean-Pierre."

I fell in love with Jean-Pierre. He was only 5'4" but he had a booming voice with which he would argue with wild intensity only to stop, throw up his arms and laugh. He had sharp eyes and dimples and a front tooth that was chipped in half, which I thought gave his face jagged character, but Jean-Pierre thought it looked like "one side of my face is warring against the other."

Jean-Pierre had a girl friend named Claire who was from Salinas and looked like Jean Seberg in *Breathless*. She wore her blond hair in a boyish cut. Jean-Pierre had taught Claire how to cook for him. "Claire," he barked good-naturedly, "prepare the chickens!" As Claire walked barefoot in a crepe de Chine robe, Jean-Pierre came up behind her and touched his lips to the back of her neck.

That evening we ate a languorous meal: onion soup, mushroom omelets, chickens roasted in Grand Marnier, and crepes suzettes, along with many bottles of beaujolais. Jean-Pierre and I talked about Sartre's *La Nausée* while Hank played Charles Aznavour records and slung his big arm around me.

Hank came to see me the following three nights and on the fourth, after we had watched Tony Perkins in *Phaedra,* he kissed me hard in the car in the parking lot and told me it was time to "quit playing stop and go." I went back to his apartment and did not return to my own for the rest of the semester.

Darkness. I lay on my back on the fake Danish modern couch in Hank's living room and felt only a dull pressure. I stared at the ceiling. I thought, I'm going to be one of those women who only make love as a duty, to have children? There was nothing thrilling about it; it was like a medical procedure for which I had been told: *"This won't hurt."*

The dull pressure was to change, however, into sensations I craved and could not keep my mind off. In the supermarket, in my adviser's office, during an exam, I would start to twitch in my chair and want nothing but to find Hank and the nearest bed.

My secret terror was that I was insatiable, a nymphomaniac— like the girls in stories I had read and only dimly understood in magazines like *True Confessions,* girls who went to ruin because they craved being "touched." I asked Hank, "What if I'm a nymphomaniac. Is that possible?" He stuck a finger between his molars and chewed on it reflectively. Then he laughed. "No, Sara. A nympho can't come, that's what drives her crazy, and that sure isn't you."

I saw the world with new eyes. In the elevator of the Student Union, I would look around and think, is there anyone here besides me who's just made love? I liked answering the door of Hank's apartment in a nightgown. I liked stumbling with him, bleary-eyed and rumpled, onto the Avenue at four, and I especially liked it when girls from the sorority would whisper and stare. Poor foolish hens. They didn't know what they were missing.

But it wasn't Hank alone, it was the setup: Jean-Pierre and Claire and the sumptuous meals and the cozy musk-ripe apartment where the four of us slept in two single beds. As a unit we were balanced. Two were tiny and two were tall—"the minnows and the whales" we would call each other teasingly. In the evenings Jean-Pierre and I would argue about existentialism while Claire cooked and Hank painted bad water colors.

On weekends, we would stock up on food, turn off the clocks and drift from the table to the bedrooms to the sundeck and out to see Laurence Olivier in *The Beggar's Opera* and then to take a sauna bath and back to bed. Jean-Pierre would bark from the kitchen when a meal was ready, *"On mange!"* And Hank would yell from our bedroom, *"On baise!"*

I was eager to try making love everywhere—on the floor, in the shower—and I could not help wondering how I was able to throw myself into such hedonism and feel no guilt. How could my upbringing have been so easy to cast aside? What I did not understand was that I was paying in other ways, for I was never free from a conviction that at the end of the month I would learn I was pregnant.

After my first night with Hank I had made an appointment under a false name with a gynecologist on College Avenue. Although I followed the doctor's instructions vigilantly, I would stare at the calendar with alarm as the twenty-eighth day of my cycle came up. In April, when I was a day late, I went into a panic. Five days late and I ran about collecting names of abortionists reputed to be "safe." Ten days late and I was inconsolable. I cried all day in my bed at Hank's, getting up to stare with red eyes at my breasts in the mirror. I met Susie at our cottage and sobbed so hard my breath came in ratchety gasps.

"I'm so scared."

Susie sighed. "Didn't he use anything?"

"I did."

"Well . . . shit then, what are you worrying for?"

"I could have put it in wrong."

As I walked back to Hank's, I remember looking at the blue water in the bay and thinking, it's wasted on me. I can't see it. That beauty. I'm pregnant and I'm going to die.

Blood! It came on the fortieth day, ending the siege and enabling us to continue feasting and celebrating clear to June. I knew that when our foursome broke up, Hank and I could not sustain things. He was overpowering in bed but in an essential

way I felt superior to him and did not like it. So it was with
some relief that I saw him off to Puerto Rico where he was to un-
dergo training for the Peace Corps.

Back in Los Angeles for the summer, I fell into a torpor. I
could not relate to bridge games and barbecues. I lay on the
beach, turning brown, waiting for September when Tasha and
Candy would return from Europe and Susie from Crossroads
Africa and we could all get back to the action up north.

II. BLOWING IN THE WIND

1963–1965

6. SARA

The times were changin', the waters had grown. President Kennedy was shot. The Beatles arrived. We'd better start swimming or sink like a stone. Timothy Leary and Richard Alpert were run out of Harvard for fooling with LSD. Negroes sat in at Woolworth lunch counters. Buddhist monks set fire to themselves in South Vietnam (where was that exactly?) while Madame Nhu went on tour, declaring that Vietnam would soon win its war against the Communists, providing U.S. aid were not withdrawn.

In September of 1963, Berkeley was the place of all places to be. It was an enclave where things happened first, where the rules of middle-class society did not apply. Susie, Tasha, Candy and I rented a two-bedroom house on Blake Street. It was our hope that the house might become a salon. Tasha claimed the largest bedroom in which she hung a painting of a nude woman reclining, a gift from an Italian artist. Candy and I shared the smaller bedroom. Although Susie stored some of her clothes in Tasha's room, she was planning to live a block away with Jeff Berman, an arrangement which would have been seen by her family, by all our families, as a scandal.

The house on Blake Street came with a green couch, a green

rug and one orange ash tray. We sewed floor pillows and used transparent colored paper to make a standing Japanese screen that was supposed to look exotic. Candy rented a piano on which she practiced, nude to the waist, Debussy's "Claire de Lune." I loved to watch Candy, everything about her was round and pink: round arms, round breasts, round pink-spotted cheeks. I resurrected a violin I had not touched since I was thirteen, and our highest musical moment came when we played a duet of the Blue Danube Waltz.

We looked very different than we had two years before. Gone were the loafers and Peter Pan blouses. We were seniors and wore grown-up clothes: dresses we had bought in Europe, nylons and stacked heels. We parted our hair in the center and when it was clean, wore it down, when it was not so clean, piled it artfully on top of the head in the manner of Jeanne Moreau. Susie and I used ice cubes and a turkey trussing needle to pierce each other's ears, an act which disgusted Tasha as barbaric until she started coveting the earrings we collected.

We stocked our refrigerator with wine and cheeses and the new diet soft drinks that had just come on the market. We were learning to cook: Tasha's specialty was veal; mine, as Tasha would remind me years later, was flank steak marinated in soy sauce; and Candy's meals were extravaganzas.

On the day before the ordeal called "pre-enrollment," when we had to fight for space in desirable classes, Candy started baking at 10 A.M. and put up water for a "pure pure consommé." All day she cooked and strained vegetables. I kept telling her it tasted no different from a bouillon cube. "Sare, you're so practical," she said with a laugh. "I don't care how it tastes, I'll know it's pure."

When Susie arrived for dinner—Jeff was off in Delano on some mission that involved grape pickers—the kitchen was a disaster zone. A mist of flour covered the floor and at the stove, Candy was struggling with three pots: the consommé; a chicken being poached in gin; and a sauce for cherries jubilee.

Susie was wearing her bohemian clothes—a man's shirt over a black turtle neck and white Levi's—but her hair was neatly combed and she looked, as she always did, fresh and pretty. She sat on pillows on the floor and began reading to us from a new

SLATE booklet that gave advice about how to beat the academic system.

"Listen," Susie said. " 'Most students at Cal perform like trained seals . . . ' "

"Oh no!" Candy shouted from the kitchen. "I just poured the cherries jubilee into the broth."

"There goes dinner," Tasha said. She stood before the mirror, brushing her white-gold hair down over her shoulder. Idly she said, "Maybe I should cut my hair."

Susie and I exchanged glances. Susie said, feigning sincerity, "Oh no, Tasha, don't cut your hair, it's too beautiful."

There was a Pakistani student I began to notice around campus who dressed flamboyantly and cast such a fierce gaze that when he stepped around a corner unexpectedly, I jumped. If my life were a novel, I thought, this fierce Pakistani would be a symbol of something. I wondered if he was evil. He had a blue-black beard and wore clothes that clashed: a yellow madras jacket, a green shirt, pink pants and a red polka-dot tie. I did not know his name but I came to know him by sight—a phenomenon peculiar to Berkeley. An itinerant writer, Thaddeus Golas, used to joke, "I lived in New York twenty-five years and knew four people. I lived here two years and knew three thousand people."

Everyone and everything came together on the Terrace, an outdoor cafeteria next to the Student Union. On sunny days the Terrace felt like paradise. Sitting at large round tables with pots of geraniums, you could see the water of the bay and the milk-white skyline of San Francisco. Dogs splashed in the fountain on the mall and there was continual music from guitars, flutes and drums. I often sat there whole afternoons, composing short stories on a yellow legal pad.

One day in October, Tasha, Candy and I decided to stage a dramatic entrance. Inspired by Renoir's "Déjeuner sur l'Herbe," we packed a wicker basket with fruit, cheese and wine, walked to a table in the center of the Terrace and spread a red checked tablecloth. Two boys sat down and introduced themselves as Psi and Kahuna. They were hitchhiking to Nicaragua to found a utopia.

A skinny boy with glasses interrupted them. "How can you guys cop out like that when there's so much to do here? I spent the summer in Americus, Georgia. Do you know there are Negroes in the South who can't vote . . ."

Thwack! A stack of leaflets hit the tablecloth followed by Susie and a revved-up Jeff Berman. He and two friends had just formed the Anti-Digit Dialing League to fight the conversion of Bay Area exchanges like YUkon, SUtter and KLondike into numbers. "The corporations are trying to dehumanize the phone," Jeff was saying as he spread papers around the tables.

We had finished our lunch and were packing up the basket when a young man wearing a corduroy jacket with elbow patches came up to Tasha. "Hello," he said with an odd smile. His lips pulled apart but his eyes looked serious, unsmiling. "I've been watching you for some time. I want to tell you this, you're my vision of the ideal woman."

Candy and I stood up to go to class. That was the thing about Berkeley. You never knew what the next moment might bring, what new person, idea, book or piece of music would enter your life and deflect it in unexpected ways. As we walked across the Terrace, I noticed the Pakistani sitting with a boy I knew named Don. I stopped to talk to Don but he did not introduce us. Later I learned from Don the following: the Pakistani's name was Ravi; he was a graduate in political science; he had grown up in England; he was not, to Don's knowledge, evil.

A week later at a party, I spotted Ravi across the room and asked Don to introduce us. Don took my hand and we cut a path through couples dancing to "Heat Wave" until we reached the corner where Ravi was talking. Don shifted back and forth, waiting for an opening, when suddenly Ravi turned and stepped toward me. "Hello, Sara," he said.

Friday, November 22, 1963. I was cramming for a mid-term in the "Age of Milton" when Candy came to find me in the General Reference Room. I had not noticed that the hall was emptying. I had been oblivious to the scraping of oak chairs.

"Sare! Haven't you heard?"

Candy's face was puckering. Her close-set eyes wobbled helplessly.

"What?"

"The President somebody shot the President he's dead!"

No. No. We walked outside and I searched for a sign that it
was all a mistake. I passed a professor I barely knew. He did a
strange thing: he bent down and kissed my cheek.

At the Student Union we stood before the television monitors,
watching flat images: Jackie in shock, bloodstains on her suit.
Lyndon Johnson speaking into the microphones: "I will do my
best. That is all I can do. I ask for your help—and God's." Something immeasurable had been snatched from us and although I
could not have said what it was, I knew that we would not see it
again.

"Who could ever take his place?" someone asked.

"Bobby?"

"Thank God for Bobby. But it'll be years."

We met Tasha and walked home. Susie called from Jeff's
apartment where she said the blinds were drawn and Jeff and
four boys were cursing at the television. Jeff had been a member
of Fair Play for Cuba, the group with which Lee Harvey Oswald
was thought to be connected. Susie said, "Jeff thinks the police
are gonna round up everyone on the Left."

"My God, don't tell me, I mean, did Jeff know . . . ?"

"Of course not," Susie said. "I have to go."

I hung up irritated. Everything I said to Susie lately was
wrong.

Years later, I would learn that Susie had put down the phone
and locked herself in the bathroom to cry. She didn't want John
Kennedy dead. She felt sorry for Jackie and the children but she
couldn't say that in front of Jeff.

On Blake Street, we decided to drown our sorrows in tacos.
We ordered a banquet from La Fiesta, then we fixed ice cream
sundaes and then for some reason we were worrying about getting married.

Candy said, "If nobody great comes along in three years, I can
always marry Bobby Moss." He had been a close friend in high

school and she said that wasn't so bad, marrying your best friend.

I was concerned because in my whole life I had never met a man I wanted to marry. Ravi? For weeks before we had slept together, I had been afraid that when he took off his bright Western clothes, he would be wearing some kind of dreadful Indian underwear. What relief to see his thin brown legs emerge in a pair of jockey shorts.

Ravi introduced me to avocado milk shakes and curries and the films of Satyajit Ray. In the middle of making love he would raise himself up and with his fierce stare say, "I want you to come." Sometimes it worked. But Ravi did not react well the night I told him I thought I might be pregnant. He started cleaning up his room. Whenever he saw me after that he called me Sharon or Susan.

The hell with him. I had just read *Who's Afraid of Virginia Woolf?* and decided I would marry someone like Edward Albee.

Tasha was lying on her back, drawing a lock of hair across her lips. "You know what my Russian grandmother's advice was? 'Natasha, you should marry a man who loves you a little bit more than you love him.'" She burst into laughter. "I've got just the opposite now." She was referring to Steven Silver, the mystery man in the corduroy jacket who, it turned out, had a poetry fellowship and was giving his ideal woman a lot of trouble.

"What are you doing for birth control?" Candy asked.

"I'm going to try the pill."

"So am I," Candy said. She had gone to see a gynecologist who had informed her about the difference between vaginal and clitoral orgasms and advised her to practice having the vaginal kind.

I was mystified. "I don't think there is any difference," I said. I had felt the same sensations when Hank was thrusting inside me as I did when I was masturbating. "The way of getting there may be different but the feeling is the same."

Tasha said, "Oh, I think there is a difference."

Candy: "I'm positive there is. My mom told me it took years for her to have vaginal orgasms. This doctor said you could practice by putting a plastic shampoo bottle in you and pulling it out fast."

"That's crazy!"

Candy ran from the room and came back waving a plastic bottle of Breck. "All right," she said, "who's gonna be first?"

During the Christmas holidays I went skiing with Rob Kagan, whom I liked more than any boy I knew but who was an inch shorter than me and therefore not a romantic possibility. Rob was to become a major figure in my life, someone I would think about through the years, for he went rushing off down roads I found both luring and frightening.

Rob had blue eyes in which there were flickers of delight, and a large, powerful nose which seemed to give his head a forward motion. He liked to answer a question with a question. When you spoke to him, he would raise his dark eyebrows like two peaks as if to say "Oh?" or "Tell me more."

When we met in 1963, Rob was planning to become a civil rights lawyer; he was also interested in sculpture, skiing, magic and music. He loved what was strange, eccentric, fantastical. He had learned about alchemy from his father, a maverick businessman who would buy anything cheap and try to turn it around for a profit. Rob's father once bought a warehouse of burned artificial flowers. Another time he bought the parts to nine incinerators. He never bought anything unless it was a deal. When Rob was little, his grandmother had sent money for Christmas and told his father, "Buy your son a new bike." Rob's father had gone out and bought used bicycle parts. Rob's mother had thrown a tantrum. "That's the last straw," she had said and filed for divorce.

Rob, like his father, always looked for the way to get more out of something ordinary. Rob would dig a dozen crescent wrenches out of the dump, set them on a suitcase and present them as a sculpture because the old wrenches looked so . . . significant! He had a knack for drawing people together for adventures: going ice skating and taking pictures of everyone falling. When I went to his house, I never knew what I would find: Rob and four friends nailing a Christmas tree to the ceiling, or listening to Nepalese yak-herding music.

It was in Rob's car driving home from Squaw Valley that he

told me about his discovery of LSD. He had already smoked marijuana six times and had tried to initiate me. He had come to our house with a joint and said, "Ready for an adventure?" He showed me how to drag, sucking in air along with the smoke and holding it down deep, but I had never been able to inhale cigarettes. After three puffs, I started to cough. "Feel anything?" Rob asked. I went to the sink to get a drink and noticed that the running water sounded a bit louder than usual. Nothing more. It was all psychological, I decided.

But LSD was something else, it seemed. As we drove down the freeway past Sacramento, Rob said he had eaten a sugar cube doused with the chemical and afterward, "I felt stabs of pain like pins and needles all over my body. I couldn't move. I thought I was going to die, really, when suddenly it stopped. Then came the thrilling part. I walked outside and the whole world was oozing. The ground was alive with snakes and vines. I saw a girl on the street and I shouted, 'Hey, wait a minute. Where are you going?' She said, 'Home,' and I don't know why but I pulled down my pants. I said, 'What do you think of that?'" He laughed. "If you can believe that."

"No!" I cried. "What did she say?"

Rob raised his eyebrows. "She didn't know what to say. Her mouth fell open, it looked like a little circle. So I pulled up my pants and told her, 'It doesn't matter.'"

Rob went on talking about serpents and vines but I had stopped listening. Instead of Rob's words, what registered was the rumbling of trucks on the freeway.

In February the four of us on Blake Street had our birthdays accompanied by heavy depression. Although we were not aware of it then, we are all Aquariuses. This year was our twenty-first and it felt bad. The fact that it rained the entire month did not help. Candy wandered in the downpour without shoes, brooding, as she was to recall later: "One, truthfully I wanted to die, and two, there was something superior about me because truthfully I wanted to die."

We divided people into two groups: those who knew, and those who didn't know. Aldous Huxley and Carson McCullers knew. Roy Rogers and Doris Day didn't. A crazy singer called Bob Dylan knew. We saw Dylan with Joan Baez at the Berkeley Community Theater and afterward, played his record on which he sang over and over in a cracking voice, "The times they are a-chayn-gin'."

In the early spring Negroes appeared on the campus. There was a demonstration going on at the Lucky Market on Telegraph. CORE had declared war on all Lucky Markets for failing to recruit and train Negroes for good jobs. After a week of picketing, the demonstrators had invented a new tactic: a shop-in. This is how it worked: students would wheel shopping carts down the aisles, load them to the brim and abandon them at the check stand saying coyly, "Oh, I forgot my wallet." Others went around rearranging the shelves and dropping food on the floor.

By the third day of the shop-in, the store was a shambles. Broken eggs, rotting vegetables and smashed loaves of bread were piled four feet high on the check stands. When I walked past the market with Tasha, I felt sick. Tasha was angry. "Those kids are acting like animals. It's disgusting."

A friend of ours who was a law student said he was organizing a group to help clean up the market. "I'm not against CORE, but their tactics are absolutely contrary to the law. It gives CORE a bad image."

One of the demonstrators brayed, "We're not interested in our public image. We're interested in stopping business for a discriminatory employer."

I said I was going in for some tomatoes. Trying to look blasé, I picked my way through the wreckage but as I was clearing the check stand, I spotted Susie, who was throwing potatoes on the floor and shot me a look of such patronizing scorn that I felt exposed.

The truth was—and this was a secret I had told no mortal except Candy—I didn't like Negroes. At my high school, half the student body were Negroes, which meant that my friends and I could not go to the bathroom alone or dawdle in the halls without asking for trouble: knife fights, hair pulling, cigarette burnings, who knew. I had one class in which a Negro greaser sat in front of me. Every day when the bell rang, he took out a jar of cream that had a foul, sickly-sweet rotting stench. I thought it was lard and felt nauseous watching him goop it on his finger and smear it through his hair. Whenever I passed Negroes in the hall, I thought I could smell lard.

We had never mixed socially in high school so I was not happy when the door opened at a party in Berkeley and a contingent of Negroes cruised in. I remember feeling especially pretty that night, wearing a lavender spring dress, my hair up and a pair of amethyst earrings from my grandmother. A tall Negro named OB asked me to dance. I refused. A song from the brand-new "Meet the Beatles" album was playing. When the Beatles sang, "I'll Never Dance with Another," all the kids threw back their heads and wailed, "Wooooo!" But OB stood apart. The pupils of his eyes were so small that it looked as if he had no pupils, just two flat brown disks. "Do you know what it's like?" he said.

"What what's like?"

He did not move. "Like, bein' a spade." The flatness of his eyes was unnerving me. "I can't get no job. I can't go to school. I can't live in a decent house."

When a slow number came on OB put his arms around me. Over his shoulder I saw Candy beaming approval. My body went rigid and it was not until the dance was over and OB was gone that I wondered if he was right, maybe I didn't know what it was like at all.

My political education began at the feet of OB and other street hustlers from East Oakland. We would meet on the steps of the Student Union and they would talk about going hungry in the slums and seeing their sisters turn tricks and their brothers shoot junk. I remember how it felt to hear, for the first time, how unfair it was. Something had to be done.

By the time I learned about the demonstration to be held at the Sheraton Palace in San Francisco, I was ready to go. Everyone was going. The demonstration would be the biggest social event of the semester.

The Sheraton Palace was one of the great old hotels; it

covered an entire block and employed 550 people, but only 31
Negroes. An Ad Hoc Committee was asking the hotel to sign a
no-bias hiring pact. The hotel was refusing, so a massive demonstration had been called for Friday, March 6, at 6 P.M.

It was 8 P.M. when I drove across the Bay Bridge with Tasha,
Steven Silver, Candy and four others in Tasha's red convertible.
We had decided to dress nicely, the boys wearing suits and the
girls in dresses, so people could identify with our cause and not
be alienated by a beatnik atmosphere. Because of the traffic we
had to park a mile away. As we walked hurriedly, we began to
hear roaring, like the muffled cheering that erupts from a distant
sports arena.

> What do we want?
> Freedom!
> When?
> Now!

We rounded the corner. I had never seen anything like it! An
army of kids, two thousand or more, was circling around and
around the Palace. The night gleamed with lights. Policemen
rode horses. There were three picket lines on three sides of the
Palace, each line sending its chants into the air.

We joined one line and I was handed a sign, "Jim Crow Must
Go." What does that mean? I asked Candy. She wasn't sure. Her
sign said, "Tokenism Is Not Enough." I waved to my friends and
gossiped and sang as loud as I could, "We Shall Overcome."
After I had checked out all the faces in the line, I grabbed
Candy's arm, we ran around the corner and joined the next
picket line.

"You guys, isn't this astounding!" We turned and saw Susie.
"Where's Jeff?"

She motioned with her head. Jeff was a monitor, directing the
line; he wore a white arm band over his jacket.

At 10 P.M. one of the monitors announced over a bullhorn that
we were moving inside. There was a court injunction barring us
from entering the hotel. I looked at the policemen reining in

their skittish horses and said to Susie, "I'm scared." She whispered, "So am I."

"Okay," yelled the monitor, "Pair up, a guy and a girl, and let's go, but keep it quiet, no singing, shhhh!"

Jeff appeared and took Susie. A strange boy linked his arm through mine and another took Candy's arm. We formed a double line and shuffled up the steps and through the doors into the lobby. Tourists backed away before us. We sat down, a thousand shiny-faced students, on the red Chinese rugs among potted palms. We looked at each other, not knowing what was coming. It grew hot, we took off sweaters. I was becoming very nervous. I didn't want to go to jail. I didn't want my future ruined. What would my parents think? Every few minutes a troublemaker in our ranks would stand and cry out, "Time to escalate!"

"Shhhh! Keep it down."

I kept plotting my escape. OB would say I was chicken but I didn't care. At two in the morning, a Negro girl, Tracy Sims, stood on a marble table and shouted, "Okay. The hotel has broken faith. Are you ready to go to jail for what you believe?"

"Yes!" the crowd roared, but Candy and I looked at each other and mouthed, "No." On the pretext of having to go to the bathroom, we walked through the lobby and straight out the door.

From the sidewalk, we watched as demonstrators started blocking the hotel doors, inviting arrest. "Pack in and lock arms, hold on!" They went limp and sang "We Shall Not Be Moved." (Where did they learn all this? I wondered.) After more than a hundred had been carried into paddy wagons, the leaders decided bail money had run out and the demonstration should continue legally.

Students poured out of the hotel and we all continued circling. I spotted Susie and Jeff, they hadn't gone to jail! The sun came up. Saturday shoppers appeared on Market Street and I could see from their startled mouths, they had no idea what to make of us. How proud I felt. I belonged to a great new body of students who cared about the problems of the world. No longer would youth be apathetic. That was the fifties. We were *committed*.

I had taken six food breaks and was heading for the car and a nap when, at two the following afternoon, Tracy Sims jumped on

a speaker van and shouted: "We won! The hotel has signed a
no-bias hiring pact. Let me hear you. What do we want?"

In the din that followed, Candy began to cry. Susie looked
dazed. Jeff clasped his hands and shook them above his head like
a boxing champ. I laughed and screamed with my last stores of
energy:

"Freedom!"

May was full of whimsy. Songs by the Beatles could be heard
everywhere, happy songs that made you want to whistle and
skip. "I Want to Hold Your Hand." "All My Loving." "Love Me
Do." At a party one night, Rob Kagan informed me that the Beatles sounded "even more incredible on pot."

"It has no effect on me. Remember?"

Rob raised his eyebrows. "This time I know just what to do.
There's no doubt about it, I'm going to turn you on."

He took me to his house near the Oakland line and did just
that. Sitting on the floor, Rob opened a cigar box and removed
the implements, holding the pieces up lovingly to the light and
placing them down like surgical instruments. Strainer. Zig-Zag
paper. Metal roach clip. All the while Rob nodded as if he were
keeping time. He licked two pieces of thin white paper, made a
fold and filled it with marijuana. He rolled it and twisted the
ends. We smoked it down. I began to cough.

"It's not working," I said.

Rob kept on nodding. "Okay, we'll do another. He lit a second
joint and before I had taken one more puff, it struck me that
there actually was a state of being stoned. We began to giggle
and could not stop. We rolled on the floor like golden retrievers.
I was to notice all the things people notice on a first trip: how
good food tastes; how hilarious and how profound things can
seem. We listened to an old song by the Coasters, "Smoky Joe's
Cafe," and I was exhausted by the emotions evoked by that simple song.

The next time my parents called and asked what was new, I
told them about this great discovery. Their reaction shocked me.
My mother lost control, screaming, "Is this why we worked and
saved to send you away to college? So you could smoke pot!"

I said I had no intention of doing it again, but for the rest of the semester, I met with Rob to blow pot and see where it would take us.

In June, just before my parents arrived to drive me and my belongings to Los Angeles, I gave Rob the coffee table we had scavenged for our house in September. Tasha, from whom Candy and I had become estranged because she never did her chores and was impossibly self-centered, became furious. She walked over from Steven Silver's and said, "Thanks for asking me. I found that table and carried it here myself."

"I'm sorry, I didn't know. If you insist I'll ask Rob to return it."

Silence.

"When are you leaving?" Tasha asked.

"Tonight."

"Aren't you even going to say good-by?"

"Good-by."

She packed her things and left me alone, the final roommate to move out. My mother arrived and combed the place to make sure nothing would be left behind. I lay on my bed which had already been stripped and stared out the window at Blake Street. I felt infused with melancholy; I was leaving Berkeley for good.

I heard my mother opening the refrigerator and the door to the freezer compartment. She cried out, "There's a clock in here!"

"What?" Foggily I walked in the kitchen and saw my mother holding an ice-covered clock. She held it away from her body, as if it might be dangerous. Suddenly I remembered. I turned my face away and laughed. The night before, Rob had come over for dinner and we had smoked some Acapulco Gold. We had decided to put my alarm clock in the freezer to see if we could stop time.

7. TASHA

That year on Blake Street was one of the roughest in her little life. She wasn't happy at all. She was completely unhappy. All the others were having a good old time and she was being done in.

It had begun with a cozy, homey feeling. She had liked living with girls who had been to Europe and knew how to sit and have a good cup of coffee. But there had been omens. Like Steven Silver popping in her life, telling her on the Terrace, "You're my ideal woman."

Sure, she had thought. And what do you want from me?

The second time Tasha had seen Steven on the Terrace, he had been wearing a cobalt-blue sweater and again, he had stared at her. This time she stared back. She saw that he had a slim, good build, dark brown eyes that had pain in them and black curly hair. He was constantly checking his hair in the glass. Tasha thought there was something effeminate about him. Oily and sly. He turned her off. Friends kept warning her: Silver destroys women. They said he had done in his last two girl friends. One had tried to jump off the Campanile and the other had ended up in Camarillo State Hospital. Tasha was intrigued. Maybe she could do *him* in.

Steven walked over and without asking, pulled up a chair. "I'm going to see a film this afternoon, a film in German about Rilke," he said. "It's supposed to be special. Want to come?"

Tasha turned her face so the sunlight caught her eyes. "I don't understand German."

"That's all right. I'll help you understand it."

His arrogance was amazing. "I'm not interested," she said.

He smiled as if to say, "You will be."

Steven refused to be deterred. He pursued and pursued her. His very persistence began to be seductive. He wrote her a hundred-page single-spaced typed letter, telling her about the poems he was working on and quoting Wallace Stevens and going on and on about the duality of experience and the fallibility of words. It sounded eloquent but what did he want?

Steven learned her schedule and one afternoon in October, stood outside the door of her Greek art class when it broke at 6 P.M. Tasha had a headache. She had been staring at slides of splinters from Greek vases until she couldn't tell the birdseed painter from the olive tree painter and wondered, was this to be her lot as an art historian? To spend her life picking over horrid fragments?

"Hi," Steven said. "I've come to rescue you, take you out to dinner." "Good God!" Tasha laughed. "I give up." She called Blake Street and told Candy she wouldn't be home for dinner. She was supposed to have cooked dinner that night.

Tasha went to Steven's apartment after they had eaten in a matchbox-sized French restaurant where he had splurged on a bottle of Taittinger. She wasn't worried about being alone with him. He was amusing, she thought, and had an interesting brain, but she was in no way attracted to him.

She had managed, while in Paris, to break the spell of her freak pregnancy. Through friends of her family she had met a law student from Stanford, George Kramer, who had a job delivering the Paris *Herald Tribune*. He was patient and Tasha came to trust him and believe he wouldn't knock her up. The sex was only mildly pleasant but Tasha was exultant. "I'd broken the ice in me." There might even be a future. George was back at Stanford and came to visit her on weekends.

Steven Silver lived on Euclid Avenue on the North Side of
campus, which was quieter, more sedate and refined than the
South Side. His building was eccentrically shaped with balconies
and a courtyard surrounded by studios, all occupied by male
graduate students whom Steven knew. There were several acous-
tic guitars in Steven's front room. After pouring cognac, he sat
down and played jazz improvisations in a quiet, teasing mood.
Tasha sank back on the couch. She was surprised at how well he
played.

They had another glass of cognac. He read her passages from
Robert Lowell and J. V. Cunningham. "To What Strangers What
Welcome." Steven was making each piece come alive, especially
one by Wallace Stevens, "The Idea of Order at Key West."
Steven said the poem could have been about her.

> She sang beyond the genius of the sea . . .
> And when she sang, the sea,
> Whatever self it had, became the self
> That was her song, for she was maker.

Tasha was flattered. She liked the idea that she was the maker
of her song, the creator of her life.

He poured cognac again.

"No, really, I've had enough." Her body was growing warmer.
Something about Steven reminded her of a painting by Matisse,
"The Piano Lesson." The air of solitude in his face.

He stood up to look for another book.

"Come in here a moment," he said.

The book was in the bedroom. She sat on the bed and he sat in
a leather armchair. He read to her from Stevens' "Sunday Morning" and his voice caught when he reached the part about feeling
"gusty emotions on wet roads on autumn nights."

He paused.

Tasha's whole body was hot. She could only see brilliant light
across the room. Then he was next to her. Kissing her. Sighing.
Then her blouse was undone but she wasn't worried about being
flat. She felt cherished and adored. He knew intuitively what
would please her. She knew intuitively what would please him.

66   BLOWING IN THE WIND   1963–1965

There was no awkwardness about zippers, no my turn, your turn.
Everything was natural. "Like a body wholly body, fluttering its
empty sleeves." She came when he came. Then it was all over.
She was never again to feel that she had any choice about
Steven, or any control. She was hooked.

On the first of November, Tasha's parents came to San
Francisco on a business trip. Tasha asked George Kramer to
drive up from Stanford and have dinner with them. She had
thought of asking Steven but her parents already knew George.
It was safe.

Before dinner, she spent an hour alone with her father in his
suite at the Mark Hopkins. She was overjoyed to see the color in
his cheeks and the familiar laugh lines around his eyes. After his
coronary, the doctor had warned him his health was fragile. Just
two nights before, Tasha had had a dream: she and her father
were walking in the hills of Tuscany when he suddenly went
limp and lost air like a tire. Thank God it hadn't been prophetic.

The four had dinner at La Bourgogne and talked for hours
about life's meaning. Tasha said good night to her parents outside the restaurant. She would see them the next day.

What Candy remembers:

It was 1 A.M. when the phone rang. Candy answered it and
heard Mrs. Taylor's voice, empty and brittle. "Ben's dead," she
said. "He collapsed in the room right after dinner. Let me speak
to Natasha."

Candy clutched at the night stand, dreading what she had to
say next: "Tasha's not here."

"Oh?" Mrs. Taylor said. "Would you tell her then, Candida,
when she returns? Break it to her and have her call me."

But Tasha did not come home that night. She slept with
George at Stanford. Candy remembers, "She was in bed with another man at the moment her father died. That was the most terrible part of all."

What Sara remembers:

Tasha did not sleep with George that night.

It was 1 A.M. when the phone rang. When Candy hung up she

started to cry uncontrollably. Sara shook her by the shoulders. "What is it, tell me."

"Tasha's father had a heart attack. He's dead."

Sara started to take care of details. She called Susie and a boy named Russ Levy, who had known Tasha since she was five, and asked them to come over. She called around to borrow a car for Tasha. She arranged to spend the night away with friends, she would give Tasha and her mother the house, give them privacy.

When Russ and Susie arrived they all discussed how to tell Tasha. They decided Candy should do it alone. The rest of them would wait in the bedroom.

Tasha walked in around 2 A.M. She opened the door and saw Candy standing in her nightgown in the hall.

"It's my father," Tasha said.

Candy nodded, yes.

"Is he alive?"

Candy shook her head, no.

The others walked out of the bedroom. Tasha's voice was like a stab: "Russ!" He went to her and she flung herself against him. They sat on the couch. Susie offered her a cigarette but Tasha wouldn't smoke, her father didn't like it. She was not crying but her body shook and her foot was clacking on the hardwood floor.

What Susie remembers:

It must have been 1 A.M. when the phone rang, because it was 1:30 when Susie arrived at the house and in no time Tasha was there and then her mother. One of them was wearing a red dress. Susie felt blank, she didn't think about the death of her own parents when she was ten. She was worried about Jeff. He hadn't come home from a meeting. Who was he fucking. Margie Rice?

She saw Tasha standing in her underpants in front of the mirror, brushing her hair. It was 3 A.M. but Tasha had stepped in the shower and washed her hair, "as if everything were normal."

What Tasha remembers:

She knew at once when she saw Candy's face. She couldn't deal with any of the arrangements. She left it to her mother and her two brothers, who flew in from schools in Boston and Yellow

Springs, Ohio. While the others went to the hotel room where Ben had died, she stayed by herself in an apartment on Nob Hill owned by friends of her parents. The apartment had a panoramic view of the bay, Alcatraz, San Quentin and the Golden Gate Bridge and everything was pearlized through a blue-white mist. Tasha pulled the blinds shut. It was so unfair! Her father had worked himself to death and for what? To live in the hills and have a pool and new Jaquars? This had led to the early death of a deep man who didn't fulfill himself? What a disappointment life was. Nothing meant anything.

She put her hands to her head. She could have saved her father. She had taken a life not so long ago—the baby—and now her father was taken. She choked back a scream. She called Steven Silver. He said he would be right over.

When Steven reached the apartment, Tasha's mother and brothers had returned and all of them had been drinking Bourbon. Each time someone spoke they laughed, but it was manic, involuntary, convulsive laughter. Steven had a drink and laughed politely with them. He asked Tasha if she wanted to take a walk. For three hours they walked and talked of other things, down Nob Hill to Broadway and Chinatown and North Beach, all the while Steven kept his arm strongly around her.

When she returned to Berkeley the week after the funeral, she began to spend every night with Steven. The two of them made a home in his bedroom. It was a simple space filled with air, light and no furniture except for a double bed and Steven's desk, which was covered with books and poetry magazines in neat piles. There was one print on the wall, a blue and green still life by Matisse which felt serene and contemplative.

"Such love I felt in that room," Tasha says. They rarely went out. She cooked and studied. He studied and played guitar and read her his poetry and she was his sounding board. She couldn't understand why people said he was a lady killer. Those people just didn't know him.

Steven liked to write while she slept in his bed. On weekends, his friends who lived in the building gathered in someone's kitchen and cooked mussels in wine or chicken in wine or some other student recipe in which the key ingredient was sour cream or wine.

One boy liked to read from Thomas Nashe:

> Brightness falls from the air,
> Queens have died young and fair . . .

Tasha burst into tears. Steven held her and knew when it was best to distract her and when it was best to let her cry. He told her, in time, how his own mother had died. When Steven was sixteen, his mother had driven her car off a cliff and left a note that said only, "My act was intentional."

At the same time Tasha was depending on Steven, she set out to prove she could be independent. The week after the funeral she found two jobs—as a salesgirl at Nicole's, which carried the most stylish clothes in Berkeley, and as a researcher in the art library, binding slides. She made one hundred dollars a week. She would never be a burden on her mother or anyone. But it was not easy. In addition to working, she was carrying a full load of studies, keeping house, shopping, cooking and doing laundry for two and being there when Steven needed her.

She was smoking again and living on black coffee. She developed an ulcer and had to eat Gelusil. In February, Steven was awarded a grant to teach a poetry workshop at Pomona College. His plan was to teach there two days in a row and live in Berkeley the rest of the week. Tasha cut classes to go to Pomona with him and felt so proud, walking across the Quad with the poetry professor. She wore a dress from Nicole's, a red voile dress with tiny blue flowers and ruffles at the neck. Steven told her, smiling, "When you wear that dress, I see you as the mistress of an artist in Paris."

The following week, though, Steven said he thought it would be better if he went to Pomona by himself. From then on, in the middle of every week Tasha returned to the house on Blake Street but she couldn't sleep. She felt empty. She wasn't wanted. She didn't trust Candy anymore, Candy's outpourings of emotion were pure theatrics. And Sara, good God, she was brainy but cold, you wouldn't want to discuss a problem with her. Susie was all right, Susie was like the earth, but all three of them were jealous of her, Tasha thought, "because I had Steven."

When Steven came back, they picked up their life of poetry and music and wine and deep talk and intense love-making, in the course of which Tasha always came and always when Steven did. Then in early April, he told her he needed to spend a whole week at Pomona.

Reluctantly, Tasha moved back to Blake Street, and on Wednesday night, found herself alone. It was spooky, a wind was blowing and the window shades were flapping. She shut all the windows. She hated the house, the horrid green carpet. It was the ugliest place she'd ever lived.

She got in bed with her book of Wallace Stevens but she couldn't concentrate. She couldn't sleep well either. Around midnight, she heard the door open. "Candy?"

Silence. Footsteps down the hall.

"It's me, Sara."

"Oh." She wished it were Candy, but when Sara came in the room she was smiling, she looked like a friend.

"I'm glad you're home," Tasha said. "I had the worst nightmare. I dreamed I saw Steven in a restaurant with another girl, a super attractive blond waif type.

"Sara, what's wrong? Where have you been?"

"The Steppenwolfe."

"You saw him, didn't you?"

Sara hesitated.

"Come on, you've got to tell me! We're like family."

Sara said she had been in the Steppenwolfe with Rob Kagan when Steven had walked in with a blond girl. "I was shocked. I thought he was in Pomona. When he saw me, he came over and said, 'You keep your mouth shut about this or I'll kill you.' He's going to be furious . . ."

Tasha interrupted, "Was she more beautiful than me?"

"No. Of course not." Sara looked strange. Was she lying? Tasha put her hands over her stomach. "My ulcer," and she began to cry. Sara brought her a glass of warm milk and sat on the bed. "How can you stay with somebody who's such a shit? He's not the only person in the world."

The doorbell rang. "Steven." Tasha slipped on a bathrobe and went to the door.

"I want to explain . . ."

"You have nothing to explain!" Tasha hurled a book at him, a book he had given her, Hauser's *Social History of Art*.

The next day they took a drive along the bay. He said he was sorry he had lied, it was stupid, the other girl didn't mean anything. The odd thing is that Tasha remembers feeling pretty that day. As she sat in the sunlight with her legs tucked beneath her, she believed Steven and she forgave him.

But seeds had been planted. Before long, Tasha was picking her way through webs of suspicion, half sentences and choked-back fear. Steven was loving and distant, sentimental and icy. He made her feel she was irreplaceable and that she could never be enough. He told her it was important for a woman to have her own life. If I work hard, Tasha thought, I might someday be interesting.

During Easter vacation Tasha went to Los Angeles. In her dreams she traveled to Scotland and China but at some point in each journey, she saw a cameo of Steven walking down Euclid with another girl. When she returned to Berkeley she made inquiries. Two of her friends had seen Steven with Sandra Jason. Sandra was a distant friend of Candy's, and a year younger than Tasha.

Steven was shocked. How had she found out? Tasha told him her dream. "I don't like it," he said. "I can't do anything without your seeing it in a dream." He took her to a bar on University Avenue where they sat beside a fake log fire and drank martinis.

"You know I love you," he said.

"Then what are you doing with Sandra?"

"Okay, I'll be honest. There's something about her I'm drawn to. I can't help it, I feel terrible about this. I don't want to lose you, but I must have my freedom."

"If you must then you must." Tasha felt her stomach lurch. She was going to have to transcend this. She had to be more than a girl now, she had to be a woman, to push herself into adulthood. Adults have complicated passions. She believed that

Steven loved her, she would focus on the love and transcend everything else.

She and Steven went back to Euclid Avenue and made love with such force, they had caught each other's rhythm as never before. In the morning, Steven kissed her. "You're a real woman," he said. Tasha felt she had won.

So began the Tasha-Sandra period, in which both girls believed they were going with Steven. Each thought she was his woman and he was her man and the other woman was a temporary interference. At other times each believed she had lost.

Sandra had met Steven, as Tasha did, on the Terrace. She didn't like him at all—he was sneaky and greasy. But while Tasha was away over Easter, Steven brought Sandra to Euclid and seduced her with sympathy and cognac and brilliant-sounding talk. The sex was so powerful Sandra was stunned. Steven told her he loved her and believed they were fated. He told her about Tasha. "I can't leave her right now because her father just died and she needs me. Be patient. Give me time."

Sandra began to watch Tasha from afar. She wanted to become invisible and follow her so she could learn everything about her. Sandra thought, if I were Tasha and walked into a room, everyone would look at me and want me.

Tasha couldn't bear being anywhere near Sandra. She thought Sandra was "much better looking than me. She had money. She was secure. She had a good figure and big breasts, so as far as I was concerned I was whipped."

Tasha's friends told her she was crazy to put up with it, but she couldn't imagine being with another man.

Her ulcer started bleeding. She worried about Steven, worried about money, worried about her mother and excelling in the art department so she could win a scholarship to graduate school. The hardest time for her was sunset. She hated being suspended between day and night, with no way to break from one to the other.

When she had been in grammar school, she used to come home and play outside—hopscotch, four-square, Red Rover—until she heard her mother's special whistle. The whistle meant dinner, time to go inside, the day gone and life passing too quickly. She was afraid to go to sleep. Monsters were hiding in the closet or under the bed.

In Berkeley the sunset lasted three hours and they were impossible. "At five, the bells in the Campanile started to ring. At six the libraries closed. I remember heading for home, to Euclid or Blake Street, and either way I'd see people stopping in little stores. Lights going on. Women rattling pans. The big orange sky. The crickets starting up. The whole lengthy performance that nature puts on with the light gradually, gradually changing color and fading. But the sky was never going to turn black. Twilight was going to drag on forever and I was stuck in neither place, the land of day or night."

The affair with Steven was never resolved. He was either living with Tasha and sneaking out to see Sandra or living with Sandra and sneaking out to see Tasha. They never broke up, the emphasis shifted. Steven would lie to Tasha, then he would confess and apologize. "Then he'd do something horrible again, and at any point in the cycle, sex was very good. Some nights we couldn't talk because of the tension but we'd go to bed and sex was incredible. There was heavy oral intercourse, but so tender and well synchronized. I had orgasms without effort, the way I haven't ever since."

She tried, at several points, to leave him, but he would call her and beg, "Please don't hang up. Poems have been pouring out of me and I need you to hear them. It's important, Tasha."

"Don't you dare call again!" Two days later he walked in her bedroom. "What are you doing here?" she said. He was wearing the corduroy coat he had worn the day he had told her she was his ideal woman. His eyes were sad, longing and frightened. "I want to go away with you. I want to get away from Berkeley and all this confusion."

"No you don't," she said. "You like the morass you're in. I can see it in your eyes. You're unwilling to pay prices. If you really wanted to change, you'd go off and face yourself. But you're afraid to be alone. You need an audience for your pain."

"You're right," Steven said, "you've always been right. That's why I want to spend a week with you and talk."

So they went to La Honda to stay at Ken Kesey's ranch while Kesey and his Merry Pranksters were off on a bus trip. They smoked grass and rode horses into the hills, "laughing and telling stories and just kind of rocking. It was so sensual—the smell of the horses and the redwoods, the pinkish sunset, the beauty of the day." When they returned to the cabin they ate everything in sight. They made love and listened to Bob Dylan and Steven read her poems he had been working on. One was about golden eagles at Big Sur. Another was about his mother and was titled, "Evil Is Playing with Possibilities."

"Do you want honest feedback?" Tasha said. "The one about the eagles sounds like Steven Silver writing poetry. I don't like the slick edge. It's eloquent but self-conscious. The one about your mother sounds as if it's coming from a deep place within you."

Steven listened intently. Then he sighed, fell forward and pressed his face into her stomach.

The week they stayed in La Honda, Tasha felt as happy and as nourished by Steven as she had during the first months. They didn't talk about Sandra, Steven's lies or Tasha's needs. She felt hope again—she might win in the end. But when they drove back to Berkeley, Steven dropped her off and went to Sandra's. Tasha didn't cry this time, she was inured. She realized he was thriving on the juggling. "He didn't care that he hurt me, he only cared if he got caught."

In December Steven left for New York for two months to do research for his thesis. He called Tasha and asked her to visit in January. He called Sandra and asked her to visit in February. He asked both of them to live with him in March when he returned. But both knew what was happening now. Berkeley was too small. Tasha resolved to get out.

When Tasha left Berkeley she made a judgment about the place that she believes to this day: "Berkeley was a town full of traps. It was a jungle, all the forest creatures were there, seductive characters who could tempt you to the high roads. You could taste a lot of worlds, go mad in a hundred ways, involve yourself with a million nuts. I involved myself with one."

When she graduated in January of 1965, she left for Paris to study French and relax until graduate school would begin. She stopped over in New York. Steven met her at the airport. She was underweight and anemic "so it was a close time with Steven because I was sick." Steven moped about her going to Europe for so long. She sailed on the *Queen Mary* with her childhood friend, Beth Warren, and for seven days sat on deck, reading Dostoevsky's *The Idiot.*

In London she and Beth found a room in a pension near the British Museum. There was a cranky pay phone in the lobby which rang one morning at five. Tasha was summoned. A transatlantic call. Steven had tracked her down.

"Can't you come back?" he asked.

Tasha said, "It's touching of you to call, but if I came to New York you'd only tell me to turn around and go back to Europe."

"That's not true."

"All right," she said. "If you feel this way in three weeks, call me again."

8. SUSIE

Susie was swept into a completely different world. Early Marx and late Marx. Thomas Paine. Jeffersonian and Hamiltonian democracy. For a year she had been attending a leftist study group with Jeff. It all sounded right. She believed in a moral way but belief wasn't the important thing. Being with Jeff was. And doing all the interesting stuff he came up with. Screenings of films smuggled out of North Vietnam. Baseball games with Old Lefties. Classes on Tuesdays and Fridays in a Victorian church that had pink and green rooms. She was often the only girl and while the men argued about neocolonialism she thought about whether she should defrost hamburger or stop by the Co-op, and if Jeff would want to make love that night and did Jeff's friends think she was too straight, too Los Angeles. She still liked to dress nicely.

She hardly ever spent time with people who were not in Jeff's group, the clique of the movers and shakers. During the shop-in at the Lucky Market, she had felt uneasy throwing food on the floor because nice girls don't mess up stores, but she knew that Jeff and his friends were right. With them she felt special, more moral than everyone else because they were fucking doing something and the others weren't.

In the fall of '64, she was starting graduate school in political science. The house on Blake Street had broken up. Sara had left for New York, and Tasha and Candy had found new roommates for their final semester. Susie wanted to live with Jeff openly, but she still had to make up stories for her mother. What her mother didn't know wouldn't hurt her.

When school started, the mall by Sproul Hall was a circus. Card tables. Leaflets. Shouting matches. Kids who had come back from Freedom Rides were collecting money to send to the South. The university announced it was enforcing a rule banning the use of its grounds for off-campus political causes. Were they crazy? The students wouldn't fold up their tables. On the first of October, a policeman told a student named Jack Weinberg that he was breaking university rules by sitting at a card table collecting money for CORE. Weinberg argued with the cop. A noisy crowd formed.

"You're under arrest," the cop shouted at Weinberg, who went limp and was carried by three police to a patrol car parked on the mall. The crowd followed, chanting, "Release him." Susie let herself move along with them after Jeff. The police and Weinberg got in the car. The door slammed shut.

"Jeff!" He dove in front of the wheels and in seconds, three hundred kids were on the ground. Holy shit! Susie worked her way to where Jeff was sitting and squeezed beside him. "What now?"

The students held the police car immobilized for thirty-two hours, during which Susie ran home for blankets and food and Jeff's notebooks. On top of the car, Joan Baez sang and Mario Savio, a big, shambling, coarse-haired young man who wore a battered sheepskin coat, said, "We're struggling against the same enemy in Berkeley as we did in Mississippi. The enemy—and this is the greatest problem of our nation—is depersonalized, unresponsive bureaucracy."

As Mario spoke, he brought pictures to Susie's mind: the classes she had taken in huge auditoriums. The professors who had never learned her name. The Kafka-like feeling of Sproul Hall itself, with caged windows for filing registration packets and fee cards. Mario was right. The university was a machine.

Mario seemed to have emerged from nowhere to become the spiritual leader of the Free Speech Movement. He stuttered badly but when he faced a crowd, words came in a silken flow. Jeff thought he was one fucking genius of a speaker. Susie thought he was a great man, a prophet. She heard kids compare him to Moses, who had also stuttered. "Mario could never lie," Susie remembers. "He had this morality thing, right and wrong, no compromise on your principles." He inspired universal respect, but by the following spring, Mario was to give up his role in FSM because he believed having a leader made the group undemocratic. Mario dropped out of school, got married, went to England, had a son who was born retarded, returned to Berkeley, drifted through marginal jobs and upon the tenth anniversary of FSM, was reportedly a patient in a mental hospital.

But what he saw in Berkeley in 1964, and the vision he articulated for a generation to follow, was a future in which the only hope for salvation rested with "movements to change America." Mario said, "The 'futures' and 'careers' for which American students now prepare are for the most part intellectual and moral wastelands." He laughed, as everyone did, when Jack Weinberg said, "Don't trust anyone over thirty." He squeezed Susie's arm when Jeff vaulted onto the police car and announced: "This generation sees the world differently than its predecessors!"

A heckler screamed, "Down with beatniks," and hurled a sulphur bomb.

Jeff wiped his eyes with the sleeve of his sweater. "We're supposed to search for the truth at this university but once we find it, we're not allowed to do anything. Well, we don't want to be armchair intellectuals. We're going to speak out and advocate!"

The sit-in around the police car lasted until an agreement was reached between the administration and the protest leaders. But it was not many days before the agreement went sour. Rallies and meetings were scheduled round the clock. Jeff ran from Leaflet Central to Telephone Central to Legal Central and Susie ran with him. FSM was creating its own bureaucracy. Susie could no longer follow the logic, but she felt she was part of a great stream.

The high mark came on December 2. At a noon rally, Mario

told the crowd: "There's a time when the operation of the machine becomes so odious, makes you so sick at heart that you can't take part . . . and you've got to put your bodies on the gears, upon the wheels, upon the levers, upon all the apparatus to make it stop. You've got to indicate to the people who run it . . . that unless you're free, the machine will be prevented from working at all!"

"Stop the machine!" Susie threw her arms in the air. She loved every person in the crowd that moved up the steps and into Sproul Hall. "We're going to stay here until all our demands are met." She had come a long way in a short time, she thought. She was no longer afraid of having a black mark on her record. No one can hurt us, we're all in this together.

Giant placards that said "FSM" were raised in front of the white marble columns. The floors filled wth activities: movies, hootenannies. In dark corners, couples were making it in sleeping bags. Susie and Jeff settled on the second floor with the FSM Steering Committee.

When night came, police locked the doors and draped black cloth over the windows so the students couldn't see outside. It gave them the feeling of being trapped. Some began walking out. Susie spotted Tasha leaving, and later Candy. It figures, Susie thought.

Rumors were flying: the police had tear gas and dogs. At three in the morning, Jeff whispered, "I'll be right back, babe, don't worry." He climbed up a fire escape to the roof, from which he saw floodlights, buses parked in a circle like covered wagons, squads of police trooping across the mall. He raced back to FSM Central and in minutes word was passed: "Go limp." Jeff told Susie, "It's crazy. We're a bunch of students and they're coming for us like it's war!"

Susie covered her ears to drown out the screaming. Jeff was one of the first of eight hundred to be arrested. He thought going limp meant scrunching his body in a ball and flexing with all his might. It took six police to bounce him down the stairs. Hours later, when he spotted Susie at the Santa Rita Rehabilitation Center, he ran up, caught her in his arms and kissed her while an AP photographer snapped the picture. As soon as they were released, they hurried home to see if they had made the evening news. They had.

Within twenty-four hours the national press had arrived. Susie and Jeff were interviewed by *Look* and filmed by a crew from NBC. Susie let Jeff answer all the questions. She was sitting with Jeff and a Newsweek reporter when the phone rang.

"Hey, Jeff, it's Sara! From New York." She said into the phone, "How are ya, kid? Oh, we're keepin' busy." She laughed. "So how's New York? Wait, hold on. Jeff wants to know if you'll organize a support demonstration at Columbia."

Sara mumbled something about the Journalism School being isolated and the kids being ultraconservative. Susie couldn't be bothered. She hung up and the phone rang again, it was always ringing. Now it was her mother in Los Angeles. Mrs. Hersh had seen Susie and Jeff's picture in the paper. "I've been thinking," she said, "isn't it about time that you and Jeff got married?"

"What the! . . . what are you talking about?" Susie said. Had her mother found out they were living together? Did she think Susie was pregnant?

That night when she and Jeff went to bed, Susie told him what her mother had said. Jeff flicked on the light. "Sure, let's get married. We're already living like we're married. Let's do it. Let's buy rings."

Susie scrunched up her face. She felt pleased and all mixed up. She had never thought about marriage. She never thought about the future. She ran on hunches and faith in her own luck, "just plain dumb luck," she once said. "I'm a gambler. I'll calculate the odds and if the risk is within reason, I'll do it."

She said to Jeff, "You really want to marry me?"

"Why not?"

She could not conceive of a reason. Jeff was the brightest star in the history department. He knew important, glamorous people who paid attention to what he said. He wanted to get married. Both their parents wanted it. You were supposed to do this in your life. It felt like there were doubts somewhere in her mind but she couldn't get hold of them.

"We'll still be free," Jeff assured her. "My parents have other lovers. You can have your cake and eat it too."

Susie nodded. She didn't want to sleep with only one man in her life, but she made Jeff promise to wait until she was ready. "Promise me you won't sleep with anyone else until I can handle it."

"I promise," he said. "Oh wow. I've got to move." He jumped out of bed and in his excitement, knocked over the lamp.

Susie told her mother to plan a wedding for semester break in January of 1965. Jeff kept pressing Susie to keep things down and her mother started escalating arrangements until it was a reception for two hundred at the Beverly Hills Hotel. Mrs. Hersh flew north to take Susie shopping and bought her hundreds of dollars' worth of clothes. While having lunch at Magnin's, they had a fight about a wedding photographer.

"I don't want some stranger taking pictures," Susie said.

"Oh, Susie, why do you have to be so extreme. Do this for me, you'll thank me afterward."

Her mother was right. "I'm really glad I have those pictures," Susie told me in 1972 as she dug them out of a bag. In the pictures Susie is wearing a white crepe sheath from the House of Nine, three-inch heels and a veil she had specially made because everything else was too fancy. She is smiling with enormous confidence and her hair is teased in a bouffant.

Jeff is spruced up, wearing a suit. "Doesn't he look kind of like Beaver Cleaver?" Susie said. Her mother, standing beside Susie in the picture, has a look of unmasked fear. But Susie didn't see her mother's face that day. She and Jeff had been preoccupied with their friends from FSM, who had put on nice clothes to look respectable.

That night Susie and Jeff left for a "honeymoon" in Palm Springs. They were supposed to go away together after the wedding but he, she, they didn't believe in all that shit. When they checked into the El Mirador Hotel, Susie felt strange and sort of shy. In her suitcase was a white nightgown her mother had bought her. She looked at it and thought, fuck, man, we don't wear pajamas in bed. But a part of her wanted to wear a lacy nightgown and be romantically initiated. Jeff ordered a bottle of Kahlúa from room service and proposed they celebrate by pouring it on each other and licking it off. Let's just go to sleep, she wanted to say.

The next morning they read the Sunday papers and ate lox and bagels, but the sky was overcast and there was nothing to do but play gin rummy in the room. They almost always played cards before going to sleep. It was the only thing Susie did better than Jeff. He fought hard and cheated but she always beat him, then she had to console him and then they were supposed to make love.

Susie spent a lot of time thinking up excuses not to fuck: having a cold, a headache or an infection; having a test; going to bed early; staying up late. In public, she flirted and made suggestive remarks like a child saying things she knows will titillate the adults. At a formal dinner, she said to a professor who offered her a plate of Camembert, "Doesn't the smell remind you of cum?" Jeff laughed and winked at her. Susie smiled mischievously but inside she felt a stab.

Jeff taught Susie about sex as he had taught her about everything. The second time they made love, he asked if she'd had an orgasm. She had never heard the word. Jeff explained that women have orgasms like men do only women can have more. Susie did not feel anything that matched Jeff's description, but she didn't think to question him. Sex was no different from politics. He was her teacher and she wanted to please him, so she started pretending.

Jeff would begin slowly, then raise himself up on his elbows and move fast. At this signal, Susie would raise her hips and do some moaning. "Half the time I was moaning from pain. I was never turned on, never got aroused, but I didn't believe other women had orgasms either."

Afterward, Jeff would ask, "How was it?"

"Fine." Both of them were afraid to say anything further.

In Palm Springs, the weather stayed cold and it was boring so they flew to Boston to visit Jeff's parents. The Bermans, Paul and Elaine, were infamous in Boston. Paul was a sculptor who cast heads in metal. Elaine taught Oriental philosophy and yoga at

Boston University. They made films together, wrote articles and appeared on local television. The outside of their house looked no different from its neighbors on a cul-de-sac in the suburb of Newton, but the inside was a jungle: beaded curtains, artificial flowers, sculpted heads, thousands of books, newspapers, Polish cinema posters, colored lights, mirrors, pictures of Trotsky, Freud and Rosa Luxemburg.

Because his parents were so wild, Jeff felt luckier than all his friends in Berkeley. For years, people in their crowd agreed that Jeff was the least fucked-up person around. He had never had to rebel against his parents' values. He was not sexually inhibited or burdened with guilt. He was not jealous. He had nearly had an affair with his sister. He did not have bourgeois hangups about privacy, neatness, body odor and hair. He never seemed depressed. He did not talk about what he was feeling but no matter, he was perpetually excited and high.

Jeff's parents welcomed Susie as their daughter and gave her the warm, emotive family life she had never had. While her own mother disapproved of Crossroads Africa, the Bermans encouraged her to live in a Bugandan village, to be a beatnik and go without make-up. The day after Jeff and Susie arrived from Palm Springs, Paul said, "You know how to keep this girl happy?" He put his arms around Susie. "Keep her laid."

When they returned to Berkeley for the spring semester, Jeff and Susie became a showpiece couple. They demonstrated and went to jail together, they did everything together. They were always overscheduled, making plans and changing them at the last minute, having car trouble, rushing in and out of pay phones, grabbing junk food and eating it on the way.

When they came home, Jeff flipped on the television and the radio and buried his head in the newspapers. Susie cooked dinner unless every plate in the house was filthy, at which point Jeff washed dishes while listening to KPFA news. Right after their wedding they had moved into the top floor of a ramshackle house on Ellsworth. Susie painted the floor green and hung bamboo curtains. They used a redwood picnic table for a desk and floor pillows for furniture. The most prominent place in the living room was given to a lithograph Jeff had bought Susie as a wedding present. Susie used to joke, "That's Jeff's idea of our marriage." The print showed a couple standing side by side; both were smiling but the man had an ax stuck in his head.

Susie nagged Jeff about taking a shower, using deodorant, buying clothes and keeping track of checks. He put on a fresh shirt every day and when he came home, stripped and left his clothes wherever they fell. The bedroom was carpeted with dirty clothes, containers of half-eaten food and yellowing newspapers. They never did laundry until everything they owned was dirty; then they rushed to the Laundromat and ran ten machine loads.

Susie was afraid to complain about the mess because Jeff would say she was bourgeois. She didn't want to be bourgeois. If Jeff thought this was how they should live, he was right. He was always right. When they went to a movie, she would pick up his opinion by the time they had left the theater and that would be her opinion.

The times she liked best with Jeff were the walks home from school, when he would rehearse his political speeches for her and there was no possibility of fucking. Jeff liked to hear Susie talk about people. "I'd be catty about other women so he wouldn't sleep with them. He loved it when I would nail people down. He'd laugh and say, 'Oh, babe, you're so right.'" The longer they were together the less she saw of her girl friends. Tasha and Sara were much too conforming. Even Candy was not political enough.

Jeff's male friends envied him because of Susie. They thought she was the most terrific girl in the Movement—sexy, smart, full of fun. But the women complained that Susie was a princess. When Susie and Jeff walked into a room, Susie was sure to break whatever mood existed. She would interrupt, tell stories, clown or organize a game. She didn't listen and was impossible to talk with because she didn't talk, she recited lines.

The only time she kept quiet was when Jeff and his friends were talking politics. One afternoon on the Terrace, they were arguing about whether Bobby Dylan had betrayed them with his new album, "Another Side of Bob Dylan." In "My Back Pages," was he denouncing all his protest songs, saying he was older then and younger than that now?

Susie was thinking about what she'd make for dinner. Jeff had asked Barry and Margie over. "C'mon Jeff," she said, "we gotta go clean up the house."

They went home and began picking up debris. While Jeff was washing dishes, he told Susie he had the hots for Margie, and in fact that very morning Margie had brushed up against him with her enormous tits, and wouldn't it be outasight to get between those legs of hers?

Susie dropped her head. "I wish you wouldn't flirt so outrageously in front of me."

Jeff shrugged. "That's the way I am."

"But it makes me feel bad."

"You can't ask me to be different. I like women, I like having fun with people."

At the dinner table, Susie was silent and did not eat. She was thinking, Margie will be better in bed. Jeff will know I'm a fake.

Barry leaned over and placed a finger under her chin. "Hey," he said. Susie smiled. She had the feeling Barry understood her. He came from back East. He was a grad student in English and he knew how to be still, unlike her loud flamboyant husband. She and Barry had once played with the idea of having an affair in faculty glade some afternoon while Jeff was teaching, but Susie had been afraid. Jeff was talking about sleeping around but he wasn't doing it yet. If she started . . .

The four of them passed around a joint. The Beach Boys were singing on the radio, "Help Me, Rhonda." Barry pulled Susie up and took her in his arms in a mock-formal, ballroom-dancing position. He rocked her back and forth, holding her close. She liked the way his cheek felt against hers. She wished he would kiss her. She wished he were staying, she wished she could wake up beside him. She had a feeling he would be gentle, he wouldn't pound while she lay there enduring it.

When Barry and Margie left, Susie started clearing the table. Jeff said, "Leave all that shit. Let's ball." He pushed inside her and it hurt, it burned. When it was over, she stood up and walked to the kitchen.

"Susie?" he called. "What are you doing?"

"Nothing."

"Are you okay?"

"Yeah." She hugged herself against the cold. What could she tell him? "This is all a shuck. You don't even turn me on. How will I make it through the next fifty years?"

She went back to bed and somehow started screaming. Jeff was scared but he held her. "I love you," he said over and over. "Poor Susie. Listen, we'll skip classes tomorrow! We'll go to the zoo. We'll go to Chinatown. We'll go see five movies. Everything will be groovy."

9. SARA

When I left Berkeley in the summer of '64, I read every book by Negro authors I could find: *Another Country, Black Boy, The Invisible Man, The Fire Next Time.* I infuriated my parents by passing out literature at their bridge parties supporting the California Fair Housing Act. My parents were afraid that if Negroes moved into their neighborhood, property values would drop, and I was contemptuous of their fear. I could not talk with them about Negroes, civil rights, pot or sex or we would end up screaming. I had to pretend I was a virgin, but I was not planning to stick around long.

A summer job in Los Angeles, then a vacation in Mexico, then off to New York where I had a scholarship to the Columbia University Graduate School of Journalism. James Baldwin told me what New York would be like: real ghettos and stoned horn players and men who made love with other men as well as women and interracial couples fucking in the bowels of Greenwich Village. I could hardly wait.

I had no patience for my friends who were still dawdling around Berkeley, suffering from what I thought was failure of will. Like Candy, who postponed graduating a year so she could do more research on the authoritarian personality. Candy wrote me letters every week, describing all the things she wanted to do and the reasons she couldn't do them. "You really are lucky, Sare," she said, "because you are moving and sure of your prospects."

I kept copies of the letters I wrote back to Candy but I never looked at them until I was thirty-two, when I came across the following passage: "I've always been so rational, so damn well adjusted. My problem is that I don't have any problems."

Could I ever have been so cocksure? I remember, only dimly, the girl who wrote those words. This same girl flew to New York in a state of such excitement that she dropped her bags at a friend's and went straight to the Cherry Lane Theater to watch a white woman stab a black man to death in LeRoi Jones's play *Dutchman.*

After the play, I met a friend from Berkeley, Sherry, and we walked across Greenwich Village and over to Little Italy for the San Genaro Festival. Everything was new and thrilling: the smell of sausage sandwiches and cannoli and firecrackers and the crowds in the streets, crowds like I had never seen. Everyone was tilting forward, walking fast, talking fast. There was a tenseness in the bodies and alert pale faces—people looked as if they spent their spare time thinking instead of lying in the sun.

I felt I was luckier than all the other girls who were coming to New York fresh out of college. I had a year to take it easy, learn my way around and make connections so I could get a job writing for *The New York Times.* And I didn't have to live with three people in an L-shaped apartment. I had my own room at International House on Riverside Drive and 120th Street, which was far from the center of town but near Columbia and overlooked the Hudson River.

The room, it turned out, was more like a cell, only five feet wide and painted institutional green. The bed was nothing but plywood covered by a pad. Above the bed was a buzzer. If anyone telephoned me, the buzzer rang and I had to run down the hall to a pay phone where I could talk standing up until someone banged on the door in anger because her buzzer had just rung. But when I ate in the cafeteria, I saw students in turbans. Most of them, I was told, would one day be heads of state.

I registered for classes and looked around the campus. Where was the equivalent of the Terrace? "Where does everyone go to have coffee and hang out?" I asked my adviser. He said he didn't know but it didn't matter because in a few days I would be dizzy with work. "And Miss Davidson," he said as I stood up to leave, "don't expect to walk out of here onto a job at *The New York Times*. You'll have to go out in the hinterlands and prove yourself before you can take New York."

The first day of classes we met in the bull pen, an overheated room with eighty desks on each of which there was a typewriter. The teachers, who were retired newspapermen, stood in formation to deliver our orders. We were to be at our desks by nine each morning, having read all three New York papers and prepared for a news quiz. We would then receive an assignment due at 4 P.M., and at 4, an assignment due at 9 the next morning. We must compose at the typewriter. No time for rewrites. No lunch hour—we should pick up sandwiches across the street at Takome Foods. We should get flu shots immediately at the student hospital because we couldn't afford to miss a day.

Then they passed out city maps and the New York green book —a guide to government agencies. A professor named Schmutter who seemed no bigger than 5'4" and always carried a yardstick jumped on a chair. "Your first assignment is to teach you how to get around the city fast," he said. "You have two hours to get a story." He called the roll and after each name gave a target: Statue of Liberty; La Guardia Airport. After my name he said, "Animal Talent House." I found the place, whatever it was, listed in the phone book and ran down the steps of the school to catch the subway.

Animal Talent House was a theatrical agency for animals. It was a three-story brownstone in which there lived a batty woman along with the Dreyfus lion, the white horse from White Horse scotch ads, a llama named Llincoln, a giraffe and thirty-six other creatures. As I sat in a folding chair interviewing the lady, a sheep dog trotted over and peed on my leg.

By the time I left, it was rush hour and the subway cars were jammed and hot as sweatboxes. The entire subway was permeated by a smell—a stale, noxious, urinal smell. The

screeching of metal on metal was unbearable—I was amazed at
the way New Yorkers could adapt. The businessmen knew how
to fold *The New York Times* in four vertical columns so they
could read it as they rode.

When I reached my desk at the Journalism School, it was ten
minutes before deadline. Schmutter swaggered over. "What's
your story, Miss Davidson?"

"I'm not sure. I saw a nutty lady and got peed on . . ."

Krrrr-rack! He slammed the yardstick on my desk and
screamed, "Go with what you've got!"

I am not exaggerating. "Go with what you've got" was
screamed at us every day. "There comes a point," Schmutter
said, "when the reporter has to stop asking questions, stop thinking and go with what he's got." At 4 P.M he ran around the room
ripping pages out of our typewriters. One girl, a timid creature
from Ecuador, had written nothing. Schmutter stared at her,
then pointed the yardstick and said menacingly, "You . . . froze!
What would happen if you were working for a real newspaper?
There would be a hole on the front page and you would be responsible because you froze."

He turned to the class. "Tonight you will write an interpretive
essay on the effects of congressional reapportionment in Dela-
ware. Five hundred words due at 9 A.M." *Krrr-rack!* And he was
gone.

Our class was a strange, unhappy blend of souls, most of
whom I dismissed as provincial squares except for one girl who
had long hair like me and one boy who had a mustache and a
sense of humor. We did not go out for coffee or smoke grass together. No romances and few friendships grew, probably because the school encouraged a tonglike spirit of rivalry as we
fought each other for the scoop.

On the third day we were sent to a courthouse in Canarsie
where trials dragged on for months and no one understood what
was happening. Schmutter clocked us in and out. "The first person back with the story gets an automatic A and the last person
an automatic F," he said.

The F went to a bony Nigerian named Meregini, who slunk
back after dark moaning, "I got lost on dee subway."

SARA   91

"What! Why do you think we give you maps?" Schmutter said.

Meregini hung his head. "I am a poet," he said. "When dis school is over I am going to run out dee door."

The fourth day we were dispatched through the city to observe President Johnson on a campaign tour. I waited at an intersection for two hours and when the limousine sped by, I dropped my pad and shouted, "There he is!" My display of emotion prompted classmates to snicker. I called up Schmutter in the news room.

"The President drove past Third Avenue and Fifty-ninth Street at 12:16 P.M.," I reported.

"What was the license plate of his car?"

"I didn't get it."

"Why the hell not! You go after that car and get the number, Miss Davidson!"

"Yes, sir!" I said and ran off down the street.

That night on a tour of *The New York Times* I got diarrhea among the printing presses. By Friday of the first week I had a rash all over my body. This was the beginning of a plague of afflictions I suffered all year: bronchitis, vaginitis, pink eye, flus and a sprained ankle from tripping on the ice. I thought my body was being assaulted by a harsh, filthy environment that, growing up in California, I had been completely unprepared for.

My reaction, at first, to the hysteria of the school was anger that I had no time to have fun. Then I decided the year was an investment in my future. It was a test, and I had never failed a test. So I performed like the most sincere aspirant but privately, I viewed each assignment with scorn. There was one other person who shared my feelings, the girl with long hair, a small brunette named Jane who had gone to Brandeis and had beautiful skin and doe eyes. We took to spending our Saturdays together and made jokes at the expense of Schmutter and everyone else. Jane coached me about New York etiquette and clothes. I had never owned a heavy coat and was frightened of winter. After looking for three weeks I bought a bright red coat that had a lining made of fake leopard fur. I was wearing the coat, trundling up Broadway, the first time I saw snow fall. I walked for hours, marveling that the cold wasn't so bad and watching the snow cover rooftops and treetops and listening to the new muffled sound cars made on the street.

"Oh I love New York and can't imagine living anywhere else," I wrote home. I wanted to eat in every restaurant, see every play, drink in every bar and know every block. I trembled when I opened the Arts and Leisure section of the Sunday *Times* because there were so many shows, concerts and ballets I wanted to see and how could I possibly do it all?

I devised a way to go to the theater on school time. We had to write a thesis on some "basic issue in the news," and I would write mine on "Negro playwrights and the race question." Half of our class was writing about Negroes: Negro artists, Negro politicians, Negro families, Negro schools. There were nine plays by and about Negroes in New York and I saw them all. One Saturday in October I took Jane with me to the Village to see *In White America*, and afterward we went next door to the Limelight Cafe. As we were eating ice cream, the star of the play, Moses Gunn, walked in and sat down at a long table. To Jane's astonishment, I walked over and tapped his shoulder.

"Hi, I just saw your play, you were terrific! And I'm a graduate student at Columbia and I'm writing a paper on Negro playwrights and I wonder if I could interview you. . . ."

He put his arm around my waist and told me to sit down and bring my friend too. "This is Peter, that's Earl, Lonne—they all actors and they all no good." Raucous laughter. "And that's Marcus, you oughta go interview him. He'll give you a story. He's havin' his first play on Broadway next month." More laughter. Marcus looked indifferent. As Jane and I were leaving, very late, Marcus said, casually, that we might want to go to a party the next night. "Roi Jones and Jimmy Baldwin will be there and you can talk to 'em. It's a party for the Actors' Studio." He rattled off the address and dismissed us with a nod.

All the next day I thought about Marcus. I broke a date with a nice young teacher from Brooklyn, bought a shocking pink knit dress and washed my hair so it fell shining and straight to the middle of my back. The party was at the Dakota, an elegant old building on Central Park West which, I did not know at the time, has more cachet than any other address on the West Side.

When the elevator opened, there was only one apartment on the
entire floor. Outside the door was a coat rack laden with minks. I
took off my red coat with the fake leopard fur lining and tugged
down my pink dress. Jane thought quite frankly that the dress
was a little too short, but I had already let down the hem.

We pushed open the door and stepped inside. Marcus spotted
us and walked over. He began introducing us, but I didn't hear
the names. I was star-struck. I had stepped into the frame of one
of those glossy photographs I had studied so often—and so long-
ingly—on the backs of magazines, photographs showing a penthouse party where a man is playing the piano and women in
low-cut dresses are breathlessly sipping martinis. At this party in
the Dakota there was indeed a pianist, a Russian who had just
performed at Carnegie Hall and was wearing a tuxedo. And
there was Keir Dullea and the three Limelighters and Mel
Brooks and Anne Bancroft and David Merrick the producer and
who, I asked Marcus, is that woman in the green sweater, she
looks so familiar . . .

"You asshole," he said, "that's Shelley Winters."

At midnight there was a buffet but I was too nervous, I would
spill something, so I just looked at the silver platters of baby
squabs stuffed with wild rice and grapes and the cut crystal
punch bowl filled with chocolate mousse.

Marcus left at 3 A.M. with a blond French actress and I left
with a producer named Marvin because he had an option on
LeRoi Jones's play *The Toilet*. Through Marvin, I figured, I
might get to meet Jones. But when we were in the cab I was
sorry, and even sorrier when we reached his sour-smelling apartment on Christopher Street so I got out of fucking by saying I
had an infection.

"Take me in your mouth," he said.

"I don't like that."

"Shit." He turned over. "Some chicks have weird inhibitions."

I eventually did manage to interview Jones, and Lonne Elder
III and Douglas Turner Ward and Alice Childress and Ossie
Davis and Langston Hughes, but although Marcus gave me
three of his plays to read he was too busy to talk. I kept calling
back. One Tuesday night my buzzer rang at 10:55 (the switch-

board closed at 11). "Okay," he said, "you come down to my place and I'll give you your interview."

"Tonight? It's so late . . ."

"That's right, baby, better catch it while it's hot cus I don' know where I'll be tomorrow."

So I put on my fleece-lined boots and the red coat and trekked through the snow to the subway and waited on the cold platform for the D train to the Lower East Side. Off at Houston Street, which was pronounced "house-ton," I looked both ways for muggers and climbed five flights to a loft with a bare bulb outside. Marcus answered the door in jeans and a T-shirt with holes. He pointed to a chair and gave a disdaining smile. "Now, what choo wanna know?"

I took out my notebook. "What made you decide to start writing plays?"

He tipped his head up and addressed the air. "I won't picket. I'm afraid to go to Mississippi. The theater is my weapon and as long as it serves me I'll use it as deadly as I can."

He sighed and for a moment, dropped his stage voice. "You want to know what made me start writing? I was walking down the street about a year and a half ago and saw a headline that annoyed me." He paused. "The headline said, 'Itinerant Negro Beggar Goes Berserk—No Apparent Reason.'" His voice was low, almost casual. "I went home and wrote a play to show exactly why this nigger, this born loser, goes berserk."

He made coffee for me. "Write this down too," he said. "Most white people feel that if a Negro thinks, he's bitter. What they have to realize is that for a Negro, the results of education is screams and always will be."

I drank two cups of coffee and he drank six beers and then I don't remember how but I was sitting in his lap and we were kissing.

"I have a confession," I said, and told him about my fantasies in high school, how I had wanted to wipe out all the Negroes in the halls.

"You mean all this time you been hatin' spades?"

He laughed teasingly and spent a long time hugging me before he led me down the loft to his bed, a mattress on the floor.

I marveled at what was happening. I had come so far. Does he like me? I wondered. He's seen and done so much. He's really a man, the first man I've met who totally and absolutely dominates me so there's just no question of who has the reins. But God, would I have the nerve to marry a Negro? My parents would flip.

His body was hard, I liked the way it felt although the taste of him was dank. He came with deep groans, and afterward, stood up to get a beer. He drank it down, looked at me and curled his lips in a snarl. "I've had what I wanted, now get out."

I stared at the floor. Of course. I asked for this.

He punched me in the shoulder. "C'monnnnnn," he said and started popping his eyes and slapping his thighs and howling. "I was jes' puttin' you on!"

He fell asleep instantly but I could not, and in the morning I took a cab all the way home. It cost me six dollars and I arrived in class a half hour late, completely unprepared for the news quiz. As I walked to my desk everyone gave me sly glances and I thought, how could they know, until I opened *The New York Times*. On the front page was a picture of faraway Berkeley, the sit-ins at Sproul Hall, the Free Speech Movement. I forgot about Marcus in my frustration. I had missed out by just a semester!

I did not see Marcus again until a year later in Boston. I was a second-string movie critic by then, and had come to review a cheap double bill at the Center Theater where Marcus appeared in a sex-sadism picture in which he played a rapist in the South who gets castrated.

When I recognized him, I nudged the young man next to me. "That's Marcus Scott," I said proudly. "I know him."

III. DAWNING OF THE AGE

1965–1967

10. SUSIE

In Susie's memory, the years from 1965 to '67 are a jumble of meetings, teach-ins, rallies, marches and talk, endless talk. Words were changing so fast. Negroes became blacks. Liberals became scum. God was declared dead. There was a New Morality, a New Journalism, a New Music, a new way of looking at everything and out of it all, a New Left!

Time magazine selected as its Man of the Year for 1966: "the man—and woman—of 25 and under." Even the establishment agreed: anybody young had more important things to say than anybody old. *Time* wrote, "Never have the young been so assertive or so articulate." This was the dawning of the Age of Aquarius and people hustled to get with it. Skirts grew shorter. Hair grew longer. The Youth of America were leaving home.

Jeff Berman was operating, during these years, as a free-lance radical provocateur. He never joined SDS, VDC or any group but he was welcomed everywhere because he possessed a talent for finding a position that many could support. When Jeff rose to take the microphone at a meeting, Susie clenched her fists and hoped he would say the right thing. He always did. He was never booed down and, more surprisingly, never attacked in the

Barb, the *Oracle* or the other underground papers being printed in the Bay Area.

Susie stayed beside Jeff and kept him grounded. She never interfered in political arguments but she thought of herself as the voice of common sense, like Jiminy Cricket. During a candlelight march to the Oakland Army Terminal in 1965, Jeff had turned to her. "What do you think? Should we confront the police or turn back?" The marchers were chanting, "Forward, forward!" But police were waiting in flying wedge formations, and gangs of Hell's Angels—the outlaw motorcycle thugs—were threatening to attack the "peace creeps."

Susie said, "Turn back, Jeff. People will get hurt. I don't want us all to get our heads bashed in."

Susie does not remember what happened next. The Hell's Angels attacked. The marchers scattered. There was another march the next morning or perhaps the next night. The details, like everything she lived through in those years, are blurred, but there is one moment that stands out. One moment is as clear to Susie as if it had happened yesterday.

It was a bright noonday in February. The year was 1966. Susie and Jeff were sitting on the lawn by the Campanile, eating bologna sandwiches from a vending machine. Susie was lettering a sign for a women's peace march: "We don't want to live in a world without men." Jeff nuzzled her neck. "That's nice to know."

Susie sighed. The Campanile bells which had been clanging for fifteen minutes suddenly stopped, and in the vacuum, subtle sounds were magnified: bird cries, insects buzzing, the fall of footsteps on marble.

Susie told Jeff a thought she had been rehearsing for some weeks. "I know I'm where I belong," she said, "but I didn't get here by myself. I didn't evolve. I'm here because of you. I might have gotten here eventually on my own but not as fast. I've skipped some steps along the way."

Jeff let his blue eyes light on her face and rest there, patiently. "It's not important how you got here. Everyone skips some steps at the beginning, when they first become radicalized. What's im-

portant, what's extraordinary, is that you're closing the gap between belief and action."

"I do believe—I know in my head these things are right, but,
oh Jeff, why do I feel so confused? It's like I don't have the
groundwork inside me. I want to help people, and I hate this
war. . . ."

He put his arms around her and told her how proud he was of
her, how much she was growing, what a beautiful woman she
was becoming. He slid his hand between her legs. "Let's go home
and ball."

In June of '66, they went to Provincetown where the Bermans
had a summer home and where Jeff had spent his summers since
he was young. Jeff's mother, Elaine, gave Susie the weirdest
book to read on the beach, *The Story of O*. At night, when Susie
went to bed she could hear Elaine moaning and shrieking in the
next room, "Oh, this is torture. Please, don't stop!"

Jeff put his mouth to Susie's ear and licked it. She rolled over
facing the wall. "I'm tired."

A few days later Susie mentioned to Jeff at breakfast that she
was thinking of getting a tattoo. Jeff dropped his fork. "Wow."
He stood up. "Hey, Mom, listen to this. Susie's getting a tattoo."
He ran around the table and with a whoop, grabbed her above
the knees and lifted her.

The remark had popped from Susie by surprise. In the years
that followed, she could only guess at what had given rise to the
idea. It seemed like a stab, an attempt to make up for a secret
lack. A tattoo might make her what she wasn't with Jeff—turned
on.

That night Susie and Jeff, his sister, Becky, and her husband,
Tom, went to Revere Beach to look for a tattoo parlor. "I was
being a perfect Berman," Susie recalls. "Bermans do crazy
things." They tried three places but in each shop, the proprietor
refused to work on Susie. "Nice girls don't get tattoos," one said.

"Jeff, I don't want to do this, let's go home."

Jeff pulled her down the boardwalk. "Don't listen to that
creep. He's full of bullshit. Let's try one more place. Oh, babe,
it'll look so cool."

So they tried the one more place and found a man who would do it. It was late by now, he wanted to close his shop and hurried Susie to pick a design. She thought she wanted a tiny daisy over her heart, but he had no small flowers.

"Here's one," Jeff said, flipping to a rose in bright red and green ink.

"It's too big, I don't like it."

"Come on, it doesn't matter that much."

Susie undid her blouse. Jeff, Becky and Tom stood together watching. Susie didn't make a sound. It hurt and seemed to take an awfully long time. She felt nauseous. She hadn't known it would bleed. At home in Provincetown, Jeff took her to the bathroom, unbuttoned her blouse and murmured, "Incredible." Susie wriggled away. "I hate it. It looks like something from the funny papers."

The rest of the summer she would only wear bathing suits that concealed the tattoo. Jeff moped and Susie began to feel guilty for making him feel bad. So one morning, before he was awake, she started stroking him. When they had finished making love, he was back in high spirits.

Dr. Annis, a silver-haired lady psychiatrist at the Student Health Service, smiled across the room at her new patient, a slender girl with long brown hair parted in the center and pulled back in a barrette. Many of the students who came in these days wore work shirts and jeans, but this girl had on a fresh white blouse, a black skirt that outlined her hips, nylons and neat black pumps. Her face, the doctor noted, had a wounded look.

"What is it that brings you here?" Dr. Annis asked.

Susie took a deep breath. She was not having orgasms. Everybody else seemed to be having a ball with sex. Everybody else thought she was. She wasn't. Every day, it seemed, there was some nude wade-in at the fountain. Susie had a model husband. She was doing well in graduate school. When it came to sex why was she so dead and dry?

She returned to see Dr. Annis once a week for the next four months but they didn't talk about orgasms. They talked about Susie's insecurity and her feeling that she was always empty or anxious. Empty was blank. Anxious was the hyper nervous wired crazy state, when it felt like she had a battery in her stomach that made her talk fast, laugh a lot and run fast.

After each session, she walked down the brick steps of Cowell Hospital to find Jeff waiting for a detailed report. Susie told him everything but the part about orgasms. He had read all of Freud's writings and could analyze neurotic symptoms although he didn't apply any of it to himself. He once said his inner life was a swampland he didn't want to get stuck in. When Susie tried to tell him about feeling anxious, he listened dutifully but she felt he had one eye on the clock and an ear turned to the radio news. "Do you understand at all?" she asked. "I feel like I'm shouting across a gulf."

He shook his head. "I don't know. Maybe I'm just more interested in historical forces than the mysteries of the soul."

Jeff and Susie had begun, during this period, to have brief affairs. Jeff had been first. At a party, he had watched a black girl from Oakland dancing to "Wild Thing." He had told Susie, "Shit, you know how long I've wanted to ball a black chick. What do you say?" Susie shrugged. She couldn't hold him back forever.

The next week when Jeff flew to Chicago for an SDS conference, he scribbled a note to Peter DuBrow on the back of a leaflet they had written together. "Dear Peter, I'm going away for a few days and if you and Susie want to keep each other company, that's cool." Most guys wouldn't have the guts to sleep with Susie without Jeff's consent.

When Jeff and Susie returned from their sexual adventures, they assured each other it had not been all that great. Everyone else seemed fucked up. All their friends' relationships were fucked up and weren't they lucky to have worked things out so well? Their marriage was like a circle that could encompass other people but the circle would never be broken.

Over Thanksgiving, they drove to the Big Sur Inn to be alone. It had been Susie's idea. They stayed in the Franklin room which had a Franklin stove and a window looking out on the redwoods, but no window glass so it was cold. The waiters in the dining room were young beatniks who played chamber music during meals. But it was funny, once Susie and Jeff took themselves away from all the demonstrations, meetings, movies and news shows, they didn't know quite what to do. They played gin, took a nap, made love, had dinner, lit the Franklin stove and Jeff started to undress Susie again. She moved his hand away.

"What's the matter?"

"I don't feel like it."

"You never seem to feel like it anymore."

"Well maybe if there weren't all this pressure . . ."

"What pressure?"

"You keep saying you want to fuck twice a day."

"I thought that's what you wanted too."

"I know." She didn't dare look at him. "But I haven't really been . . ." She stopped. "I haven't been liking it that much."

Jeff's face was wiped by a look of shock.

"No, listen, that was in the beginning. It hurt. I was afraid. It's just that if we could take things easy . . ."

He started to cry.

She was stricken with dread. She couldn't bear to see him crumble. "Please, let's make love now. Okay? Please, I *do* want it now, Jeff." She had to patch it up. It was a small price to pay: her sexuality for this lovely man. She could do a lot worse. Few women had orgasms anyway. This would be her secret she would carry to the grave.

STRIKE! On the first of December 1966, thousands jammed the ballroom of the Student Union and voted to strike. All week, navy recruiters had been manning tables on campus but when students had set up a table for antidraft literature, the police had been called. Heads had been cracked and twelve students arrested.

"Student Power" was to be the new slogan. As the meeting broke up, the chairman cried, "Implementation! Okay, you guys, let's get it together." People signed up for committees: leaflets, publicity, artwork, sound. Susie recalls, "There was always some jerky guy who'd been an electronics freak since he was little and he would take charge of the sound system." Jeff was appointed head of the leaflet committee and Susie was to organize a tele-

1. March for Free Speech, Berkeley, 1964. Mario Savio is in front, second from right. The leaders decided to wear suits and ties to make a favorable impression on spectators. (Oakland Tribune Photo)

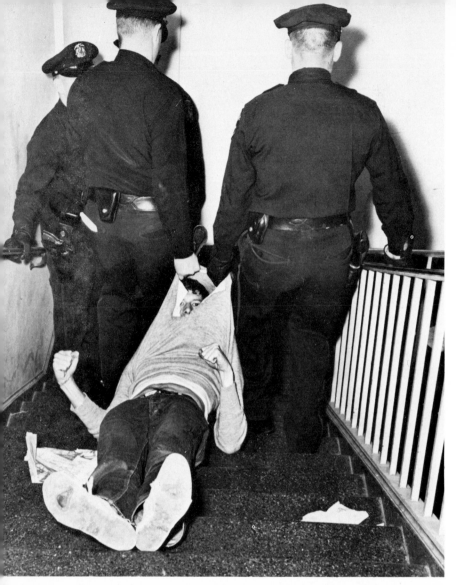

2. More than eight hundred were arrested after the sit-in at Sproul Hall, Berkeley. Susie and Jeff Berman, like the unidentified young man above, were bumped down the steps and into paddy wagons. (Oakland Tribune Photo by Jim Edelen)

3. Joan Baez and Bob Dylan, 1963. He sang about a battle outside that was ragin' in "The Times They Are A-Changin'." (© Jim Marshall)

4. The first Mass Marches to End the War in Vietnam, 1965. I covered
the march in Cambridge for the Boston *Globe*. (Peter Simon)

5. Susie and Jeff were marching in Oakland, where they were stopped by police and attacked by Hell's Angels. (Oakland Tribune Photo by Keith Dennison)

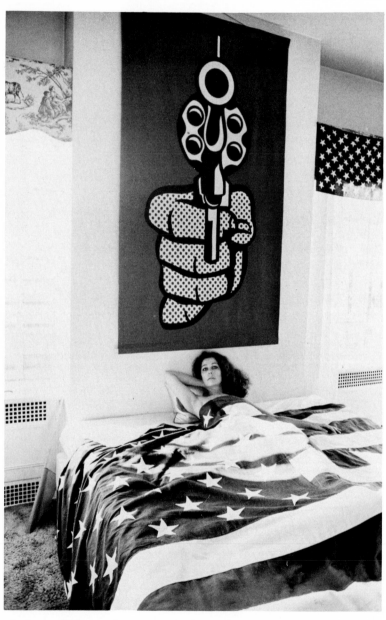

6. Art could be anything in 1965, when Tasha started working in a New York gallery. Above, Ultra Violet in a flag-covered bed under a Roy Lichtenstein wall hanging. (David Gahr)

7. The party never stopped; Andy Warhol was everywhere; people dressed themselves up to make the news. (© 1976 Fred W. McDarrah)

8. Allen Ginsberg at the Human Be-In, a Gathering of the Tribes at Golden Gate Park, San Francisco, 1967. (© Jim Marshall)

phone campaign to call up students and ask them to boycott
classes.

At noon the next day, Susie stood on the balcony of the Union
and looked out on a sea of cheering bodies. A twenty-foot
banner proclaimed, "Happiness Is Student Power." The Rolling
Stones sang from speakers, "Time is on my side, yes it is!" There
was a crack of thunder and rain poured down, but the crowd
packed in. Susie remembers feeling it was one of those moments
when the masses come together. "We were the student body
presidents, the *crème de la crème* who were supposed to inherit
the system. Only when it came time to step into power, we
would change everything."

Jeff said over the microphone: "We're giving notice today, all
of us, that we reject the notion that we should be patient and
work for *gradual change*. That's the old way. We don't need the
Old Left. We don't need their ideology or the working class,
those mythical masses who are supposed to rise up and break
their chains. The working class in this country is turning to the
right. Students are going to be the revolutionary force in this
country. Students are going to make a revolution because we
have the will!"

Susie felt goose bumps. The bodies surged in a burst of ecstasy
and it was her husband who was standing there doing it to them.
For the first time in ages she wanted to make love.

As the strike moved into its third day, however, it became
clear that students would have no allies in their fight. The faculty voted not to support the boycott. "The liberals betrayed us,"
Jeff said angrily.

Kids were starting to cross picket lines because they had to
take finals. Christmas was coming up. The strike leaders debated: should they keep up the fight and risk massive defections
or call it off and try to save face? They bickered. In the past,
they had always been able to hammer out a position to present
to the kids, but this time they were deadlocked. Jeff proposed
something radical: an open microphone. Let anyone who wanted
to step forward and talk.

The result was amazing. At a mass meeting in the Life Sci-
ences Building, a stream of people came before the microphone

to say the same thing: the battle isn't over. We may concede now but there will be another round. After three hours of testimony the crowd felt stoned. Instead of closing with "We Shall Overcome," they grabbed hands and sang the chorus to "Yellow Submarine." They would not use a black song, they would use their own culture, the youth culture.

Leaflets for the next day pictured a yellow submarine and said, "This is an unexpected symbol of our trust in the future and our longing for a world fit for all of us to live in." It was signed, "We love you." On the back was a yellow mask that people could cut out and wear to class.

Jeff and Susie wore the masks all day. Susie remembers, "It was like saying, fuck you, you're not gonna get us. We'll call off the strike but we'll wear masks like outlaws. We're outrageous and wild. We'll outlive you all."

The leaders, the heavies, now realized they had absolutely no idea how they were going to change the system. To find out, they would have to blow their minds.

January 14, 1967. Blow their minds! When Jeff and Susie saw the posters for the Human Be-In, "A Gathering of the Tribes at Golden Gate Park," they knew the time was right. They would go with Barry and Margie and take LSD. Their first acid trip. All the way in one day.

On the morning of the Be-In, this is the scene: Jeff slips on a pair of clown pants that bag around his spindly legs, a green flak jacket and a Liverpool cap. He keeps telling Susie he wants her to look outrageous. She wears red granny glasses and wraps a lace tablecloth around her as a shawl but she feels a little silly.

Margie arrives wearing black leotards with a pink feather boa. When they reach the Polo Field, the four of them place blue tabs under their tongues.

"How long will it take?"

Barry is the expert. "Half hour, maybe more."

Even before the drug comes on, the scene looks spinny. People dancing on the grass. Allen Ginsberg all in white, chanting OM. Hell's Angels parked about the stage like gunmen, guarding the sound equipment. The Angels and the hippies are friends now, thanks to Ken Kesey who convinced the Angels that both groups are outlaws from straight, washed America.

Susie notices a buzzing in her head. Girls with bare, jiggling breasts are carrying babies on their backs. Balloons, soap bubbles and hair, hair everywhere! Astrology, tarot, leather capes, Grateful Dead, Sufi dancing, body painting, Hare Krishna Hare Krishna.

Jamming on stage are a succession of rock bands with names that must have been conceived while tripping: the Freudian Slips; Big Brother and the Holding Company; the Hedds; the Chosen Few; the Jefferson Airplane; the Electric Train; A Sopwith Camel; Earth Mother and the Final Solution; Moby Grape; the Only Alternative and his Other Possibilities.

A lull in the music. Timothy Leary ascends the stage and chirps, "What I have to say can be summed up in six words: turn on, tune in, drop out!" What's happening? Susie thinks she is hallucinating. Before her walk twelve men dressed in tuxedos and each of them has the same face. They pass, turn around and snake by her again, but this time the first man stops in front of her. She is scared. He is taking off his face! No, it's a mask. They're all wearing masks. The face turns out to be Rob Kagan. His eyes are all twinkles. Susie bursts into tears.

Incense and marijuana. Kittens popping out of a basket. So many funny hats: porkpies, stovepipes. A black man in a loincloth is juggling yellow balls. A toy collie leaps up and catches a ball in his mouth. The crowd slithers and laughs. They are passing around food, crusts of sourdough bread, oranges and jugs of wine. Everyone is photographing everyone else. Flash. Flash. Flash. A man in trunks is boxing to the music. Mimes in whiteface are flouncing through the crowd. The scariest is a girl with black spider hair and a comb of red feathers like a rooster's on top of her head. Here she comes, look out! Jeff! We gotta get out of this place.

Back in Berkeley, safe in Barry and Margie's house, Susie lies on the rug, shuts her eyes and sees a picture of the plane crash that killed her parents so many years ago. It is a picture that is usually censored from her mind, but the censor isn't working and the picture springs up. She sees her mother all smiles at the airport. The black funeral car. She wriggles and screams, "Mommy, Daddy," but in some recess of her mind, she knows it's safer to cry for her parents than talk with Jeff about what's wrong.

Barry and Margie nurse her through it, resentful that as usual, Susie is hogging the stage. Jeff is sitting close by but not listening to his wife. He feels one with the struggle of the people of the world. He wants to go back to the park and wash everyone's hands. The people with their hands can build a better world, a socialist world. He weeps from joy.

The next day, Jeff tells Susie he had thought taking acid would be like going to the circus and watching pink elephants. What amazed him was that the show happened inside. Susie does not say this but she had been afraid that the drug would be like truth serum. She is relieved, her secret is safe.

1965. Tasha was in Paris when she learned she had been refused the scholarship to Columbia. What a huge, huge blow. She couldn't afford to pay $3,000 for tuition at Columbia when she could go to Berkeley for free.

But she couldn't go back to Berkeley. She was fed up with the art department, the incestuous community, the endless sunset and most particularly Steven Silver. She wanted a new life. She thought of Paris, London, Rome, New York. That was where the jobs were. She decided on New York. She would mix it up with the art world for a year, have a fling and then go back to graduate school.

In September she packed a suitcase with clothes and mementos: a water jug she'd bought in Casablanca on her first trip to Europe when the boat stopped there; her pillow; poetry books —she didn't go anywhere without Wallace Stevens—a picture of her father and a list of thirty people to call.

She flew into Kennedy Airport alone and took a taxi to what sounded like an address on Mars: 333 East Thirty-fourth Street, where she was met by a friend of her mother's, Iris Lawson. Everything in New York looked fabulously strange. The colors were brown and gray: brown buildings, brown stone. There was green in Central Park but it was an old green, a green that contained insects and secrets.

The day after she arrived, Iris told her about an apartment opening up in a rent-controlled building across the street. Tasha hurried over to see it. She had to climb four flights of stairs where moths and spiders made their home. She opened the door and found a railroad flat: one room after the other with no doors separating them. From the outside hall you stepped into the kitchen, then you hit the bedroom, then you walked through the bedroom into the living room which had a window looking out on a brick wall. The floor was covered with greasy linoleum, and the walls had seven layers of paper and paint. It was dark as a cave.

Tasha took the apartment. The rent was sixty dollars a month and she was lucky to find it. The first thing she did was pull up the linoleum. "Underneath it was the whole cockroach army of New York. I ran to the hardware store and bought Black Flag, covered my face with a scarf like a bandit and sprayed. Then I left and stayed with Iris. When I came back I found the corpses. Ugh! I swept up hundreds, then I started on the walls."

She bought gallons of white paint to blitz the place. Iris gave her dishes, old furniture and a cot on which she slept in the living room. It was grim, but she was being brave, "like a pioneer lady." The place was so dark she had to call up the weather to find out if it was sunny or if she needed a coat. But it didn't matter, she was only going to be there a year.

She made the rounds of museums and galleries looking for a job. She had a special outfit for job interviews: an olive green straight skirt by Ardee of California; an olive green cotton blouse with no collar, long sleeves and a zipper down the back; and a pair of lapis lazuli earrings. With her rosy tan and long blond hair, she looked like Miss California "and I was playing that to the hilt. People would ask, 'Did you go to Sarah Lawrence or Vassar?' I'd pause and say dramatically, 'Berkeley.' That was a turn-on. They'd come out from their desks and ask if I knew Mario Savio and had I been arrested at Sproul Hall?"

She met dozens of people who took her number and called her, not for jobs but for dates. Then she heard there was an

opening at the Hilda Carson Gallery. She put on her olive green
outfit and hopped on the subway. The gallery was in an elegant
old brownstone on East Sixty-fourth Street, but the opening was
for a receptionist. All right, she thought, I'll be a receptionist for
a year. She was told to wait in Hilda's private office. The room
was glossy white and decorated with paintings by De Kooning,
Jasper Johns and Mark Rothko. Tasha posed herself in a Mies
Van Der Rohe Barcelona chair. The phones on Hilda's desk
began to ring. A half hour passed. The phones rang and rang. Finally in walked Hilda, carrying a minah bird in a cage.

Hilda was a stiltlike woman in her late fifties, who kept her
gray hair cropped short and bright lipstick smeared unevenly on
her lips. She was wearing a wrinkled Davidow suit, alligator
shoes and nylons in which there was an unsightly run. Her voice
was like a parrot's.

"Hello," she trilled. "You're not aggressive enough for this job.
I rang the phone in your office and you didn't pick it up." She
plunked the cage on the desk and the bird squawked. "I rang it
to see what your phone voice was like."

Tasha stared back at Hilda. "You're wrong. I didn't answer the
phone not because I'm not aggressive enough but because I have
good manners. I don't work here yet. This isn't my office. I have
no business answering that phone."

Hilda narrowed her eyes. "Maybe you are aggressive enough."

She asked about Berkeley and Tasha's major. Finally she said,
"We-el, we'd like to have you work here. But you know, most
girls work here for nothing, just for the experience."

"That couldn't be me," Tasha said. "I have to support myself."

"We-el," Hilda said, "we'll pay you sixty-five dollars a week."

Tasha figured: since her rent was sixty dollars, it would work!
She started the next day. "I acquired an instant life—four hundred friends, none of whose last names I knew. I went to every
opening, loft party and underground film. I kept busy every
night because I couldn't stand my apartment and couldn't bear
being alone."

There was, in 1965, a rush for newness in the art world. Art
could be anything: Campbell's soup cans; Brillo boxes; hot dogs
made of plaster of Paris; a blank canvas in front of which a live

woman sneezed. It was mad! It was fabulous! Every day brought something new. Pop Art, Op Art, put-ons and camp. Splashy openings at Castelli's and the Jewish Museum. *Paris Review* parties. "The party never stopped," Tasha says. "On Tuesday nights, my 'friends' and I would go in a gang from gallery to gallery, drinking wine and taking pictures of each other."

The people at the openings were dressed to make the news. Rich ladies competed for attention by wearing pop clothes made out of flags or lunch pails or chain mail. Andy Warhol and his superstars would show up, sallow-faced, wearing black leather suits and carrying whips. At churches in the Village, Charlotte Moorman played the cello topless and Yoko Ono staged her happenings.

What Tasha loved about New York was that there was no twilight. Night fell like a curtain. She walked out of the gallery at six and it was black. "Nothing stopped. You continued moving as fast as during the day. I never felt suspended until the next morning."

She was taken up by a group of young artists from different countries. When one of them had a show that sold out, he threw a party and the whole gang ate well. Most of them lived in lofts. A loft was an entire floor of an industrial building. You had to ride up in a freight elevator and use a bathroom in the hall, but the loft was an undivided space where the artist could work, assemble sculptures, cook and sleep. They were super for parties. They held hundreds of people, and there was always a scruffy band of film-makers shooting 16-mm movies of it all. The characters were fantastic: men in bedouin robes, Russian countesses who carried turtles in their pockets, young painters on the skids running hashish from Tangiers. "I can't get no . . ." Mick Jagger sang from loudspeakers, "no no no . . ." girls in feathers and slouch hats who had long necks and stuck their pale heads in the air like cranes . . . "no satisfaction!"

Saturday was the busiest day at the gallery. It was the day the Beautiful People came out to promenade up and down Madison Avenue, ducking into galleries where they met absolutely everyone they knew: socialites, actresses, wives of politicians, fashion designers, hairdressers, interior decorators, writers for *Art News* and photographers for *Women's Wear Daily*.

On fall days, the avenue was bathed in ocher light. Everything in the shop windows looked rich and golden and the light made it richer. There were Bokhara rugs, Louis XV chairs, crewel pillows, Fabergé Easter eggs, Florentine leather bags, French patisseries, boxes of brilliant red fraises des bois, truffles, grouse flown in from Scotland and oils by Degas and Renoir.

The ladies strolled in Pucci dresses, Gucci shoes, black mink, Chanel bags and gold bracelets from Van Cleef and Arpels.

"Tamara!"

"Marsha!"

They called as they passed.

Tasha sat at her desk near the front window, and her face in the ocher light was what most people noticed before they looked at the paintings or each other. She welcomed customers and showed them around. It became apparent very fast that she was a good saleswoman. She had warmth, believability and this golden emanation. Customers invited her to have lunch in their penthouse and help decide where the new painting should be hung.

One Saturday in November, she awoke in her dark room on Thirty-fourth Street and thought she would try to sleep a little longer. As she drifted back under she heard a voice, "Someone will ask how much you are today."

She got up, made coffee and took the subway uptown. About noon, she saw two men in British suits.

"Gregory!"

"Gustav!"

They embraced, touched cheeks and kissed the air. The one called Gregory asked Tasha about a new artist. She led him upstairs. He stood in front of a canvas a moment, then fixed an appraising eye on Tasha. "You've told me about the price of the painting, but how much are you?"

She blanched.

"Are you all right?"

"I knew that remark was coming today."

He took a silver box out of his pocket. "How old are you?"

"Twenty-two."

He opened the box and held it so she could see the cache of thin pink pills inside. "I was exactly your age when I developed epilepsy. Before I did, I used to have déjà vu experiences. I suggest that you have yourself checked."

Tasha said curtly, "I don't have epilepsy," and turned her back. "I'm sorry, I can't help you anymore."

As the afternoon progressed she felt sicker and sicker. That night she went to a happening at Judson Memorial Church. She was sitting between two men, neither of whom she knew well. Pictures of limbs and entrails, rice paddies and green berets were flashing on overhead screens. Lights swung on and little mirrors were passed around. Tasha held up the mirror. Her face looked green. She asked the man on her right, "Is my face green?" He laughed and said no, how absurd. She looked again. "It was white with an apple green tint," she recalls, "and my lip was truly quivering. I hadn't been drinking or smoking. It wasn't the lights. It was a picture of me that was not visible to anyone else."

She started to reread *The Idiot*. November was the season of her father's death and Kennedy's assassination. The previous November she had had heart pains and shortness of breath. She had gone to have an EKG, convinced she was having a heart attack. This November she worried that she would have an epileptic fit on the subway and no one would know to stick a pencil in her mouth.

What disturbed her was that "everyone saw me one way and what I saw in the mirror was so different. On the outside, I'd succeeded brilliantly. I should have felt good but I felt lousy. It didn't add up to meaning anything. The friendships were shallow. The job had no substance. I was sleeping with six men, which was not my style. Nobody was close to me. I could have died on the subway and no one would have cared."

When she sat at her desk she used to stare, sometimes, at a man who ran a gallery across from Hilda Carson's. She learned his name was Bob Goodson. She recalls, "I thought he was super attractive and very married." One Saturday she saw him in Central Park with his wife and two small children. They were sprawled on the grass, wearing Shetland sweaters, listening to a Puerto Rican steel band. Tasha felt a pang. She wished she had a family and a husband like Goodson.

Instead of a family, she had romances: with a painter from Argentina, a Dutch sculptor and a novelist from Brooklyn who was an inpatient at a psychiatric hospital. He drank too much but he seemed to understand Tasha. He knew about faces in the mirror. "What I remember most about those men is their work—talking about their work—and the way we ate." The novelist took her to Italian restaurants in the Village. "He had an interesting brain but what a slob." The Argentinian was built like a bull, hyperexcitable and lusty. "The best sex was with him although his work was the least interesting."

The Dutch sculptor lived in the Chelsea Hotel. Tasha liked him the most. "There was a wholesomeness about him and his bright wood sculpture." His best friend was a Dutch novelist who was going wth Betsy Johnson, the hot young designer for Paraphernalia, the hottest new boutique on Madison. The four of them would meet in the Don Quixote bar of the Chelsea, which was a zoo: people popping acid into strangers' drinks. They bought sandwiches and beer and ate them on the roof of the hotel, or else they went to Max's Kansas City.

Tasha was at Max's three or four nights a week. Max's was a hangout where artists could eat for free by trading their work with the owner. Tasha would go with one of her boyfriends around 9 and at 2 A.M., they would still be there, buried in noise and smoke. "I loved it. I'd get butterflies when I walked in, wondering who'd be there and who we'd end up sitting with." She had a handful of little dresses from Paraphernalia that she liked to wear with patterned tights and high boots. She was taking birth control pills and her body was changing. "I developed breasts, I had a voluptuous little figure."

She wrote Steven Silver chronicles of what she was doing and how fabulous it was. He wrote back, "I want to hear about your inner landscape." She whipped him a typed note: "My inner landscape has a lot to do with my outer landscape. As usual, Steven, you're the master of the eloquent phrase but it doesn't add up to meaning much."

She was swinging between feeling lost and trembling and feeling she had the world by the tail. At work she was responsible
for so many sales that the older staff began to snipe behind her
back. Hilda liked to pit people against each other. At staff meetings, she placed the minah bird on her finger and said to its beak
in her singsong, "I have too many people working here. I can't
afford this many employees." She scanned the table with her
squinty blue eyes and stopped on Tasha. "I hear that you don't
type very well."

Tasha said, "I don't type all that well but you don't pay me
that goddamned much. In fact I was thinking of asking you for a
raise." The next week her pay check was ten dollars higher.
Tasha knew that "if you barked back at Hilda she loved it. I
think she loved me very much."

Tasha applied to Berkeley for graduate school the following
year, but she had an idea. She wanted to set up a graphics department, to open a new world of collecting for young people
who could afford to spend $200 but not $2,000 for a work of art.
At the time, none of the major galleries had graphics depart-
ments.

By the spring of '66, Tasha's railroad flat was brightened by oil
paintings, sculpture, drawings and water colors given to her by
the men she was seeing and artists in the gallery. She had people
up for brunch every Sunday. There were Italian markets near
Thirty-fourth Street where she bought butterfly cookies dipped
in powdered sugar to set out in a basket with flowers. She liked
to cook scrambled eggs with fresh herbs and serve them with
"Tasha's super-duper stuffed tomatoes," smoked fish and Colom-
bian coffee.

On Easter Sunday she invited one of the older sculptors at the
gallery, Mark McCall, to come with his wife and daughters. It
was an impulse. Mark did not fit in with her crowd. He and his
wife, who was a painter with another gallery, wore fur coats and
bought first-class airline tickets. Tasha's friends hung out in jeans
and found Mark and his work both unctuous and phony.

Mark arrived with a gift of Easter cakes from Little Italy.
While his wife, Roberta, sat pretending to be relaxed on the bol-
stered bed, Mark watched Tasha break eggs. He clasped his

hands. "Roberta, come in here and look at Natasha. Doesn't she remind you of the women we saw in the Caucasus? It's true, Natasha, there's something magnificently Russian about you, in spite of your fair coloring."

Tasha brushed her hair off her face. "My grandparents were Russian. And you're right. There's a heavy peasant slob in me who loves schmaltzy sentiment and a good sobby book and corny violin music and heavy soup."

She laughed. It sounded like the ringing of triangles. Mark laughed with her which set her off higher. Mark didn't look so pompous when he laughed.

He asked her to do some work for him in exchange for which he gave her sculpture. Keep track of his mail while he was in Paris, type lists and make inventories. Order new metals.

When Tasha stood before one of Mark's pieces, she wanted to be silent. She thought his constructions were records of powerful struggles, as if an arrow had been shot or two cougars had fought and the metal and worn-away stone recorded the impact.

When Mark was in town, he took Tasha out for lunch and long walks. He could cover the same block every day and each time, spot a detail that inspired him: the carving on a window, the arch of a dog's paw, a slit of sunlight seen between skyscrapers. He was always finding omens and interpreting signs. He fished a worn tool out of a trash can and said it meant the end of a cycle. He and Tasha liked to rummage in thrift stores like Mary Tarsh's, where he bought her a set of eight blue place settings. "He figured I was a rich girl trying to live the down life. He didn't realize what a big deal it was for me to have dishes that matched."

Tasha still didn't like his stagey manner but she was warming to his spirit. The crackle of energy when he walked. The eyes of ocean blue which never stopped seeking and sorting. The texture of his hair, thick and prematurely silver.

One Monday, which was the day the gallery was closed, he came by her apartment for some papers. They drank wine. He kissed her hair. She was excited and repulsed. She moved across the room. He moved right after her. There was a willfulness about him that made her bend, but with annoyance. He was married. He was exactly twenty years older than she. Tasha didn't like the way she felt afterward.

The next time he came over she said, "Look, what happened last week was a one-shot deal. Let's not repeat it."

He agreed, and they resumed their lunches and walks as friends.

12. SARA

After my year at Columbia, it had not been easy to find a job. Most newspapers and television stations did not want to hire women reporters. They had reasons: women would quit to get married; women couldn't be sent out alone at night or into the ghettos; women couldn't carry heavy equipment. I sent off a hundred applications and was offered three jobs: in Portland, Oregon; Sarasota, Florida; and Boston. I picked Boston because it was closest to New York and because Candy would be living there.

Candy had just married Bobby Moss, a graduate student at Harvard. They had been friends all their lives and in June, without warning, friendship had turned to love—magical love that set them apart from all others. When they had called me with the news, I felt devastated.

I envied Candy for her bright, devoted, funny, lovable husband. Yet I knew she envied me for my work, my adventures. She often edited my articles and she shared my nervous anticipation the night before I began my job as a reporter at *The Boston Globe*.

I was to work on the night staff, from 2 to 10 P.M. I wore a tailored blue suit and pinned my hair on top of my head so I would look older than I was—twenty-two. I found, my first night, that I was the only female in the city room, except for a woman named Selma Moran about whose temper I had been warned. I liked being the only girl, the exception. I was also one of the few people not of Irish Catholic descent, I discovered, as I met Claffey, Connolly, Doyle, Driscoll, Healy, Murphy and Monahan. When I picked up the phone to take an obituary, I could absolutely not understand the caller. "Mash-field," he said, which turned out to be Marshfield, and "Bill-a-rick-a," which was Billerica, and "frappe," which was a milkshake. I studied a map of Greater Boston. The towns had names like gray mashed potatoes: Mattapan, Milton, Dedham, Dorchester, Scituate, Braintree, Belchertown.

I typed the obit and took it to the desk, then waited for someone to scream or bang a yardstick. A half hour passed. I watched the city editor, Charlie Claffey, who had a pale and moonshaped freckled face, read it and toss it in a basket.

"Was that okay?" I asked nervously.

He looked at me as if that were the silliest question he had heard.

My next story was a suicide. "Call our man at police headquarters and see what he's got," Claffey said. I called our man, Minihan, who said, "All I know is, he's still alive."

But no, I said, he died at six o'clock.

"He did, huh? Well, you scooped me kid." Minihan said he'd check on it and call me back. Two hours later I called him back. His voice was slurred: "All I know is, hessh shtill alive. . . ."

That night, a group of reporters took me to dinner at Pete's, a newspapermen's hangout downtown. Pete's had red checked tablecloths and good cheap food and martinis that came in a water glass and cost fifty cents. So many of the foods were new to me: Boston scrod, steamers, quahogs, "chowdah." The men coached me about how to pad an expense account and how to talk to priests and police sergeants. What surprised me was how much of the time they spent sitting around, playing cards, reading mystery novels and griping when Selma Moran was given crack assignments like the trial of the Boston Strangler just to keep her out of everyone's hair.

My second week at the *Globe,* the new managing editor, Ian
Menzies, called me into his office. "Tell me about yourself," he
said. "What are your interests?" I told him I was interested in the
new student political groups. "Good idea for a story," he said.
"Tell Claffey I've given you a week to do research."

The story turned into a four-part series on the "committed generation" which had to be read by six editors and rewritten each
time. In retrospect it looks very tame, but at the time it started a
controversy because I did not say SDS was infiltrated by Communists. As a result, every leftist group in Boston started calling
me to get their statements in the paper. I became close with a
girl named Phyllis who headed the W. E. B. Du Bois Club, and I
started going out with Carey, an SDS leader from Harvard, who
was fixated on California girls and his walkie-talkies, which he
liked to take apart and put back together. He went to sixteen
meetings a week and came in two seconds flat but when I
suggested (apologetically, not wanting to seem critical) that he
was awfully fast, he shrugged, "That's how I am."

On a beautiful fall day I walked next to him, backward, at the
head of the first Mass March Against the War in New England.
It was October 16, the same day Susie was marching with Jeff to
their appointment with the Oakland police and the Hell's Angels.

In Boston the air had the scent of crisp apples and falling
leaves. As I stood beside Carey, he shouted into the walkie-
talkie, "Here they come and it looks good!" That evening I
argued with the editors of the *Globe* until they agreed to play
the story up big.

I began to think of myself as an agent behind the lines. At the
office I wore suits and heels but when I got home, I combed my
hair down and changed into jeans or a shift and black tights. I
found an apartment four blocks from Harvard Square and two
blocks from where Candy and Bobby were living. My place was
in a basement but it had brick walls, a fireplace, a kitchen pan-
eled with barn wood and a bathroom down the hall with old
marble fixtures. Ninety-five dollars a month furnished. I acquired
two kittens whom I named Nicholas and Alison after the charac-

ters in *The Magus,* an important book to me because it captured our generation's ease with sex and difficulties with love.

I kept a miniature orange tree to remind me of California and the radio tuned to WMEX, the Good Guys, who played the music to which I was addicted: "Good Vibrations," "Do You Believe in Magic?" "The Eve of Destruction," "Nineteenth Nervous Breakdown," "96 Tears," "Help I Need Somebody," "Like a Rolling Stone," "She's Just My Style."

The *Globe* sent me to be interviewed by a psychiatrist at Harvard; they said this was standard procedure before they would place an employee on permanent staff. The doctor showed me a copy of his report to the publisher: "Don't be misled by this young woman's tendency toward beatnik dress and liberal thought. The data from her past indicates that she is a competent, systematic achiever."

Before long I was writing about an astonishing range of subjects: insurance scandals, Playboy bunnies, State House politics. I was fascinated by Boston "pols," the little men with cigars who shuffled pigeon-toed around the State House and called each other "sweet-haht." When the General Court adjourned for the year, these distinguished legislators sailed paper airplanes and stood on their chairs singing, "Aba daba daba," which came out, "Abber dabber dabber."

I became the assistant film critic and once a week, reviewed all the terrible movies that the critic, a dotty, lovable lady named Marjory Adams, didn't want to bother with. *Beach Blanket Bingo. The Return of Fu Manchu.*

When the Beatles came to Boston, I was assigned to cover the concert. This was the year John Lennon said, "The Beatles are more popular than Christ now." At the stadium, I spotted a row of Kennedy children, fresh from Hyannisport, jumping on their seats and screaming. Joseph Kennedy III, who was thirteen and was wearing a flowered mod tie "as a joke," told me he wanted to grow his hair long, like Lennon, "but I don't think my parents would let me."

I had an eye for detail and a naïve ignorance of the rules, so that even when sent on the most routine assignment, I'd write it with a twist that led the editors to put the story on page one for "color." One night when there was nothing much happening, Claffey sent me to a cocktail reception for Leonard Bernstein. There was no news angle but Bernstein was a local boy, and I saw his mother standing in a corner with her fur coat folded over her arm. She reminded me of ladies I used to see in temple on Jewish holidays. I walked up and asked her what it was like, raising Leonard Bernstein.

She looked at me and shrugged. "Take any genius. If you don't give him the right upbringing, he'll fall by the wayside."

Sometimes my eye for detail got me in trouble. In 1966 I rode with a lady named Poppy Laurence and three of her friends in a caravan of Mothers Against the War. As they drove from Chestnut Hill to Boston Common, the women talked about how nervous they were—someone might throw a rock—and how violent this country was, and Poppy said she liked best to march in Washington in the spring because the cherry blossoms were out and it was so pretty. Later she got into a screaming fight with a heckler named Joseph Mlot Mroz, a Polish house painter who showed up at every demonstration carrying a cross and a sign that said "Communism is Jewish."

I wrote a lot about the ladies and very little about Benjamin Spock's boring speech at Boston Common. The next day Poppy called me in tears, saying I had made a laughing stock of her. I had undermined the whole point of the march and all the members of Women's Strike for Peace were canceling their subscriptions. The men reporters had a great laugh about it but I felt dizzy, went in the bathroom and threw up.

Before I had been at the *Globe* a year, Tom Winship, the editor, stopped me in the hall. "If you could write your own ticket at the *Globe*, what would you do?"

"Be a correspondent in Europe or Russia," I said.

"Jesus, you want the moon." He laughed gruffly. "I don't have a European Bureau."

"Then send me to California. Ronald Reagan, an actor, is running for governor and he might win, and I'm from California . . ."

So he did.

I found that I could pursue any subject I was interested in by proposing a story about it. And I could pursue men. When Ralph Nader came to Boston I studied his picture and asked to be assigned to interview him. Mrs. Ralph Nader, I thought, until I shook his hand and felt his unmistakable indifference to women. Mrs. Roman Polanski, I thought, until I met him for lunch and found he was two heads shorter than I.

Mrs. Gideon Bockner, I thought, when I met him at a friend's house. Gideon was an Israeli who was studying film-making at Harvard, and making love with him was so sweet and so charged that we could not sleep because we could not stop touching.

On Wednesday, the day I went to movie screenings, Gideon came with me. He waited while I typed my reviews and then we had dinner at Felicia's in the North End, chicken cooked with lemon and hearts of artichoke on pewter plates. "I love you," he said. "I am saying that to only one other girl, in all my life."

Most nights when I came home from the *Globe*, Gideon was in my bed, reading magazines. We unleashed in each other such pure physical joy. Neither of us was very sophisticated. We knew nothing of oral sex or esoteric positions. It was all completely simple and completely enough.

We had been together five months when, on a Friday, he did not come by my place at the hour we had arranged. I called his house. No answer. At ten, I started to worry. At midnight, I drove by his place to see if his motorcycle was there. It was. I knocked on the door. No reply.

("What happened," I had asked him that night at Felicia's, "with the other girl you loved?"

"We are together four years, we decide to get married, but at the City Hall I escape.")

I broke out in hives and my eyes swelled up so badly I couldn't sleep. At eight in the morning I started calling Gideon's friends. They hadn't seen him but said I shouldn't worry. He sometimes took off on crazy impulses.

When my phone rang at 4 P.M., I jumped for it. "I am on Cape," Gideon said in a faraway voice. "A guy ask me late Friday."

"But I could have gone with you. I have the weekend off."

Silence.

"Look, I am in private home. I can't talk. I see you in few days."

Oh God, I thought, I drove him off. I was just like my mother. Too critical, too demanding. I would change, he would see. For two days, three days, I called his house on the hour and drove by to check for lights. On the fifth day he answered the phone.

"Don't you think you owe me an explanation?" I said, still praying there *was* an explanation.

"Yes," he said.

Long silence.

"It just seems to me that it's over. And it's all right."

"What do you mean it's all right!"

"It's just . . . all right."

"I know nothing about you other than your name," Dr. Simpson said.

Where do I start, I thought. There's a horrible, weighing-down pain in my chest. I look at the trees blooming along the Charles and wish I were dead. When I get on an airplane I pray it will crash.

Dr. Simpson crossed his legs. I watched his knee swing. "Perhaps you could write me a brief biography?"

"Okay," I said. "The only biographies I've written have been applications for schools or jobs. They were elaborate lies. It'll be interesting to tell the truth."

The doctor smiled. He was British and had an all-knowing manner that made me uneasy. "After we've worked together for a time, I think you'll find this biography to be a different kind of elaborate lie."

What the hell could he mean? I considered the possibilities. I believed that I loved my parents. Did I hate them? I believed I was strong and independent. Was I weak? I believed I had overcome the guilt my mother drummed into me about sex. Perhaps I was still ashamed.

I definitely was ashamed to be seeing a psychiatrist. I was supposedly the girl with no problems. "I've always been so rational,"

I had written to Candy just a year earlier. I needed to be rational, to have my actions make sense.

During this season, I used to go to Candy and Bobby's house for refuge. Their arms were always open, their refrigerator always full. But when I could see past my own fog, I noticed signs that something was awry with Candy. She walked in her sleep. She lost keys, she burned food. She fell sick and became so weak she could not hold up her head, even to read. Two months passed and no doctor could diagnose what was wrong. She talked on the phone with her analyst in California. As her strength returned, she resolved to leave for London to train with Anna Freud. Bobby still had another year of courses at Harvard, but then he could join her and write his thesis in England.

I was shocked at her decision. "They just got married and she's leaving the country for a year," I told friends, who said, "Candy's gone crazy. That marriage is done for."

In February of 1967, Governor Ronald Reagan gave the nod and Clark Kerr was suddenly, unexpectedly fired as president of the University of California. That night the *Globe* dispatched me to San Francisco and as the plane took off, I prayed it would not crash.

I drove directly to Berkeley and could not believe my eyes. Telegraph Avenue was changed utterly. On the walls were posters announcing rock concerts at the Fillmore and the Avalon Ballroom but you could hardly read the message because the letters rippled about the page. Hippies, before *Life* and *Newsweek* discovered them, were lying on the sidewalk wearing headbands, beads and leather-fringed vests. They were smoking joints and waving psychedelic God's eyes and hawking pipes and the *Berkeley Barb,* all of which I bought.

I searched for familiar faces. A small girl, barefoot, with long frizzed hair was approaching me and waved. I squinted. We drew closer, she beaming and snapping finger cymbals. I realized we had never met. As we passed she whispered, "Salami."

"What?" But I was smiling back, it was infectious.

"John the Baptist said to Salome, if you will dance I will love you." The girl tinkled and twinkled and padded on.

Then I bumped, literally, into Susie Berman, who was passing out leaflets protesting Reagan's "political interference with the university." I had not spoken to her since our awkward phone call at the height of the Free Speech Movement. She looked exactly as I remembered: pretty, fresh. Unlike the street hippies, she was dressed neatly in a white sweater and navy wool skirt.

"Sara!" To my surprise, she threw her arms about me. "What are you doing here?"

"I'm working for *The Boston Globe*. They sent me out to write . . ."

She wrinkled her nose. "That's a shitty newspaper."

"No it isn't. It's the first major paper that's come out against the war."

Susie shrugged. "I gotta go. Jeff's waiting. Come to the march on Saturday, see ya."

It was just like the past. Whenever I said something Susie disagreed with, a switch would flicker in her eyes and she went off. I didn't want to see her again.

I called up Rob Kagan. "Well well," he said, "you're here in perfect time for a very special party. Come on over." I walked to his house on Kelsey Street where he was living with a lambent-eyed painter named Kris and her sister Jane and his best friend, Billy, who told me, "Our scene is so groovy. It satisfies all my emotional and sexual needs without pinning me down to anyone."

Fuck you, I thought. But then Rob burst through the door and caught me in a bear hug. He had been the first person to turn me on to grass and I wondered, what did he have in store next?

Rob's hair was clear down to his shoulders, so that all you could see was the hair and the nose that gave his head a forward motion. He was wearing jeans and a green velvet jerkin.

"Tell me about New York," he said.

"I live in Boston now. Tell me about law school."

"I'm in art school," he said. "The biggest thing in my life, even bigger than taking LSD, was learning to dance. Do you dance in New York? We've been going to dances where you can take off your clothes and there are strobe lights and liquid projections on the walls. The combination of acid and nude dancing to rock

music and liquid projections is thrilling! Like, how could I get up
the next morning and go to a classroom and talk about torts?"

We laughed and Rob began rolling joints. He told me about
the new art form he was creating. "I call my pieces 'events,'" he
said. "They're like a movie, only they happen in real time and
space, and they're staged for one person, an audience of one. Before the event I do research on this person. I talk to his friends
and collect mementos from his childhood. I learn about his fantasies. On the day of the event, the person comes home and suddenly finds himself in the middle of an adventure. He's taken
various places—in the streets, to special rooms—and different
things happen. There are actors and actresses. It's sort of like an
initiation into a secret order—like Hesse, you know? The Magic
Theater?"

I shook my head, wishing Rob would stage an event for me,
when I noticed he was staring at my dress, my new red and
white Mary Quant mini-dress.

"Where did you get that dress?" Rob asked.

"Why? Don't you like it?"

"There's nothing really . . . special about it." He raised his
eyebrows like two peaks. "On the other hand, I don't know your
life-style in New York. Maybe the dress is perfect there."

People began arriving for the party and I saw what Rob meant
about "special" clothes. They were wearing Edwardian velvet
gowns, spaceman suits, African robes, cowboy regalia, Donald
Duck hats and Indian war paint. I felt shy and out of place. I
took out the pad I always carried in my purse and made notes—
the note-taking was habit by now. I wanted to remember all the
details. The living room had walls covered with aluminum foil.
Rob's bedroom looked like a madman's attic. The room was so
dense I wondered how he could live in it. There were antlers,
cuckoo clocks, railroad signals, mirrors, flashing lights, paintings,
two stuffed peacocks, twelve bowling balls and a cannon ball.

The party room on the top floor was carpeted with hot pink
fur. A light show—colored blobs that squiggled and oozed—was
being projected on the wall. People were lying on the floor with
stereo headphones. A bearded figure pulled me down, handed
me a headset and a joint. "It's a tape," he said, sucking in his

breath and croaking so he wouldn't exhale: "Rob spent weeks preparing it." Shooooo. He exhaled. The tape contained every song the Beatles had recorded on a loop so the music played continuously: "Penny Lane," "Ticket to Ride," "Norwegian Wood," "I'm a Loser," "Please Please Me," "Drive My Car," "Eight Days a Week."

I stayed in the pink fur room for six hours, nestled with strangers, puffing on joints while the Beatles sang right inside my skull. I thought it was the most fantastic party I had been to in my life.

In the following days I wrote stories about Clark Kerr; the two Berkeleys—the hippies and the politicos; and the rise of the Haight-Ashbury in San Francisco where the Diggers gave away food. Then I went to see Hank Smith, my first lover, with whom I had had no contact since the breakup of our four-way ménage. He said he had been flunked from the Peace Corps because he lacked the proper attitude. He was working as a surveyor and he was exactly the same: big and brawny with his eager, goofy smile. We made love in his apartment near the Fillmore and when I didn't come, he asked what was wrong.

"Nothing. I don't have orgasms all the time."

"You used to." He shook his head and grinned. "Sara. What have they done to you back East?"

By the time I returned to Boston, carrying posters from the Fillmore and a record of the Jefferson Airplane, I was plotting my escape. Not back to Berkeley. The people there were playing and I liked it, it was fun, but I had deadlines to meet. I had to go to New York and make it nationally, or I would end up embittered like Selma Moran.

On my days off I started job hunting in New York. I told Ian Menzies I was planning to quit the *Globe*. I was moving to New York because I was in love with a man there and wanted to get married. "It's a shame for us to lose you," Ian said thoughtfully.

What happened, subsequently, was exactly the reverse. Ian arranged for me to be the *Globe*'s correspondent in New York, and a month before I was due to leave town, I fell in love with a man who lived in Boston.

13. TASHA

In the summer of 1966, California, to Tasha, seemed like a haven, a way off the treadmill of going to Max's and loft parties and openings that didn't add up to anything. The gallery was closing in June for the summer, and she kind of wanted to see Steven Silver. She sublet her apartment on Thirty-fourth Street and when she flew home, she says, "My ego was in great shape. So many men had been interested in me. I felt prized, even if it was by people who were married, psychotic, whatever."

The day after she arrived in Los Angeles, Tasha had dinner with Steven. He told her he had been taking LSD with a man who was coaching him in classical guitar. He was troubled by the strange feelings he had for this man. He had stopped writing poetry. He was devoting himself to music. He thought Tasha looked more beautiful than before.

As they lingered over coffee, a wave went across the table. Tasha's heart was all achy and trembly as they drove to Steven's house, "but it wasn't the same," she recalls. "I wasn't prepared to take the shit and he was prepared to give it."

Steven hinted that he was still seeing Sandra Jason. He asked Tasha out Saturday, then called back and switched it to Sunday, lying about his reasons. Tasha said, "Forget it, I'm busy Sunday."

She went to a party with her oldest brother where she met a young man named Jay Rosen. He could have been her twin. They were both twenty-three. Jay's eyes were the same color blue as Tasha's, his hair the same color blond. Tasha thought there was a farmer in him. He had been a swimming champion at Yale and had worked for the Peace Corps in Tanganyika, living in a red clay village, teaching English. In the fall he was starting medical school in Seattle.

Going out with Jay was like being a teen-ager again. Driving down Sunset in his white convertible with the top down and the radio blaring "Good Lovin'!" Eating chili burgers and milk shakes at Delores's on the way to a movie and a drive along the beach. On their second date, as they were necking on his couch, Tasha placed her hand on the zipper of his pants.

Jay was upset. "Have you done this before?"

"A couple of times. Why, haven't you?"

Jay folded his arms. "I take this seriously. If we do it now I'm afraid we'll do it all the time and it will lose its meaning." Tasha raised her eyebrows as if to suggest she had a different view. Jay said, "I wouldn't want to marry someone who just threw it away."

"You don't mean you want your wife to be a virgin?"

"Why not?"

She had to stifle a laugh. "I didn't know anybody still felt that way."

Jay shrugged. "I don't mind being at variance with my culture." He began kissing her again and Tasha thought, he'll get over it.

Jay's parents were divorced. His father was a dental surgeon and his mother was a screen writer who lived in the Hollywood Hills. In July his mother left the city for two months. Tasha moved into the house with Jay and for the rest of the summer, they were inseparable. They spent their days lying in the sun by the swimming pool, listening to the Beach Boys. They played touch football and wandered around the grounds, picking tangerines and avocados. Tasha made tangerine marmalade. Jay made notes for a novel he was writing about Tanganyika, called *The*

Drums of Morogoro. At night they barbecued steaks and watched television, or went out to baseball games.

They slept nude in the master bedroom, took showers together, hugged and kissed but hardly ever made love. When they did, it was tense and quick. Tasha decided that Jay had "a bourgeois streak in him that wasn't in me. I'd made the mistake of being honest with him. He knew about my abortion, so as far as he was concerned I was damaged property. But we were falling deeply in love and everything else felt really right."

What Tasha remembers most about the summer is "how peaceful we felt and all the laughing we did." She became close to Jay's younger brother, Artie, and his grandfather, "a wonderful old man who'd been a tailor in the old country and kept a scissors in his pocket so that if he was in a restaurant, he could snip the ribbon on a packet of saltines."

She read *The Drums of Morogoro* as Jay wrote it. She thought he was a good writer and should fulfill himself. The only work she did all those months was to teach with a black artist she knew from New York, Ed Beasly. It was the summer following the Watts riots, and Ed had a grant to run an art workshop in the ghetto.

Toward the end of the summer, Hilda Carson called and asked her to come back to the gallery in September to organize a graphics department. She offered her $140 a week—double her previous salary. Jay was leaving for Seattle and Tasha knew she couldn't stay in Los Angeles without him. She would languish from the sunsets and the freeways and the palm trees.

Jay drove her to the airport and at the ticket counter, said suddenly, "I'm coming with you." When they arrived at her apartment on Thirty-fourth Street, the air was stale and sooty because there was no air conditioning. He hated her apartment. He hated the dark building. He hated New York. How could she stand it?

He stayed two weeks, and the night before he left, she cooked a rib roast with shallots and wine. When she set it on the table, the table cracked and the roast fell on the floor. Tasha burst into tears. "I would have gone away with him if he'd asked me. I was ready to get a dog and a job in Seattle." But Jay said he thought he should get settled there first. He was also worried about sex. Making love had been easier and better in New York but not all that better. He was thinking of seeing a doctor.

When Jay left, Tasha threw herself into her new job and for two months, was chaste. She came home at night and wrote Jay letters. Every few days he called, and they made plans for a reunion in Los Angeles at Christmas.

In November, Mark McCall returned from a trip to India and came by Tasha's place on Monday with a vial of Panjabi rose essence. The perfume was so strong that a touch on her wrist lasted all day. Wearing it gave her confidence. The fragrance was so close to that of actual roses that when people walked by her desk, they turned to see where the flowers were.

She and Mark fell into spending Mondays together. By Thanksgiving they were lovers. "I felt guilty because of his wife, but the sex was super good and it was a relief not to feel rejected. I didn't have the doubts I'd had with Jay, like maybe my breasts weren't big enough. Maybe my thighs were too flabby. Maybe he didn't like my body. I certainly didn't like it."

The affair with Mark wasn't serious anyway. It was forbidden fruit that couldn't last, Tasha decided, and started to prepare for Christmas. She spent weeks tracking down the perfect gift for each person. An engraving for her mother. Cashmere sweaters for her brothers, and for Jay, an antique white-gold pocket watch she found on the Lower East Side. She packed her best clothes, Christmas presents, jewelry and some lithographs she planned to sell in Los Angeles to pay for the trip.

Jay was waiting at the gate with two dozen roses. They sat down because they were shaking and just wanted to look at each other. When they walked, finally, to the baggage claim area, they could not find her suitcase. It had been stolen! All her clothes. The presents. And the lithographs, which were worth $1,000. The insurance only covered $600.

Jay pleaded with her not to worry. "I'll buy you new things. I don't care about the presents." That night he made love to her so naturally and wholeheartedly that she was bewildered. Had he changed? Had she?

The Christmas trees on Wilshire Boulevard were bright orange and garish. The smog made Tasha's eyes burn. Mark called her from New York, which she had specifically instructed him not to do. She took the phone in her father's study so Jay couldn't hear.

"I've decided to tell Roberta about us," he said.

"What are you talking about? What is there to tell?"

"That I'm falling in love with you. That I need to keep seeing you. I love Roberta but you're important in my life."

Tasha was stunned. "Don't you think this is premature, to make so much of it?"

"I'm making of it what it is. When are you coming back?"

The next night, Tasha and Jay were at his mother's, walking outside by the swimming pool. "Sit down. I want to tell you something," Jay said. She sat on a chaise longue. It was damp but she ignored it. Jay's face looked so fresh, so unconfused.

"I want to marry you," he said.

Tasha gave a nervous laugh. "Let's not joke around."

A sting of hurt in his eyes.

"I'm not kidding, Tasha."

She couldn't look at him now. I've got a whole new life in New York, she was thinking. And Jay's such a kid. He has bourgeois ideas. The sex is no good. I'll be trapped, I'll never grow, I'll suffocate in Seattle with the rain and the fog and the twilight that reminds me of my father dying.

But she looked in his eyes and knew: my father would have loved me to marry Jay Rosen.

"We still have a lot to work out," Tasha said. "The sex . . ."

"I've overcome that. Haven't you seen?"

"I have a big job to finish in New York. I have to go back, at least until the summer."

"Then you're not saying no?"

"No."

For the rest of the holiday Jay made love to her at every opportunity. When they parted, it was agreed he would visit her at
Easter.

In New York, Tasha resumed spending Mondays with Mark.
Jay's letters came furiously. Tasha brooded: one person is wrong
for me and one is right for me, but maybe the one who looks
right is wrong.

She recalls, "I wasn't sure I could learn anything from Jay. But
Mark was married and twice my age. He was the most bizarre
person. We were the oddest couple. He looked much older than
he was because of his white hair, and I looked like a waif because of my long hair. When we walked into a room, I could see
from people's faces what they were thinking: that girl must have
a father thing. That man must be strange, probably dumped his
wife for this child.

But she couldn't stop seeing him. Every day was an adventure.
They shared a fascination with seeing and perceiving and when
they took walks, their eyes would be drawn to the same detail.
They talked about the light that objects give off, and searched
for the color within a color. Mark taught her how to scan "out of
the corner of the eye so you perceive the abstract elements of nature. When I do this, I see beams of light, parabolas, chasms,
colors and shapes moving unceasingly."

What Tasha loved most was that Mark was constantly celebrating life. "Nothing was out of reach of his imagination." What
pained her was that he always had to leave at two in the morning. "What if somebody broke in here and I needed you?"

"You can always call," he said. "Roberta works in her studio
and she sleeps there most nights. Even if she's home you can
call. She knows."

Roberta's way of dealing with the affair was to discount it.
Surely it would die out within a year, so why disrupt their lives?
She asked Mark to go out with her socially and keep up appearances. Tasha didn't protest because "I didn't want the responsibility for this man. I didn't want to be with him the rest of my
life."

Because they had to live under veils, they spent most of their time in Tasha's dark apartment. There was something unclean and thrilling in their love-making. Nothing was out of reach. She thought about Jay, how easily shocked he was. Yet she felt for Jay with her heart. Jay offered her a chance to have a family like Bob Goodson's, two small children and picnics in the park and everyone wearing Shetland sweaters.

Mark had the unstable life of a sculptor. He had weird ideas about the cosmos and a willfulness that was infuriating. When she opened her eyes on his face up close she saw a skeleton.

Suddenly he rolled with her like a horse going over with its rider in a stream. He held her below, then on top so she could see the reversal of light on their bodies. He could sense when she was drifting and knew how to coax her back. His hand was persistent, relentless, victorious.

She was awash in sunlight.

Then it clouded over.

If I marry Jay, I'll spend my life trying to break out of a cast. But is Mark right for me? She was fighting with Mark, struggling to get up and he was with her, pushing her, he wanted her to burn. She was out in the ethers now, out where the sun is pure pure gold like the gold that comes from the rumblings of the earth and she came, he came, gone beyond.

Late in the evening, they would bathe and go out to an expensive, out-of-the-way restaurant like the Cafe Argenteuil. Mark ordered lobster and an exquisite bottle of wine that slid over the tongue. They loved ritual and ended their evenings with coffee in an expresso bar in Little Italy.

She continued writing Jay about the prospects of marrying him and living in Seattle. She thought back to Steven Silver and Sandra Jason. Now the roles were switched. She was in the middle, unable to commit herself or give up either man. And she felt for Roberta. "I'd been in her position and I knew her pain."

She told Mark about Jay one Monday late while they were drinking Bourbon and eating herb omelets. Mark said in a flat voice, "Marrying him will be like stepping in a box. You'll be a prisoner, even if he makes you comfortable and gives you all kinds of privileges."

"But I feel peace with Jay. With you it's pure turmoil."

"Of course," Mark said. "There's no peace in me. There's a labyrinth, there's light in darkness, and the deeper I go the darker it gets and the brighter." He took out the flask of Bourbon he carried and poured another glassful. "What you see as peace in this nice young doctor is mere sleep. He hasn't explored the inner realms. He hasn't embraced a fraction of his selves. Each of us has a thousand selves. That's what Gurdjieff said: 'There is no permanent and unchangeable I.'"

It annoyed Tasha when Mark talked about weird Eastern stuff like Gurdjieff and the I Ching. It was superstitious, not rational, but something in that spooky talk reached her and made her flinch at the idea of a Jewish wedding in Los Angeles.

As Easter approached Mark stepped up the pressure. "Are you going to marry this man or not? Are you going to give up your life here and me?"

Jay, on his part, started asking why Tasha was rarely at home nights when he called. The week before Easter, she telephoned Jay and said she'd been given an unexpected project. "I'll be working day and night. There's no point in your flying all this way because we won't have a minute to spend together."

Jay's letters fell off. What Tasha had told him was partly true: she was working day and night. She had her own office now on the second-floor landing and she had power. Her department was the busiest in the gallery. She was courted by artists who wanted her to sell their lithographs and by customers who wanted first options.

She started wearing expensive suits by name designers that she bought wholesale on Seventh Avenue. She went out to lunch at the Right Bank with museum directors and customers from out of town.

"A big sale turned me on. Forty prints to American Can Company. A series of twelve to the Museum of Modern Art. A sale so big you needed an adding machine to total it. But there were times when I detested the job because you succeeded so much on your charm. I knew I could make sales to men who came in by themselves. I had a little more trouble with couples. I'd have to play to the woman."

Tasha remembers that some nights, she had to massage her gums "because my face had been frozen in a smile. What was the point? I was losing ground, losing track of something but I didn't know what. When I wrote letters, I thought, they could have been written by anybody to anybody. They had a business tone about them."

She talked about her frustration at weekly encounter sessions that Hilda was requiring everyone on staff to attend. One of the salesmen asked her, "What would make you feel back on the track?"

"Do something creative, on my own."

"Like what?"

A ridiculous idea came to her. "Start a film department. Make movies of the gallery artists."

So she did. And although it meant longer hours, she was absorbed again in her work.

In May, Mark went to London for a one-man show. Tasha drove him to the airport and gave him a gift—a piece of red jasper. "If the show goes well, take the money and have an adventure."

The show sold out. Mark chartered a helicopter to fly to Stonehenge where he watched the sun rise, shocking pink, between two slabs of prehistoric stone. When he returned to New York, he went straight to the studio and worked for seven weeks. When he felt himself lagging he took out the red jasper. "It has healing powers," he told Tasha.

He assembled hunks of marble and rock and pounded into them rivulets of polished metal. What resulted was an enormous form—twelve feet high—grainy and jagged at the base with fine, smooth fingers at the top. The piece buckled upward. Tasha felt there had been an explosion in the rock and the rivulets of metal were the fault lines. After Mark had slept and meditated with it, he titled the piece, "Natasha, Stone."

Tasha found an excuse to sever her link to Jay Rosen. A girl friend in Washington wrote and said she had seen Jay at a party.

"He was with a nursing student and they were making out like crazy." Tasha called Jay. "I know about you and the nurse. What kind of person would do what you've done? You're supposedly engaged to me."

"Nothing's happened. . . ."

"You're just like your father. I don't want to see you anymore. It's over, period," and before he could respond she hung up.

She spent the summer of '67 back in Los Angeles. She had received a grant from the Ford Foundation to set up a lithography workshop in Watts. She and her mother rattled around the big house by themselves and it was lonely. She learned that Jay was in Israel. "I had a brief flash of jumping on a plane and going to meet him, but that passed," she says. "Mark was calling every week."

At the end of August, she was sitting in the back yard with her grandmother Helena, who had grown up in Russia and had never cut her hair, which she wore in a braid coiled around her head.

She was showing Tasha how to crochet. She made a clucking sound. "Of all my grandchildren, you're the most beautiful. I just can't understand, why aren't you married? All the others are married. I thought you'd be the first one to be snatched up."

Tasha smiled.

Helena set down her needle and in a shy voice, asked, "Natasha, do you like the company of men?"

14. SARA

A month before my departure from Boston, I was assigned to write a story about a new marine research center funded by the federal government. When I called the center, the press spokesman told me the staff was about to fly to Mexico to trap fish. "Want to come along? You can write your story from there."

Apparently I caught my editor in an expansive mood, for he agreed to send me and two days later, I was on a small plane that flew from Mérida in the Yucatán peninsula to the island of Cozumel. The research party was a hale, raucous group of marine biologists and former navy divers, who always seemed to have their hands filled with dip nets, shark sticks and regulator hoses. They taught me how to snorkel and I wrote to Candy, "I've discovered an astonishing new world—under the sea." I took notes and photographs and swam and wore my hair in braids. "What a racket," they kidded me. "You get paid for this?"

In the evenings we would gather to drink rum and smoke grass on the veranda of an old hotel that had wooden fans and in which we were the only tenants. Most of the divers were so earnest about science that I found them asexual, but there was one who intrigued me. His name was Jack Hanson. He was a full professor and yet there was about him a spirit of hijinks. It was most unusual for a man of his generation, his standing in the community, to smoke dope and sing rock songs. For reasons I was at a loss to understand, he would not look at me or speak to me directly, so I took the liberty of studying him. I liked to listen to him tell stories; he moved his eyes around and spoke in funny voices that made everyone laugh. He had sparse brown hair and was balding on the crown, but his body was tight and fit, like an astronaut's.

One night, I must have been staring with unrelieved intensity, for he suddenly looked at me across the room. "How old are you, anyway?"

By the end of the trip, we were sitting together at meals and taking walks by the sea wall, and he was telling me about his wife of twenty years, his three sons and his marriage in which "there was never any magic. We got married because that's what everyone did." For years, he said, he had been living in Boston while his family stayed in the house he had built in Ogunquit, Maine.

"So, I'm just the lug who rolls home once a month and makes trouble."

"If there's nothing there, why don't you get divorced?" I was twenty-four. The situation seemed simple.

He was forty-one. He sighed. I turned away, but he pulled me back to him with unexpected urgency.

During my last weeks in Boston, Jack and I spent every night together. He lived in a converted customs house whose windows looked out on the open sea. We cooked shellfish chowders and made love listening to the foghorns but mostly we laughed and acted silly. We brought out in each other a lightness and mirth. He said what he loved most was my smile. That was strange, because all my life, people had been telling me that I had sad eyes and looked as if someone were chasing me.

Because Jack saw me differently, I began to be calmer and happier. He was the first man I had known who took care of me, and who talked about the possibility of marrying. He came very quickly and I rarely did but that was not important. I felt peaceful and loved.

The day before I was to leave for New York, he tuned up my

Volkswagen and helped me pack. Then I sat on the floor by his tank of tropical fish and cried. "Jesus," he said. "How do you turn your back on your family after twenty years? It's not that I shouldn't have done it long ago. It's just that it's not easily done, and I don't know if I have the backbone."

I got up and pulled my coat tight around me, walked out the door and drove to Manhattan. Jane, my friend from Columbia who was now a reporter at *Newsday*, had found us an apartment on Seventy-fifth Street by the East River. I was appalled when I saw it. The apartment consisted of two narrow rooms, side by side, and two closets, one of which was a bathroom and one a kitchen. When I flicked on the light, cockroaches skittered. What am I doing here, I thought, as I crawled in a wretched sleeping bag on the floor. I had left a wonderful man, good friends, a job and a cozy apartment—all for this?

The next day, the daughter of Josef Stalin, Svetlana Alliluyeva, defected to the United States and held a press conference at the Plaza Hotel. That evening I filed my first story from the "Globe New York bureau," and from that point I had so much work there was no time to look back. Jane lived in one room of our apartment and I set up the "bureau" in the other. I bought a desk, a bed and file cabinets and considered installing an AP wire machine in my closet, but the thought of all that yellow paper spewing onto the floor made me ill. I had to run the operation on a shoestring because the publisher of the *Globe* didn't think he needed a New York bureau.

All I had to begin with was a letter from my editor, which enabled me to get a press pass. The minute I woke up I would flip on the radio to the all-news station and, my heart racing, tear through *The New York Times* to see what stories I had missed. I became a slave to the news. Any riot or strike would cause me to cancel all plans for the evening and scurry into the street. I felt strange and nervous with no office to go to, no boss to see daily, but I loved New York again. I was becoming friendly with the press corps and they were calling me with tips and I was making page one regularly when Jack's letters began arriving.

"I thought if I fell in love with a writer I would at least get a little mail," he said in the first.

"I miss you terribly," he said in the second.

"I love you! Write or I will shoot myself? I love you, write or I will jump out a window? I love you, please write and send me that wonderful smile. I think that's what I miss most of all."

I started flying to Boston every weekend on a forged youth-fare card. It was May, and Jack took me diving on the Cape. One Saturday at Falmouth we put on our wet suits, weight belts, tanks, fins and masks and were lumbering over the rocks to jump in when Jack said, muffled through the mouthpiece, "Where shall we get married?"

I wanted to run throw my arms around him but I couldn't move under the weight of the gear.

Jack tilted forward and, laughing through the mouthpiece, smashed into the water.

On a sticky weekend in June, Jack flew to New York and met me in the East Village where I was covering a three-day cosmic love-in. Sergeant Pepper was everywhere and the Fugs sang free in Thompkins Square Park: "Coca Cola Douche," "Wet Dream," "Slum Goddess" and "Kill for Peace." A boy in a wizard's hat was selling bananas for ten cents with a three-cent deposit on the skins. Anyone who heard Donovan sing "Mellow Yellow" knew why. Smoking banana peels could get you high. Outtaaaaa-sight! Louis Abolafia, a black-haired artist who reminded me of Rob Kagan in Berkeley, was campaigning for President. He kissed me on the cheek and punched Jack's shoulder and handed us a flier showing him nude under the legend, "What have I got to hide?"

Jack laughed and laughed. He bought us matching purple T-shirts from the Naked Grape. He sang to himself in a melodious tenor that rendered rock lyrics ridiculous, "Will ya still need me, will ya still feed me, when I'm sixty-four?"

We sat in the park and I interviewed sixteen-year-olds who had run away from home because their parents didn't understand them. Jack watched them paint flowers on each other's cheeks. "I'm too old to be a hippie," he said, "but there are teeny-boppers. I could be a forty-bopper. Here's how it works: I come up on the plane in my businessman's suit. I take a cab to the East Village, I open my attaché case and wham! I take out the dope, the beads. . . ."

The Fugs started singing "She's my slum goddess of the Lower East Side." Andrei Voznesensky, the Russian poet, railed and flailed his arms while the "Group Image" used axes to destroy the stage and then out came His Holiness Swami Bhaktivedanta in an orange robe with a cue card so everyone could sing along:

> Hare Krishna
> Hare Krishna
> Krishna Krishna
> Hare Hare

But things were not all beautiful in the Summer of Love. I had to write about Linda Fitzpatrick, an eighteen-year-old runaway who was slaughtered with her boy friend Groovy in an East Village basement. On Fifth Avenue, 70,000 patriots came out for a "Support Our Boys in Vietnam Parade." At the reviewing stand, an ABC cameraman warned me, "Watch out, your hair is too long and your skirt is too short." The marchers were chanting, "Death to the Communists!" Two hippie girls who tried to pass out daisies were knocked to the ground. The Teamsters Union waved signs, "If your heart isn't in America, get your [a donkey was pictured] out of here!" A boy in a scout uniform set fire to a red flag but police put it out. "Burn it, burn it," the mob yelled. "Why not?" shouted one man. "The peaceniks burn the American flag. What are we, Americans or rats?"

I had seen enough. I was starting to walk home when a flatbed truck with a load of men rolled by. Suddenly they lifted a garbage can full of tar and dumped it onto a twenty-year-old boy, selected, probably, because his hair fell below his ears. The boy let out an unearthly scream. Feathers were rained onto him. I stumbled into an apartment lobby and put my head between my knees. I was incoherent when I called the city desk. "They tarred and feathered a boy right in front of my eyes. It's ugly. Madness . . ."

Charlie Claffey said nothing except, "Oh yeah? Keep it short, we have a tight paper tomorrow."

Very late that night I sat down to write Jack. In recent weeks he had gone to see his family twice but each time he had returned without telling his wife, Chris, about us.

I drew squiggles on the paper. When I'm thirty, he'll be . . . forty-seven. Will he still go diving when he's forty-seven? I shielded my eyes so I wouldn't see the rug. It was an Oriental carpet I had admired in a thrift shop but when I brought it home it made the room depressing. Why hasn't he told her? She's not as disinterested as he thinks. He's got to tell her.

I gave Jack a deadline. If he didn't tell Chris over the Fourth of July weekend, I wasn't going to wait around any longer.

Jack did manage, on the last night of the interminable four-day weekend, to tell Chris he wanted a divorce. She reacted with hysteria, swearing she would never agree to it. She would go see a marriage counselor. She would go to Weight Watchers. When Jack told me this, I became hysterical and cried so hard my nose started bleeding.

"Are you going to leave or not?" I sobbed.

"Listen, we're dealing with people, who are very tricky animals. You can't expect things to go according to a schedule. I can't tell you the exact moment this will be wrapped up, but I love you and it's got to work out, for both of us."

When I hung up the phone, I went in the bathroom and wept into the sink for what must have been an hour. Blood ran from my nose and tears from my eyes and the watery mess converged in the basin. Then there was a moment in which everything snapped. The blue of the bathroom walls became brighter. The sound of running water became distinct. I looked in the mirror at my swollen, bloody face and said aloud, "Why are you doing this? He's only . . . he's only a man. *One man.*"

The next day I called Jack and told him I was feeling better. He let out a rushing sigh of relief.

"You goon. Do you think you could be the one to stay calm?"

"I'll try."

"Well, it sure would be appreciated."

In the same week that Jack asked Chris for a divorce, the week of July 4, I accepted a blind date with a writer in New

York named Michael. He had been given my number by a friend, who had told him I was a "no-nonsense girl" and was built like Carly Simon, whom he had known since childhood. Of Michael, the friend had told me only this: "He's amusing," which made me assume he was not attractive.

What struck me, then, when Michael walked through the door was how unexpectedly attractive he was. He had black eyes, black hair and dark skin that made me think of the color of a sorrel horse. He had brought with him a literary quarterly that contained a short story he had written. I was impressed. Within the next twenty-four hours he was to flood me with his work. He was twenty-nine and had been writing on his own for ten years, completing many stories and a novel.

When he walked through the door, I remember feeling as if I were letting in a hurricane. The small apartment shook with laughter and motion and word play and sexual expectancy. I stayed with him that night, and from the outset, sex with Michael had a texture radically different from anything I had known.

It was scary. There were a hundred horses in his corral and they were raring and pawing. Michael would not hear "no." He wanted me to do things I hadn't done or dreamed of and didn't think I wanted to do. "You'll like it, trust me," he said and pressed on. The threat of a stampede over and in me was frightening and exhilarating and violently addicting. I had trouble concentrating on my work, and by the weekend, I was ready to close the door on the world.

It was a steaming night of thick summer rain. The Doors were singing "Light My Fire," seven minutes of electrical spiraling down and down and down and down. The air-conditioner was humming although the machine was old and could only take the edge off the heat. We lay without clothes on top of a sheet. My cat, Nicholas, was sleeping beside us in a pose of surrender. His paws were spread-eagled and his white stomach was exposed, pulsing faintly.

"Amazing," I said. "I could never be like that."

"Yes you can," Michael said. "You can be just like that cat. I want you to, lie back now." It was difficult but I stretched out my arms and legs. "You're so feminine," he said, as if savoring what he saw. "Those downcast eyes of yours are very, very feminine." Stroking, soothing, he worked his way down until his head was between my legs. I flinched. I had never let anyone do this. . . . "Just relax." His voice had the most persuasive cadence. He began, very slowly, to flick his tongue against me and I was surprised, it was pleasant. Warm lazy ripples.

Try to set the night on fire. Then, although he did not change what he was doing, the sensation was changing. I had an image of children, beautiful happy children, wearing crisp black and white dresses and suits. It was a gathering of children at a birthday party, and cakes were being brought to them on silver trays.

Could I actually come like this? I wondered. I was beginning to recognize signs—the tension, the straining and huffing to reach a destination. My eyes were shut and everything—the room, the rain, the Doors—was blanked out. It was exquisite, torturous. I must have release, I thought, please don't stop. *Please*, I know you must be tired but please it's so close. I was shaking, wound up like a hunt dog ready to dash and still the intensity kept building until I was astounded the body could register such extreme sensations of pleasure. I screamed.

"That was lovely," Michael said and laughed softly. He looked up dreamily. "I was really into it."

Later he taught me how to go down on him and I did not mind it, although I had been sure I would. But the night ended badly, as did many of the nights that Michael and I spent together. The slightest word could ignite in him a rage and he would storm out. On this particular night, we had turned out the lights to sleep. Michael began to cough and toss. He propped himself up on pillows.

"Do you believe as I believe that Lee Harvey Oswald acted alone?" he asked me.

"No."

"Why not?"

"I'm too tired to go into it now."

He leaped from the bed, grabbed his clothes and slammed out the door. "You condescending cunt."

He called the next morning. "Hey baby, I'm sorry. I got angry, that's all. Come up here later on. Bring your tall sexy body. We'll eat and drink and fuck and suck."

Over the Labor Day weekend I flew to Boston to be with Jack. We went sailing at sunset and hit calm waters, just as the sky was turning rosy orange. We lay on our backs to savor the stillness and I felt as rosy and heated as the sky.

When Jack reached for me in bed, though, I mumbled, "I'm tired." I made excuses all weekend, and for the first time since we had met, we were bickering. At one point I slipped and called him "Dad," but if he heard me, he pretended he hadn't. He fell silent. He vacuumed, he untangled the telephone cord. He washed his socks, he changed the muffler on his car. He is fussy, old womany and silly, I thought.

On Sunday night, I told him about Michael. His chest seemed to collapse. "I knew there was something." He made the saddest sound. "Now you know how I felt driving home to Chris. Your guilt increases with every mile you get closer."

"No," I said, "it's not quite like that. This has no chance of lasting, it's mainly sexual. But somehow, I think it was over the night you found out Chris still wanted you. I let go. I didn't want to compete."

Jack's eyes were burning and I knew he could not speak. As I watched him, I realized, to my wonder, that I was enjoying his pain, for it indicated that he so loved me he could be hurt.

If what seduced Tasha was poetry and what seduced Susie was ideology, what seduced me—and what made the affair more than "mainly sexual"—was psychological perception. Michael had a rare capacity for feeling, and I thought he understood me as no man ever had. On days when I felt the world closing in, rendering me incapable of making a single decision, he would ask, "What are the problems?" Gently, he would explore and resolve each item as if moving down a check list. Then he would kiss me. "You see? There's nothing to worry about."

He liked to find the humor in a situation. New ideas and images grew out of our conversations and often, I did not have to explain things to him, we could speak in what he called "short-hand."

He understood my depressions, although in many ways his temperament was the opposite of mine. While I awoke with grumpiness and vague forboding, he sprang out of bed, cheery and optimistic. Despite debts and unemployment, he was excited to see each day, excited to read the papers and watch the latest movie and read *The New Yorker* and eat rare sirloin steak and baked potatoes with lots of catsup and a Heineken beer. "When I get some dough," he said, "Heineken will be the house brand."

His face reflected completely the mood of the moment. He had a clamorous laugh, people loved him or hated him and he never went unnoticed in a room.

But he had eccentricities that frightened me. He wouldn't blow his nose or drink out of a paper cup. He weighed himself three times in a row because, he complained, the scale would "fluctuate wildly" each time he stood on it. He rooted for the sports teams of Philadelphia and if the Phillies lost a game, he fell into a sulk, but if they won, he strutted as if the victory had been his own.

He always dressed the same in a black T-shirt and baggy khaki pants. He owned no jeans. I teased him that he was a man of the fifties. He had smoked a little grass but preferred drinking scotch. He knew nothing of radical politics and was, at the time we met, "for the war."

The first night we met he had asked, "How come you're not married?" I was only twenty-four but I had been asked this question so often I had an answer ready: "My husband died, in a car accident."

I confessed the truth less than a week later, by which time Michael had told so many lies it was to take years to unravel them. He painted himself as a world traveler, master chef, professional photographer, successful published writer and long-standing radio star in Washington. The truth was that he had never held a job longer than six months and was $3,000 in debt.

"The Bee Gees, the Byrds, Harper's Bizarre, Iron Butterfly, Cream, Lovin' Spoonful, Procol Harum . . ." I was coaching

Michael about rock 'n' roll groups. He had been hired to do a show on an F.M. radio station that was switching from classical music to rock, and had presented himself as a "rock expert." He possessed not a single rock album and I had ten, but by the end of two weeks he knew every group. He brought home hundreds of albums which we listened to and filed under the beds. "If I can just stay on the air two months," he said.

What I remember about the fall of '67 is listening to his shows while Jane and I shortened our skirts and ate low-fat cottage cheese. Every week the skirts seemed too long again until we had them so high they barely covered our behinds. With our legs swinging loose and exposed to the air, we felt frisky and reckless, but we had to diet manicly. Twiggy was the standard. Eugenia Sheppard wrote in the *Herald Tribune*:

> The new ideal leg is a round little pole. . . . It's deli-
> cately round but with absolutely no calf. To be stuck
> with legs and calves is just too crass for words.

It was my fortune, I thought, to have polelike legs. I wanted to be the Girl of the Sixties: brand-new, streamlined, groovy, daring, upfront, telling it like it is. I also wanted to stop wearing a bra, but Jane and I worried that it would cause our breasts to drop.

Michael stayed on the air two months and after three, he was signed to a two-year contract. One evening in December, he called me during a commercial. "How about meeting me at Sardi's after my show?"

"What's the occasion?" I asked.

"No occasion, just feel like having a good meal."

I wore a red wool mini, black tights and black boots and felt sensational as the captain showed me to the table. "Why don't you have a martini?" Michael said. "Okay." I was looking around happily and the two actors at the next table were staring. When the drinks came I immediately took a sip. "What's that in the glass?" he asked.

"Hmmm?"

"In the glass."

"Nothing."

"For God's sake, look again."

I peered into it. At the bottom was a diamond ring.

My parents started planning a wedding for April and engagement presents were arriving, but in the first weeks of 1968, I noticed Michael changing the subject at the mention of marriage. When I could stand it no longer I asked what was happening. "I feel like we're rushing it. I've been a bachelor almost thirty years. I've lived with women, though. Would you consider living with me?"

No, I said. Either we get married or break up. I now had to stall my parents without alarming them and nudge Michael further without blowing everything. And I was furious; why had he given me the ring if he wasn't sure?

The last week in January he came home from having lunch with Carly Simon and announced: "Okay, I'll do it. Carly thinks the world of you and she urges us to marry. But I want to do it fast, this week, at City Hall."

I jumped at the chance. A bird in the hand. The next day, a Wednesday, we had our blood tests and went to Tiffany's to buy rings and to Sloane's to buy a kingsize bed. City Hall looked grim. A sign outside the chapel said, "Please do not throw rice in hall or on stairs." The father of Michael's best friend, Bernie, was a rabbi. He could marry us Friday in Bernie's apartment overlooking Central Park. Just Bernie and his wife and Jane would come. And Michael would ask his father.

"Can I ask my parents?" I said. "I don't know if they can fly here on such short notice but I'd like to give them the option."

"Absolutely not!" Michael said. "That's the point of doing it fast, so I don't have to deal with relatives I don't know."

"But your father is coming, it's not fair . . ."

He was out of control. "All right," he screamed, and slammed his fist in his hand. "We'll call the *whole thing off!*"

The night before our wedding I wandered around the United Nations until three in the morning because the *Pueblo* had just been seized by North Korea. A French journalist asked me over drinks to go home with him and I almost did. In the morning, I went to Kenneth, who did Jackie Kennedy's hair and had offered, when I interviewed him, to give me a complimentary styling.

"Don't let him shorten your hair or the wedding is off," Michael warned and he wasn't kidding. Kenneth cut four inches before I knew what he was doing, pulled my bangs off my face and fixed little spit curls, "tendrils," he called them, around my cheeks. I went home and combed it out and did it over myself, praying Michael wouldn't notice the missing four inches. I put on a white knit mini-dress he had bought me as a Christmas present, white tights and white pumps. Jane gave me a bouquet of yellow roses. "This marriage won't last six months," I told her. By the time we arrived at Bernie's in a taxi, I was a wreck. I sat in the bedroom crying. The rabbi came in and patted my shoulder. "Brides always cry," he said, "but they're happy tears, tears of joy."

He was wrong. I was crying because I was marrying a lunatic.

Once I was standing beside Michael, though, looking out on the snowy park, I felt happy. After the ceremony, we had dinner by ourselves at L'Etoile, where we ordered a sixty-dollar bottle of burgundy, lobster crepes, chateaubriand, endive salad and chocolate mousse. We held hands and kissed continuously. Michael promised he would make it up to my parents. At the door of his apartment he stooped to pick me up. "Don't be crazy," I said, laughing. "I'm too heavy, you'll get a hernia."

"I don't care if I get a hernia," he shouted as he carried me to the bed.

9. Body painting, Sufi dancing, Hare Krishna, Hare Krishna. (© Jim Marshall)

10. Haight-Ashbury. Runaways by the Fillmore. (Andy Mercado, Jeroboam, Inc.)

11. Hardhats marching on Fifth Avenue to Support Our Boys in Vietnam. As I watched, another group in the march tarred and feathered a young man with long hair. (Burt Glinn, Magnum)

12. Hell's Angels, 1968. The Angels and the hippies were friends then.
(© Jim Marshall)

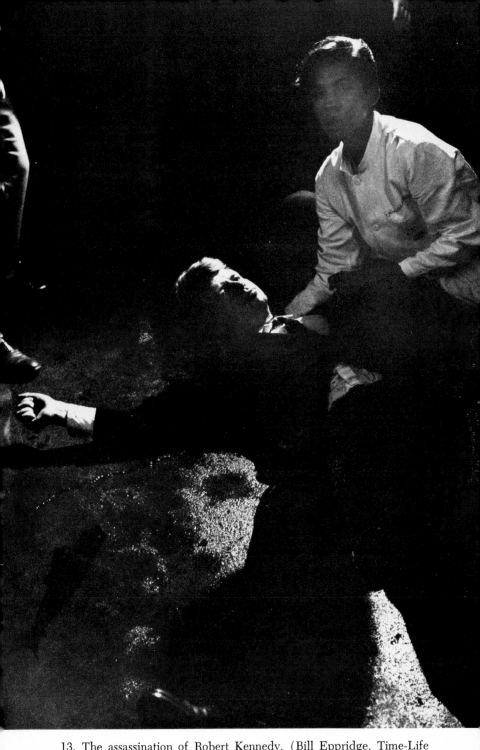

13. The assassination of Robert Kennedy. (Bill Eppridge, Time-Life Picture Agency, © Time Inc.)

14. Students occupy the dean's office at Columbia University, 1968.
(Gerald S. Upham)

15. Chicago police during 1968 Democratic Convention. Police hold Pigasus, a pig the Yippies were running for President. (© 1976 Fred W. McDarrah)

16. Chicago convention riots. (UPI)

15. SUSIE

By 1967, Susie was frustrated. How many times had she marched, lettered signs, made peanut butter sandwiches and answered phones? How many times had she watched Jeff fire up a crowd, his freckled face lit by TV camera lights?

And still the war went on. More drafted, more dead. Marches in the street were a fucking waste of time. Even housewives in the suburbs would march against the war now, and yet, in the face of massive opposition, LBJ had authorized the bombing of Hanoi.

In February, after Clark Kerr was fired, Susie had bumped into Sara on Telegraph Avenue. Sara was acting like a big-shot reporter and Susie knew it would be a waste of time talking with her. She'd go back and write what all the reporters who cruised through Berkeley wrote: the Movement was losing steam. Youth was turning inward.

Jeff said that was bullshit. In an essay that was printed in the *Barb*, Jeff wrote, "The dropouts in the Haight-Ashbury are creating new values and building counter-institutions that will serve the revolution." Susie was attracted to the hippies for different reasons: being a hippie meant you could run naked in the forest, get away from your husband and fuck everyone else.

She made inquiries about having her tattoo removed. "I wanted to shed my inhibitions, but I was embarrassed to have a cartoon on my chest." She went to see a doctor at the Student Health Service who said he could remove it surgically, and a date was set for May.

On April 15, 1967, the day of a nationwide Mobilization Against the War, Susie woke up feeling sick to her stomach. She told Jeff she thought she was catching the flu. When their friends, Bob and Roxanne, came by, Susie told them all to go along without her. "I'll listen on the radio."

When the three came home, they found Susie at the kitchen table in her long nightgown, eating Polish tomatoes from a jar. Jeff lifted her up and kissed her, then buried himself in the TV news. Roxanne asked Susie how she felt. "Awful, but it's the weirdest thing, I can't stop eating these tomatoes."

Roxanne said kiddingly, "Could you be pregnant?"

Susie was stunned. To this day, she does not know how she got pregnant. She used a diaphragm and didn't keep track of her period. Jeff was always talking about wanting to have kids, but Susie didn't think about it because if she did, she would have to think more about the marriage.

"Hey Jeff," she yelled to drown out Walter Cronkite. "I think I'm pregnant."

Jeff went crazy with excitement. "So I was hot shit again," Susie says. Within weeks, all the women they knew in Berkeley were getting pregnant. That was the flow. "I didn't know what it meant," Susie recalls. "I didn't know my cervix from a hole in the ground." Suddenly there were all these issues to confront: natural childbirth, nursing, husbands in the delivery room, rooming-in, *Thank You Dr. LaMaze*. And Susie had to face a disappointment: being pregnant, she couldn't have surgery to remove her tattoo.

For the first time since she had met Jeff, she started being friends with other women. They would talk on the phone about what the doctor said and how much weight they were gaining. Susie would shove a book at Jeff—"Read this and see if I should breast feed." Jeff would flip through it dutifully and tell Susie she looked beautiful, which she did. She was eating real meals and finishing everything on her plate instead of running all day on candy bars and Fritos. What blew her mind was that she had breasts. She could fill a B cup. She felt sexy and ripe. In the summer at Provincetown, she paraded around the beach in a gay French bikini. People stared and she loved it, flaunting her tanned belly over a shocking pink bikini.

She was sorry to be missing the Summer of Love in San Francisco but relieved that she wouldn't be taking acid anymore. Reports showed the drug caused chromosome damage. On the Fourth of July she felt the baby quicken—bubbles and rumblings in her stomach. She asked Jeff to come feel her stomach. Why did she have to ask?

Jeff was reading all the time and talking long-distance to his friends in Berkeley. Every day, they said, there were love-ins on Telegraph and it was hard to get a crowd to listen to anything serious. Kids would shout, who cares? Look inside, eat some sunshine. Work out your sex trip, man. Wasted runaways were lying on their bedrolls in the street. Sergeant Pepper's lonely Sergeant Pepper's lonely. "Spare change?" V.D. clinics, snapshots on bulletin boards: "Mary we love you please come home."

Jeff brooded, was the New Left dead? The ghettos were erupting—there were riots that summer in Detroit, Cleveland and Newark. But the blacks wanted nothing to do with white radicals. Andrew Kopkind wrote in *The New York Review of Books*, "To be white and a radical in America this summer is to see horror and feel impotence."

Jeff's friends were flipping out. At parties they devised schemes for blowing up armories and the Golden Gate Bridge, but to Jeff it was fantasy talk, diverting him from the real issue: what was he going to do with his life?

He had been fired from his teaching job at Berkeley. He had been arrested four times. He would not start a bourgeois career. But what was the alternative? Be a perennial nonstudent and end up like the forty-year-old bohos at the Med? Live off his parents? He would soon be a parent.

When Jeff and Susie returned to Berkeley in the fall of '67, they applied for welfare. Jeff took a job at the Experimental College at San Francisco State. He was paid almost nothing but he could teach what he wanted: "Youth as a Class" and "A Radical Analysis of the Week's News." Susie quit graduate school and threw out all her books. From now on, she told her mother, "I'm gonna learn from life."

She really wanted to stay home and bake bread. The baby was due in two months and she painted the spare room yellow and hung madras curtains she had shoplifted from India Imports, which was not much different from stealing cashmeres at Saks except now there was a rationale: you were ripping off the system.

She bought a basket to use as a cradle and braided ropes to string from the ceiling so the cradle would rock. She felt hurt that Jeff never offered to help. She had a splitting headache. She felt a limb kick out against her. It was astounding. The baby was turning completely around and now her stomach was lopsided. "Jeff, come look at me, hurry!"

He was watching a football game. "In a minute, I want to see this play."

She walked in the living room and switched off the set. "It's always something else. Whenever I want you to be with me you're running to the meeting or the movies or the news or to watch a goddamned ball game."

"Quit hassling me. I was up all night writing, I wanna relax."

"Sure. While I paint the walls and put up shelves . . ."

Jeff sprang to his feet, pulled the TV cord out of the wall and dumped the cumbersome set in the garbage can.

By the time Susie started natural childbirth classes, Jeff was absorbed in a new political effort—the Resistance, a group that had come together to plan a new kind of militant demonstration. They had to counteract everyone's feeling of impotence. Take the offensive, stand up to the pigs and fight. Right on! In meetings that lasted until dawn, they concocted a scheme: Stop the Draft Week. They called a press conference and announced they would shut down the Oakland Induction Center for a week "by decree of the people!"

Sometimes the Resistance meetings were held the same night as Susie's natural childbirth classes. "Please, Jeff, I need you to come," she would say, feeling hurt she had to beg. Jeff would go along but keep checking his watch and ask to leave early.

When Susie sat in on Resistance meetings, she began to be nervous. The men were talking about the "French plan"—snake-dancing in the streets, hurling smoke bombs and turning over cars to make barricades. Then the men laughed because the French plan sounded absurd. In all their meetings, they never did figure out how they were going to stop the draft. Fuck plans, the people would learn in the streets.

Susie knew they were using overkill with words. "It was shooting in the dark. They never knew what the fuck they were doing until it was over." It was Jeff's trip anyway. She was thinking about whether to use cloth or paper diapers.

Just before Stop the Draft Week, the leaders and their women posed for a picture that was made into a poster. Jeff wore a helmet and carried a gladiator shield painted like an American flag. The other men struck menacing poses, holding bricks, grenades, lead pipes, smoke bombs and acetyline torches. Susie was lying on the floor, her belly like a mountain on which Jeff had his foot planted. No one was smiling. The combination of their fresh, innocent faces with the weapons gave the picture a surreal horror.

Susie remembers that when they were posing, the photographer had told her, "Raise your fist." The two-fingered peace sign had been co-opted by now, but Susie didn't like the raised fist salute. It felt phony and mean, but if she objected, the men would put her down for being uptight. She raised her fist.

Jeff had to help her to her feet. She was enormous, the baby was due in two weeks and it felt like they were racing on two tracks: the baby and the Resistance. With one week to go, they went on a tour of Alta Bates Hospital. They were shown the labor room and the changing room where the husband goes to put on his gown. Their friend Roxanne had just delivered her baby at home and Susie was thinking, why do I have to go to a hospital? But she and Jeff agreed, "We'll do it straight the first time."

Jeff refused to let Susie go along to stop the draft. This demonstration was too rough for pregnant ladies. Susie felt pissed that she was missing out but pleased that he cared.

On Friday, Jeff left home at four in the morning. She helped him smear Vaseline on his face to protect him against tear gas. He put on a jock strap with a metal cup so the pigs couldn't smash his nuts. He wore a football helmet. Susie wore a ruffled dress from Motherhood Maternity. She had a job, her phone number had been given to demonstrators to memorize and call if they got busted, but the phone never rang.

At midnight, Jeff came home waving his fists and singing the chorus to "Alice's Restaurant." His clothes were torn and his right hand was bleeding. "Oh, babe, it was so fucking heavy, we didn't close the induction center but we closed the whole city!" He told her they had formed small groups and rampaged through the streets, painting slogans on buildings: Smash the State! Off the Pigs! They broke windows in the Bank of America and with special glee, painted over parking meters (don't follow leaders), so that no one could be given tickets.

"It felt so good to smash the windows in that bank," Jeff said. "This is a real turning point. Everybody's talking about secret armies of urban guerrillas. No more theorizing. We're gonna remake this country in the streets. We're gonna knock those motherfuckers who control this thing right on their asses!"

Susie fixed coffee, feeling blank, tuning out, while Jeff sat down to write an essay for the *Daily Cal.* "We took power yesterday and we felt very real for the first time in months. The victory of October 17 is that the lines are finally drawn: which side are you on? Either you stand with L.B.J., Reagan and the Oakland police, or you stand with the demonstrators and some claim to courage. Thirty years ago at the siege of Madrid, La Pasionaria told the troops of the Republic that you can die on your feet or live on your knees!"

"Hey Jeff, I got the bloody show," Susie yelled out the window. The first sign of labor. They timed the contractions and called the doctor, who said there was no rush, go to the hospital in an hour. In the labor room Jeff coached her. "Relax, stay with it, you're doing fine." In the transition time, Susie started to slip. The pain was astounding, nothing like what she'd expected. "I want a tranquilizer."

"No, babe, you don't need it," Jeff said, and she was enraged. He was pushing her even now. He wanted to tell his friends she had done it all naturally. Didn't he care about her?

"I want a tranquilizer!" she said. "Call the nurse, I want a shot." It was an important moment because it was the first and only time in their marriage that Susie defied Jeff. But years later, Susie was to rethink that moment: perhaps Jeff had been trying to encourage her, to tell her the worst part of labor was over.

Jeff called the nurse, who checked her and hurried to get the doctor. Susie was fully dilated. They rushed her to the delivery room. The doctor put a stethoscope to her belly and mumbled something . . . heartbeat dropping. Suddenly there were six people working on Susie. They smashed oxygen on her face. Where the fuck was Jeff? He had to run put on his gown and she could hear from his voice how terrified he was.

The oxygen failed to raise the baby's heartbeat and the doctors were going to use mid-forceps. No time for anesthesia, they had to get the baby out. No time for LaMaze. "What's happening!" Susie screamed through the mask. Nobody could hear her. She felt like her insides were being ripped out. They switched her from oxygen to gas and she was screaming, "Is the baby alive? Am I dying? Is there brain damage?"

She was on the verge of nodding out from the gas when she heard, through a mustard-yellow fog of gas and pain, a wailing and a muffled voice, "It's a boy."

A boy? She had forgotten the whole issue of sex. She heard Jeff say in a squeaky Donald Duck voice, "He's fine, he's beautiful." She tried to get her bearings. The baby was alive. She was awake. No damage. A boy, wow, thank God it was a boy! She had been scared of having a girl, another female in the house that Jeff might love more than her. They had already picked a name—Sam, after Jeff's grandfather who was still living, which meant they were breaking Jewish tradition but Susie didn't care. It was a strong, gutsy name.

She held the baby in her arms on the delivery table. He had bright pink skin and big feet and was wailing. Who was he? A stranger. She felt like laughing, she felt like crying. She was sore and wanted to sleep but she wouldn't let go of this funny-looking being who was wailing so hard. He would be in her life from now on. Sam.

On December 1 Jeff stood on the steps of Sproul Hall and set fire to what he said was his draft card but was actually a movie pass. He had lost his draft card with its 1Y deferment years ago. Two hundred men were turning in their cards. Phil Ochs sang, "I Ain't Marching Anymore." Jeff shouted, "Once you've turned in your card and said the system doesn't scare you anymore, you can start living as a free man!" Balloons hit the air. Trumpets blared "The Star-Spangled Banner." Two weeks later Jeff was arrested. The Oakland district attorney had decided to make an example of him. The Supreme Court had just approved the jailing of demonstrators who burned their draft cards.

Susie went to bail him out with Sam in her arms and was photographed by the San Francisco *Chronicle*. It was unreal, Jeff was always on the front pages and now this one happened. She didn't believe he could be sentenced to prison. They were invulnerable.

After the arrest, Jeff was running more than ever to lawyers' meetings and Resistance meetings but Susie rarely went. They could not afford baby-sitters and besides, she would have felt guilty leaving Sam.

In the first months, Sam cried continuously. "Everyone else's baby slept and went 'goo,' but Sam was always wailing and driving us nuts. I'd try singing to him, rocking him, walking him, nursing him and then he'd cry some more until I wanted to throw him against the wall or myself out the window."

Sam slept in spurts. Susie would rush to fall asleep and just when she did, he'd wake up screaming and she'd be so frustrated. "I was tired all the time and pissed that Jeff could sleep like a log through it all. I didn't know what the fuck I was doing. Should I try a pacifier? I didn't want to use a pacifier. One book said this, one book said that. All the other ladies with the babies were doing fine and I was going crazy and they were giving me advice."

As soon as Sam could sit up and crawl, though, his disposition

changed. "He became an angel," Susie says. She felt her son had
a tremendous spirit that wanted to come out and master the
world. He was a pusher, he did everything early, stood up and
talked early in a gravelly little voice. At times she was so
engrossed with Sam that Jeff seemed superfluous. But then there
were moments when she missed all the action he was still caught
up in. She made a point of listening to the news so she would
have something to talk about when Jeff came home. When
friends saw her at the Co-op and asked what she was doing, she
laughed nervously. "Nothin', being a mother."

Over Christmas she was starting to feel more and more lonely,
when their old friend Barry came to visit. He had broken up
with Margie and spent the last year on an island in the Aegean
writing poetry. Barry and Susie took walks with the baby. He
had a way of listening with his green eyes totally there that
made Susie feel appreciated. She told Jeff she wanted to make
love with Barry.

Jeff said it was cool—he would set her up that night. Jeff had
set up all her affairs. Susie washed her hair and daydreamed as
she cooked chicken with white wine and fresh mushrooms. At
dinner she avoided Barry's eyes, waiting for Jeff to bring up the
subject gracefully. When they had finished eating, she nudged
Jeff under the table. Nothing. They watched television and Barry
said he was going to sleep. When he had left the room, Susie
threw a copy of *New Left Notes* at Jeff. He stood up, knocked on
Barry's door and said, scratching his head, "Fuck, man, Susie and
I, like, if you want to ball Susie . . ." Barry laughed. "Outasight."

They smoked a joint and Jeff wanted to undress Susie and present her to Barry but she was embarrassed about her tattoo.
They began to tease and wrestle with each other. Susie pushed
Barry off the bed. He pulled her after him, pinning her down
while Jeff was yanking off her tights. She was laughing and
thrashing when Barry started kissing her. She put her arms
around Barry and they kissed more deeply and suddenly her
husband's head popped between theirs and they giggled. Neither
of the men could get it up. You go first, no you. Susie put her
hand on Barry and that was all it took. They were both so

aroused Susie thought she would faint but she was scared, she didn't want Jeff to see her this way.

The next day they all felt awkward and formal, and the following day Barry left. Susie and Jeff couldn't talk about what had happened because it would bring out unspeakable issues. On New Year's Day, they took a walk in Tilden Park. Jeff carried Sam in a backpack. He was raving about the heavy year coming up. The revolution was just around the corner! Susie told him, "Next year I want to get out of the rut we're in. I'm going to smoke a lot of dope and make a bunch of new friends."

IV. FIGHTING IN THE STREET

1968–1969

16. SARA

> *Chicago, Chicago* . . .
> You say you want a revolution . . .
> *That wonderful town* . . .
> Number nine, number nine . . .

1968. Robert Northshield, who produced "The Huntley-Brinkley Report," was to call it "the most incredible news year we lived through."

It was a year in which we followed the news like junkies with a rising tolerance for shock. The improbable—the shock—became a daily occurrence, and it all happened live in color in our homes. Two assassinations. A President dumped from office. Funeral trains, riots, campaigns, count-downs and the most unbelievable occurrence of all: a clashing of tanks and young people and police with C.S. gas in the streets of Chicago, while the Democrats met behind barbed wire to conduct the electoral process.

There were student uprisings all over the world: Columbia; the Sorbonne; the University of Mexico. ROTC buildings were burned to the ground. Yippies rained dollar bills on the New York Stock Exchange. Jackie Kennedy married Aristotle Onassis. Russia invaded Czechoslovakia. Civil fighting broke out in Northern Ireland and Biafra and everywhere we heard the sound of marching charging feet.

At the height of the summer, I sat beside the pool of the Eden Roc Hotel in Miami Beach with Tom Winship, the editor of New England's largest paper. His son was reading the *Quotations of*

Chairman Mao. Republican delegates were sipping Tanqueray. Winship said to me, with a brave, befogged look in his Yankee eyes, "Well, I think we're going to have a revolution."

I did not want to miss a second of the action, nor did Michael. He talked about the news on his shows and I flew around the country pursuing it. I kept a carry-on bag ready to go on short notice: down to Memphis after Martin Luther King was assassinated and up to Cornell after blacks carrying rifles shut down the school. Whenever I was gone from New York for even a day, Michael would call me on the phone, have me paged at hotels and meet me at the airport. We discussed what I'd seen, what he thought and what it meant. As I unpacked, he would pour himself a scotch, put on a Frank Sinatra album and announce out our window to the street, "My wife is back!"

One spring night, I was at Kennedy Airport because Bobby Kennedy was flying in from a campaign trip.

"Miss Sara Davidson, please come to the American Airlines courtesy phone."

It was Michael, calling from the station on the beeper phone. "Darling!" he said. "Lyndon Johnson just went on television. He's not running. He will not serve another term. Can you believe it? Bobby's gonna make it."

Kennedy was informed of the news en route and when he stepped off the plane, his supporters went wild. A Puerto Rican man yelled, "Bobby, Bobby, you don' have to worry no more!"

I ran up to Kennedy and asked if he thought the Democrats would unite behind his candidacy now.

"I wouldn't describe it in those terms," he said, smiling shyly as he reached out for hands to shake. "I think it's a long way to Chicago, and to November. A great deal can happen in political life. We've seen in the past six weeks how unpredictable things can be."

But I was sure Bobby would be the next President. McCarthy was an honorable man but Bobby could win. He would end the horrible war and move the country into sunlight.

Not many weeks later, the phone rang at four in the morning. Michael took it in the living room, then came and sat on the edge of the bed. He took me in his arms. "I love you very much," he said in a choked voice. "We're lucky to have each other."

"What is it?" I said. "What's . . ."

"Bobby's been shot."

Another assassination, another funeral, more crowds. Everything was starting to seem déjà vu and I could not believe. I could not commit myself to causes because there were too many and I had seen how few succeeded.

John Dos Passos wrote of John Reed, "Reed was a Westerner and words meant what they said." I took words literally. I did not know what Susie Berman knew: that most of the rhetoric uttered by the Left was "shooting in the dark." When radicals announced they were going to stop the draft, "We will actually shut down the Whitehall Induction Center in Manhattan," I took them at their word, but they did not come close. They were outnumbered by police, two to one.

By 1968, it was not possible any longer to be a spy behind the lines. If you worked for the capitalist press, you were the enemy. During the spring, when students at Columbia seized five buildings, I used my press pass to get onto the campus, then hid it away so I could mingle. I was on their side anyway. I had shivered in the harsh atmosphere of Columbia and if this was what it took to change the place, I was for it.

"Lenin won, Fidel won, we will win!" students wrote on the walls with their blood. I worried that I was in the wrong camp. I had fantasies of Mark Rudd and his henchmen storming into my house at the height of the revolution, yelling, "Up against the wall, motherfuckers!" Would they shoot me before I could convince them I was a friend?

Michael and I were living at this time on West Twenty-third Street in a four-room apartment he had occupied for ten years. The neighborhood was a slum but he had stayed because it was rent-controlled and more importantly, because he loved repetition. "I've been here ten years. I'm known in this neighborhood." He had charge accounts at the butcher's and grocer's and could cash checks at all hours. He was used to cooking and taking care of the place, but the day after our wedding, although we never discussed it, he stopped all chores and left them to me.

Each day he would call and tell me what he wanted for dinner. When he came home, he fixed himself a scotch and retired to the bedroom, which I called "the green room" because it was dark green and closed, he never opened the blinds. The green room contained our kingsize bed, Michael's desk, a stereo, a television, a telephone and a wall that was covered from the floor to the ceiling with shelves of records. Michael liked to drink and wouldn't drink after dinner, so we ate late, at ten-thirty or eleven. While I cooked, he stayed in the green room reading, watching television or talking on the phone.

After eating, he went straight from the table to sleep. I cleaned up muttering to myself, "I hate the fucking dishes, I hate the way Michael chews with his mouth open. What's wrong with you, Sara, why are you such a bitch?"

Michael went to sleep early and I stayed up late. By the time I awoke he had usually left the house, but never without sitting on the edge of our bed, wearing one of his new Cardin jackets and a wide tie. He would kiss me and whisper, "I love you, my darling." If I murmured a tender word from my sleep, I would hear him announcing as he sailed out the door: "I have a wonderful wife and a wonderful job. I'm a lucky man!"

He was a fan. He cheered when things went well for me and if somebody did me wrong, he shook with rage. He read and edited my work and always found something worthy of praise. Whenever I had doubts, he said instantly, "You're great, you can do it."

He asked that I be his fan in return, but I had had no training in this business. "Tell me you love me," he would whisper, more frequently than I felt was reasonable. He wanted approval of all his positions, everything he did and said, but I could never give it unless I meant it. "Do you have to be so fucking honest?" he would say.

What I could praise, honestly, was his radio show. He was developing a new F.M. style, in which he did not scream like A.M. disk jockeys but spoke in a quiet, reflective voice. He talked about books, sports, Mayor Lindsay. He read from Moss

Hart and told stories from his childhood. But the key to his show was the programming.

He might start with Joan Baez, "Plaisir d'Amour." A woman's voice and guitar, sweet-sounding. Segue to Simon and Garfunkel, "Scarborough Fair." The same rhythm as Baez, still sweet but busier: male voices harmonizing and electric instruments. Parsley, sage, rosemary and thyme, concluding with a ting! End of sentence. New paragraph: the Jefferson Airplane with "Lather." Grace Slick singing in a minor key, an ominous note. Something scary going on: Lather was thirty and they took away all of his toys. Brrrrrrr. As "Lather" faded, in would come the Stones, "2000 Light Years from Home." Spook-house sounds: creaking doors, skeletons, a crescendo to a nightmare. Violins wailing, it's so lonely, you're one thousand liiiiiight years from home. In the last thirty seconds, Tom Paxton's voice would come in over the shivers and echoes, Paxton singing a cappella, "Sully's Pail." By the time the Stones had faded out completely, there would remain one voice, lamenting the death of a friend, Sully. Abruptly, a violin slide and Donovan appears, "I will bring you gold apples . . ." The violin cries for Sully and Donovan offers apples. "Legend of a Girl Child Linda."

Having begun with Baez and lost love, having passed through lands of decadence and nightmare with the Stones, we would come to rest with Donovan on a hillside of velvet. From folk music to acid rock and back down to sweetness, segued so carefully no one would notice the transitions. All in twenty minutes. Without Michael having spoken.

"That's the challenge," he told me, "you don't utter a word, yet anyone truly listening can hear your voice throughout."

Every week, Michael brought home stacks of new albums. On nights when I had finished my assignments, I would sit in the green room with him and smoke a joint. Whenever I smoked, I invariably could leave whatever mood I was in and go to happy. Why, then, did I not stay stoned all day? Because I did not believe you were supposed to be happy all day. When I was stoned, the judge in me was whisked off the bench. I ceased to study Michael with a critical eye, the eye that always reserved approval. I would sing with him and laugh uproariously at his puns which, ordinarily, I found irritating. I would stroke his hair. "You're my bunny," I whispered.

He would look at me with amazement. "You're an *angel* when you're stoned."

When he took me to parties and the host asked what we wanted, Michael would order scotch for himself. Then he'd point his thumb at me and say, with comic exaggeration, "Get her stoned."

On the weekends we had dinner parties, to which we invited mainly Michael's friends and people we admired: musicians, writers, actors, producers, radio and television personalities. While they drank and laughed in the living room, I banged around the kitchen preparing a number from my repertoire: moussaka, beef bourguignon or chicken cacciatore. These were the days of competitive cooking in New York, and preparing a dinner for friends was a performance. I was always uptight, worried something would go wrong—the crust would burn or the sauce would curdle. It never occurred to me to ask Michael for help, and none of our guests came in the kitchen.

Once the meal was over, I loved the fast talking and joking that lasted until early morning, but after a few months, I began to make excuses when Michael suggested another party. "I have a story to write. . . ."

"You mean you're not going to let me have my friends over!"

"It's too much work," I protested, but then I felt guilty for being selfish and gave in.

In the early summer of '68, the editors of the *Globe* met to decide which reporters would be sent to the national political conventions. These assignments were the choicest of the year, and I was overjoyed when told I would be sent to one convention. I asked for Chicago because that's where the demonstrators were going, but the editors said, "The radicals are just shooting off their mouths." They decided I should go to Miami, because I was a "Rockefeller expert," which meant I had written several stories about Rocky's comically mistimed attempt to stop Nixon.

The minute I stepped off the plane in Miami, wearing a brown knit mini-dress and tights, I knew Rockefeller had no chance.

Nixon's minions were everywhere: crew-cut Teutons and Disney girls in dowdy knee-length dresses with straw hats that said "Nixon's the One."

I was depressed around them and depressed at Rocky head-quarters so I came up with an idea: follow a member of the Massachusetts delegation from his arrival in Miami to the voting. I went to the airport to meet the delegation and picked out a likely prospect. He was alone, he was young—thirty-four—he was tall with pale pink skin and when I introduced myself, he told me he was "honestly uncommitted." I will call him Robert McKimmey. He was a state senator and before that he had sold insurance. "I don't know what to expect here," he said, "this is my first convention."

I sat next to him on the bus to the Algiers Hotel and asked if I could follow him around. He was flattered. I could tell he had not been interviewed much and did not realize what he was agreeing to. For the next three days, I followed him around the pool and to the beach, went waterskiing with him and stood be-side him at cocktail parties. I wrote down what he drank, whom he saw and everything he said. He was not a great intellect, I thought, but nice.

What happened with McKimmey is what often happens with interviews. I listen, I nod, I seem to agree, to appreciate and ad-mire this person and believe his every word is worth writing down and savoring. He begins to bask and preen in the attention and feel sexual stirrings, which we both are aware of. What he does not know is that as I nod, I'm laughing to myself, this is great, you're giving me just what I need.

After two days, McKimmey confided his dilemma: the district he represented favored Rockefeller and he thought Rocky would make the best President, but he had "political debts." He owed his presence at the convention to Governor Volpe and his start in politics to Congressman Brad Morse, both of whom were strongly for Nixon. "I don't like doing it," McKimmey said, "but I guess I'll have to follow their lead."

I wrote up the story and Winship liked it. "It's the first piece of enterprising we've done," he said. But the day it appeared, McKimmey, his face working, grabbed my arm on the convention floor. The story was a scandal, everyone at the Algiers was talking about it. All the delegates had told him I'd made him look like "a public drunk and a patsy." His career was over. His wife would divorce him.

I was shaken. "I can't believe that," I said. "It must be sour grapes. The others are jealous of the attention you're getting." But the *Globe* reporters who covered the State House were furious with me as well. I had broken rules again, it seems. The entire delegation was now angry at the *Globe,* and for the rest of the week I avoided the Algiers.

Reporters are not supposed to react as I did. They're not supposed to care what their subjects think of an article after it's published. A good reporter must find a means, any means, to make people reveal what they should never reveal. I had watched crack investigative reporters: bullying, stalking and psyching out their prey, kicking down doors and refusing to relent until the source cracked. But I lacked the temperament. I was warm and seemed so sincere and ingenuous that people talked to me as if I were a friend. But I was not a friend. I wrote what I thought regardless of the consequences, only to sweat and suffer over the consequences. What pained me was not so much the suggestion that I may have ruined someone's career. What made me feel awful was having pretended.

After Miami and the Battle of Chicago, Michael and I flew to Los Angeles so my parents could give us, at last, a wedding reception. Michael had never been part of a family. He was an only child and his mother had died when he was eleven. All he had was his father, Phillip, a dapper man given to high and low moods, a playwright whose last hit had been in 1953.

Michael took an immediate liking to my younger sister, Terry, and ignored everyone else. He borrowed a car and drove to the beach. He came and went when he pleased, but I asked him for one favor. "My grandfather is really special. Would you come with me Friday to his house for breakfast?" Michael agreed, but on Friday he got up early and started out the door.

"We're going to my grandfather's, remember?"

Michael said, "I've got an appointment in Hollywood. It won't take long."

"We're supposed to be there at ten," I said.

"Are you telling me I can't keep my appointment."

"I don't think you have enough time to do both."

He insisted he did and left.

When he wasn't back by ten-thirty, I went to my grandfather's alone.

"Where's Michael?" he asked. I had been answering that question since we arrived. "He had an appointment," I said, and bowed my head. All my grandfather wanted was for me to be happily married.

Grandpa put away the third place setting at the table. He served me a grapefruit, apple strudel and a glass of tea. We talked about the weather and my grandmother, who was in a nursing home that depressed me because it was across the street from the Pink Pussycat School of Strip Tease. The doorbell rang.

I opened the door, glaring.

Michael said, "I thought you said eleven."

"I said ten, and I made a specific point about it."

"No you didn't . . ."

We started shouting. My grandfather hurried from the kitchen with his small steps and as he watched, Michael slapped me and knocked me into the wall.

It was not the first time Michael had hit me. In April he had given me a concussion. I had told the doctor, "A shelf of books fell on me when I was cleaning." I had to stay in bed a week, during which Michael sat with me and talked about things he had never talked about with anyone. His mother's long illness and death. His being sent away to boarding schools from the age of seven. His loneliness, his fantasy world, his troubles in school. "I was constantly running away or staring out the window. I was always being told, 'Michael, shape up or ship out.'"

He laughed glumly. "I spent my adolescence on the high seas."

At the end of the week we felt a bittersweet closeness and Michael swore he would never allow himself to think of striking me again.

That Friday in Los Angeles, I thought, he broke his word! I'll have nightmares for years. I can't bear it: my grandfather, red in the face, beating his small fists futilely against Michael, crying something inaudible, something in Hungarian. I winced. I wanted to scream.

But we had to calm my grandfather. Michael said coaxingly, "Everything's okay. Sara's all right—see? We love each other very much. We just had an argument, things got carried away."

Michael offered to go along with my grandfather on his ritual afternoon visit to the Health Club. I watched the two of them drive off, snail-like, my grandfather's head just visible over the wheel of his yellow Oldsmobile that he never drove faster than twenty miles per hour.

Then I had to meet my mother to go shopping. Listlessly, I pushed hangers along the rack at Ohrbach's. I tried to imagine what Michael was doing. I was sure my grandfather would take it on himself to try to talk some sense into Michael. "You got lotta time in New York to do what you want," he would say. "When you're in Los Angeles, listen to me, you should spend a little time with your family."

I pictured Michael: tense, not listening, thinking about the Phillies. He would press my grandfather to speed his routine: the pool, the gym, the sunroom filled with elderly Jewish bodies, the shower, the steam bath, slow slow steps, trudging behind the old man's nude buttocks.

"Okay, big fella," my grandfather would say as he dried himself. "Usually, you know, it takes twice as long."

I imagined Michael on the snail's ride home, guilty and still raging, wondering why the hell he had gotten entangled with this strange Southern California family that seemed to produce midgets and giants.

I could not look at Michael when my grandfather dropped him at my parents' home. Not knowing where to go, we walked into a cocktail lounge on Fairfax Avenue where we sat like zombies. Over the bar, a neon martini glass was flashing.

"I'll leave for New York," Michael said.

"I'll stay here."

"My lawyer will call you. . . ."

We both began to cry.

My sexual rage was the most powerful single emotion of my life, and the feminist analysis has become for me, as I think it will for most women of my generation, as significant an intellectual tool as Marxism was for generations of radicals. But it does not answer every question.

Sally Kempton, *Cutting Loose*

17. SUSIE

In the fall of '68, the new culture was in flower by the San Francisco Bay.

"Have a rilly good day!" Ankle bells, righteous weed, Free Heuy! Shambala, brown rice and bare feet singing Power to the People!

Oh sure, there were still kids in Berkeley who slept through it: kids who studied at the library, bought their clothes at Roos-Atkins and stepped over smoke bombs on the way home to lunch.

But hundreds and hundreds were living the new life. Every house was a commune, every longhair was a brother. You never had to deal with the straight world at all because freaks had set up alternatives: Resistance Repair; Movement Motors; the Law Commune; Radical Theater; Wine and the People; free schools; free clinics.

Life was free and so was sex. Mmmmmmmmm sex, the ripe scent percolated in the air. All over Berkeley, strangers would lock eyes and flash. Everyone was turned on. All the couples Susie knew had been married three or four years, the women had had babies but were still young and antsy that the sexual revolution might pass them by. The men—shit!—most of them had been going out on their old ladies for years. They were itching for their wives to screw around a little now because it would take them off the hook.

What the fuck, Susie thought, and started asking guys to sleep with her right out. When she did this with Jack Fried, he refused, he wouldn't feel right, he loved Jeff. "But our marriage is fucked up," Susie protested. Jack was gutless but there were hundreds of fish out there in the new culture.

One day she got a baby-sitter so she could go to a rally. Jeff was speaking but Susie doesn't remember about what. People came to rallies these days to get stoned, put down the speakers— bad politics, wrong line—dig the chicks, go for coffee, score and deal. A lanky boy with violet eyes offered Susie a doughnut. She thought he was beautiful. They started wandering up the Avenue. He took her arm.

"You have an old man?" he asked.

"Why?"

"I'd really like to ball you."

"Where?"

So it went.

Jealousy was bourgeois. We shouldn't have to censor our sexual desires. We shouldn't censor anything. If it feels right, do it. But while the men could ball for lust and not get attached, the women kept falling in love. What a mess.

A group of people Jeff knew from San Francisco State were talking about living together to smash monogamy. If they lived together, the women could have separate rooms and the men could rotate. But what about the kids? What about money? Maybe they should open up their heads a little first. Get together once a week and have encounter sessions.

Jeff had a line against therapy groups: they encouraged people to adjust to a sick society instead of questioning the society itself. He said therapy was self-laceration, but if it was happening, shit, he and Susie had better check it out.

So they went to encounters every Monday night. There was no professional leader because the group wouldn't put anybody above them. And the group had to be open, so new people came and went. They all brought their babies and put them to sleep in the same room. A few members who had been to Esalen and Synanon tended to run things because they knew the tricks:

"Share a secret with us you've never told a soul."

"Go around the room and tell each person what you think of him."

"Pick a partner, close your eyes and explore the person's body." Susie loved this. Her first partner was her friend Roxanne. Susie had never touched another woman's body and it was astounding to break that inhibition, to run her hands over Roxanne's enormous breasts and feel her nipples and have it be all right.

At each meeting somebody took the hot seat. The night it was Roxanne's turn, the group asked her to tell her husband, Bob, what she thought of him. Roxanne was drinking tea and her hand began to shake. "I love him . . ."

"Bullshit, you hate his guts."

"Cut the crap, Roxy, what don't you dig? Get it out."

All right, she hated his selfishness, the way he talked to her like she was stupid or something. Sometimes she got so angry she wished he were dead, but she couldn't let on how angry she was. It would destroy him, or else he would leave her. Susie was frightened when she heard Roxanne say this stuff.

A few days later, one of her friends in Berkeley, Maureen, dropped by with her new baby. She told Susie some of the women in the Movement were getting together to talk about women's oppression. Women's what? Susie laughed. She wasn't oppressed—her husband did the dishes and let her sleep with other men. Maureen started talking about how men had power and women didn't. Women were like blacks. Women were treated as inferiors and kept in subservient positions to men.

Susie still didn't get it.

"Look at you," Maureen said. "You've got a master's degree but what can you do with it. Become a secretary? Or else stay home and be a maid?"

Susie went to the meeting of women with apprehension. They didn't like her, they thought she was a snob, they were jealous because she was Jeff's wife and she was pretty.

She remembers walking into Maureen's living room and seeing

all these women sitting on the floor with their legs spread carelessly. She had not been in a room of women since when. The sorority? They wanted to go around and let each person say what she thought about other women.

The first girl said, "I don't like 'em."

The next said, "There's nothing worse to me than going to a party and getting stuck with the women."

"Right."

"I hate to say it, but I've always felt superior to other women. I think they're dumb."

They began to laugh and look at one another. There were girls in the room Susie had seen a hundred times. A lot of them she had written off as jerks, but now, as she listened to them, she understood what they were saying, she could make a connection with each of them and she felt such love.

When they met the next week, more women showed up. The group doubled, split in half and doubled again. Something far out was happening but they didn't know what. They weren't calling it "women's liberation" yet. They didn't have words like "consciousness raising." They tried to draw up a reading list but could only come up with a dozen books, so they started collecting their own data. They would go around the room and let each sister tell her story. The talk was so personal, revealing, shocking, and yet there was a safeness. No fighting for the microphone. No shouting down a sister for having the wrong line. No matter what the issue was, they would take the woman's side.

Susie felt as if the life in her were being turned on. Before long, the women's thing was all she could talk about. Jeff said she sounded like Chicken Little. He and his friends grumbled that the women's group was counterrevolutionary. It was a conspiracy of dykes who were anti-sex. Stokely Carmichael was right: the proper position of women in the revolution was prone.

Jeff came home one day laughing and waving a copy of an underground paper: "Our line on the women's trip—LET THEM EAT COCK." That did it. Susie ripped the paper from his hand. "All these years you've been shouting about the blacks and the poor, you've been fucking *me* over. You treat me like a doll, like I can't think for myself. . . ."

"What's the matter," Jeff said, "can't you take a fucking joke?" But he was starting to sound defensive. "For the first time," Susie says, "he couldn't tell me I was wrong or that I didn't understand. He couldn't quote Marx. He couldn't mow me down with rhetoric. In fact I had Marx and Engels on my side."

At her women's group, they talked about their problems in the Movement and they talked about sex. Sex, sex, the very word made Susie sweat and turn red. "I'd never heard people talk about this stuff. I didn't even know women masturbated." The group read Masters and Johnson—that was a mind blower—to see proof that all orgasms are centered in the clitoris and that the vaginal orgasm, that holier than holy super-come, was a myth!

Susie had to ask where the clitoris was. Jeff had never touched her there because Freud and his father had informed him that mature women have vaginal orgasms. Jeff wouldn't read the Masters and Johnson report. "It's men in the laboratory with plastic penises. It's a bullshit mechanistic capitalist trip, so whatever they come up with is jive," he said.

Susie couldn't read it for other reasons. When anyone in her group mentioned "orgasm," she says, "I'd feel a stab of fear go through me and I'd get all flushed, like when you're caught lying. I'd been lying for five years. Could the women see through me?" She couldn't unburden herself to the group because she couldn't expose Jeff. It would get all over town.

Jeff still said he wanted to fuck twice a day and especially in the morning, in the sun, to Bob Dylan. It was a sunny morning around the time of Thanksgiving. In the last few days Susie and Jeff had been fighting about everything: how Sam should be weaned, the women's group, Jeff's trial. But this morning they had finished a lazy breakfast like in the old days with the papers spread about. Sam was sleeping and the sun was pouring in through the bay windows. Jeff wanted to move the bed in the center of the room so they could fuck in the sun.

They smoked a joint. Jeff was kissing her. Dylan was singing,

"How does it feel . . ." Here we go again, Susie thought. She pulled her lips away. "Can't we just snuggle?"

Jeff folded his arms. "Forget it." She recognized the look in his eye—hurt and quiet.

"Look, Jeff, I've been doing a lot of things I don't want to do just so you wouldn't feel bad."

"Let's forget it."

"No. Look at me. There's something I have to tell you."

"I don't want a big hassle."

"I don't care what you want, it's always what you want . . ."

The telephone rang. Susie started. Shit, it was her mother, calling from Los Angeles. Her mother never called in the morning.

"Are you all right?" Mrs. Hersh asked hesitantly. "Is everything okay?"

"Yeah. Why?"

"I don't know, I've been getting these funny feelings."

Susie was standing a foot away from the bed where Jeff was sitting, hands on his knees. She was stoned, she was naked.

"Are you sure everything's all right?"

"Well, no, actually, Jeff and I are having problems."

"What kind of problems?"

Susie looked at the floor.

"Sex."

She looked up; Jeff had not moved. He was squinting at Susie, watching her lips.

"What about sex?"

"Well," she said, "everything's bad." And suddenly she thought, who cares anymore?

"I've never had an orgasm."

As she said the words, Jeff formed them on his lips. He looked bewildered. Susie held the receiver to her ear and stared at Jeff, wanting to scream, "Yes, that's what I've been trying to tell you." He rose and walked from the room.

It was unreal: Susie standing there naked, listening to her mother offering to pay for marriage counseling. When she hung up, Susie walked quietly to the bedroom and looked in. Jeff was weeping. What had she done?

She steeled herself. "I don't care how much it hurts you, I have
to tell you what's going on with me. You heard what I said in
there. I've never come."

"In all these years?"

"Never. I was faking it. All that moaning was an act. I'm
sorry." She started to cry. "I didn't know any better."

Jeff pressed the heels of his hands into his eyes. "You don't
have to go on. I know. I guess at some level I've known all along.
I couldn't face it either. I'm equally to blame."

"That's not it," Susie said. "There's something wrong with me.
I can't come with anyone. I'm some kind of freak." She wrapped
her slender arms around him and sobbed. He patted her. "We'll
work it out," he said weakly.

Sam was a year old in November of '68, and he was the happy,
stable link between his parents. Susie had come to know him as a
buoyant little soul. He had Jeff's cute nose and curly hair, but he
was not a mellow baby, he was constantly wriggling. His eyes
followed Susie's every movement. At the Co-op, strangers would
stop her and say, "I've never seen a baby look so intensely at
things."

In the mornings she would take him in bed with her and nurse
him while Jeff read the *Chronicle*. They were warm, cozy times,
cuddling with her husband and her son. Jeff talked to Sam
about the Revolution and the Giants—Che and Willie Mays. He
had a game: he would hold out his fingers and Sam would grip
them so tightly that Jeff could lift the baby straight in the air.

After Jeff left the house, though, the day stretched long. When
her women's group formed, one of the first things they did was
organize a play group so the mothers could have relief. The
women were reading Doris Lessing and talking about not dressing as sex objects. They decided to wear uniforms—work shirts
and jeans. They stopped shaving underarms and legs. Susie
hated it. "I'll die for the revolution but don't ask me not to shave
my legs," she joked. She wasn't ready to give up looking pretty.
That had been her high card. Without it, what would she do?

What made it so confusing was that there were two revolutions going on at once—like a circus in two rings. At the encoun-

ter group they were experimenting with sex and relationships:
let's all be free, fuck each other and get rid of our bourgeois
hangups. But in the women's group they were furious at being
desired for their bodies. They talked about living without men
and figuring out ways to reproduce the species without sex. "It
was two different messages and I was real confused because I
wanted to follow both of them," Susie says. "I hadn't fucked all
the men I wanted to yet. I still had sexual hangups. But I'd been
treated as a sex object all my life. I liked it and needed it, and
yet I didn't like it because I knew what kind of sex it produced—
that it left me feeling empty and unloved. So these things were
all mixed up and everything was changing so fast. . . ."

Years later, as she was recalling this, Susie paused. A gleam
came to her eye. "But it was sure exciting!"

"Jumpin' Jack Flash it's a gas gas gas!" There was music in
the air: "Hey, Jude," "Mrs. Robinson," "Sunshine of Your Love,"
"Foxey Lady," "Mr. Fantasy," "Take Another Little Piece of My
Heart."

Susie asked Jeff to take care of Sam half the week. "He's half
your kid."

"But I've got classes to teach and the trial to prepare for. You're
not doing anything."

Susie snapped, "I'll find something. I'm sick of getting the
shitload because your work is so important."

"Will you shut the fuck up," Jeff said. "I'll take the kid."

So Susie was sprung, but what to do now? Go out on adventures. Find people to fuck. She would brush her hair out loose to
the waist and head for the Med—the Cafe Mediterraneum—an
expresso house on Telegraph that became her second home. The
Med was dark and smoky, thick with noise and the scent of
coffee. People sat at marble tables, rattling spoons, rapping
about the pigs and last night's party. It was a place for fast
pickups and political organizing. Everybody there knew who
Susie Berman was, and before long they knew she wasn't there
for organizing.

On Mondays, Susie and Jeff went to the city for their group.
The encounters were getting heavy: major freakouts every week,

but Susie thought it was all for the good. "Why can't people say what they mean all the time?" she asked Jeff. "Why can't we be open?" One Monday in December, the energy was so high that someone said, why not run with it? Stay up all night and give everyone a turn? They took a break for an hour, during which Susie and Jeff drove home to get diapers and food for Sam. On the way back, Jeff asked Susie if she wanted to talk about her orgasm trip.

"No, absolutely not."

"Everyone has troubles."

Susie was adamant. "I'm not going back there unless you promise me you won't bring it up. It's my problem."

The group was meeting in an old Victorian mansion near the Panhandle. The house had stained-glass windows and gas lamps. In the living room, thirty or forty people were sitting on wooden crates and paisley cushions. A red NLF flag rippled down from the stairwell, and on the walls were blowups of Ho Chi Minh.

It was five in the morning when Susie had her turn. She sat with her legs tucked beneath her, ladylike, in front of the fireplace, facing the group. Jeff sat right beside her, wearing olive-drab fatigues and a cap pulled down to his eyes.

"Okay, Susie," one of the men said. "What's it like being married to a big radical star?"

"Never a dull moment," she said jauntily.

"Are you the great woman behind the great man?"

"Not exactly." The questions were coming fast and she couldn't keep track of who was asking them, but she knew it was men, they led the assault.

"You mean you don't dig cutting his pictures out of the paper?"

"I used to. I even have a scrapbook."

Everyone laughed.

"But I've always felt this pressure on me. I never had a chance to develop on my own. I had to keep up with Jeff, so I skipped a lot of steps."

"You mean he carried you with him?"

"Yeah," Susie said. She was staring at the gas lamp, searching her mind. She wanted to sort out all this shit. "When I met Jeff he was like my teacher. He knew so many things. He'd read all these books. People looked up to him. He had wonderful visions. In lots of ways, he was everything *I* wanted to be but didn't think I could be: famous, a leader, inspiring people to do good in the world."

"Why couldn't you be a leader?" a woman asked.

"I wasn't smart enough. That's what I thought, anyway. And I didn't need to be smart. I could get wherever I wanted through Jeff. I've been living . . . I'm only beginning to see this now— how much I've been living through him. I mean, fuck! *I* want to be up there speaking at the microphone. I want to write the leaflets. I'm tired of being the little voice in his ear. I want to be somebody in my own right."

She was talking so fast people hitched forward to stay with her. "Nobody takes me seriously. I wouldn't be in this room if I weren't Jeff's wife. None of you, not a goddamned one of you, gives a shit about Susie Hersh. But Susie Berman. Oh, that's something else. Susie and Jeff Berman, they're Mr. and Mrs. Berkeley. They're the perfect radical couple, loving and struggling and building the revolution. Look how wild and free they are. They're so hot they fuck twice a day."

Tears started from her eyes. Somebody threw her a Kleenex box. "That's the biggest joke of all," she said. "How free we are." She blew her nose. "Well I'm sick of the act, I'm sick of faking it. I'm not Miss Hot Pants. You want to know how wild I am? I've never had an orgasm in my life." She was choking. "I don't know what the fuck it is."

The room went dead. Nobody moved. A teacup shattered. A baby cried far away. Susie became aware of Jeff, breathing laboredly beside her. She had forgotten he was there.

A disembodied voice asked, "Is there anything else?"

"No." But she was still holding back. She couldn't say the rest —that Jeff never turned her on. That would kill him. So she lied. "That's all."

Quiet. Then everybody talking at once. A woman rushed over and put her arms around Susie. "That's the bravest thing I've ever seen anyone do. I have the same . . . problem you do, but I would never have had the guts to admit it."

Susie caught a glimpse of Jeff drooped against the fireplace.
His friend Bob was patting him. Bob's wife, Roxanne, would say
years later, "It was terrible to watch. A lot of people in the room
didn't particularly care about or love Susie and Jeff. A lot of
them were voyeurs and this was hot shit. They couldn't wait to
tell their friends. Before long it was all over San Francisco. At
the Med, nobody talked about anything else for a week.

"You see," Roxanne said, "Susie and Jeff had fooled everybody.
They really *did* look like the perfect couple, like they had no
hassles. Everyone had envied them."

To Susie, it felt as if she and Jeff had been standing on a platform and a wind had blown off their clothes. For a while they
drew closer, all they had was each other. Then Jeff got busy with
his trial and the Third World Strike at San Francisco State. The
school had been shut down. Police were firing guns at demonstrators and Hayakawa had been called in. Jeff was there more
than Berkeley. When he came home to mind Sam, Susie headed
for the Med.

One day she took acid by herself, picked up a seventeen-year-
old guitar player and spent the night with him in Tilden Park.
Susie says, "I was looking for the penis that was gonna give me
the orgasm. I knew there had to be a man out there who would
so turn me on that somehow it would happen." She was always
turned on—with everyone but Jeff. She stopped faking orgasms
and told her lovers, "Don't worry, I'm having a good time." But
still the secret doubts. Was she physically damaged? Did orgasms even exist?

Jeff started spending entire nights away from home. When he
came back for Sam he would find Susie in bed with someone else
and they would be so civil. "Jeff, this is Fred." Shaking hands
from the bed.

They had a dismal Christmas, pretending for Sam, and Jeff
said he was splitting by himself over New Year's. Fine, Susie
said. She wanted to be alone. On New Year's Eve, she cleaned
up the house by gathering all of Jeff's papers, dirty clothes and
ripe-smelling debris and dumping it in his study. She put Sam to
bed, poured a glass of wine and had an idea.

Her women's group had received an anonymous gift. A box

had been delivered to the house where they were meeting by a red-haired speed freak none of them knew. "This is what you frustrated bitches need," he had said, laughing, and split.

When they had opened the box, they had found a parchment scroll with drawings of nude women breaking their chains. Attached to the scroll was a vibrator shaped like a cock. The women had been outraged, but at the end of the evening, Susie had hooked the package under her arm and carried it home.

On the eve of the New Year, Susie took a bath, lit some candles and turned on a Miles Davis album. She got out *The Sexually Responsive Woman* and read the part about how to use a vibrator. In her twenty-five years, she had never masturbated.

Lying on the couch in the living room, she held the machine up to her and turned it on. My God, it was intense. She flicked it off. She was frightened. It sent strange buzzing waves through her body. Come on, she coaxed herself.

She flicked the switch again and the machine simply did it. Fast—one two three. So that's what it is! That's an orgasm? How 'bout that. She laughed aloud. Then she heard a crash: sirens wailing, horns honking. Were they coming to get her? No, it was midnight, New Year's Eve, 1969. Everybody was celebrating this grand event.

Susie laughed and clapped her hands. There's nothing wrong with me, tra la! She wanted to call up the world and say: "Guess what, I can have orgasms." Instead she sat right back down on the couch and had six more.

The next morning, when Jeff walked in the door, Susie was curled on the bed like a cat. She told him the news. He let out a whoop. He threw his cap in the air. He grabbed Susie and danced around the house. "Far out! Let me see it. Show me how." Then he cried. "I love you."

"I love you too."

"Oh, babe, I'm so happy. Don't you see? Everything's going to be all right."

18. TASHA

And what of Natasha? In the spring of '68, while Sara was covering the student riots at Columbia and Susie was wading out in the new culture, Tasha was organizing a major exhibit of Mark's sculpture at the gallery.

It was a season in which she paddled through fog, peering at images hidden under gauze. She was colluding with Mark and Roberta in a charade that no longer fooled people. "Rumors had started," Tasha says. "Roberta's friends were snubbing me, and the other artists at the gallery complained that I was pushing Mark's work more than theirs."

She had moved from her dark railroad flat on Thirty-fourth Street to the sanctity of the Upper East Side. She had not wanted to give up her sixty-dollar-a-month apartment. She had grown accustomed to sleeping with the hall lights on and calling the weather to see if she needed a coat. But one night in March, she had bolted awake to see a strange man edging into her bedroom. She had screamed and he fled. Two weeks later, someone else had broken in.

With Mark's help, she found an apartment on Sixty-fourth Street near the gallery for $180 a month. The apartment had once been the maid's quarters in a town house. It was up five flights and consisted of a bedroom in which there was no space for anything but a bed; a living room; and a thirty-foot terrace overlooking a courtyard. "The place was very European and totally too small, but the light in the neighborhood was like a Vermeer."

She uncrated her collection of paintings and sculpture and was feeling pleased with her little garret when she received a piece of news: Jay Rosen was getting married. His younger brother, Artie, had flown across the country to tell Tasha. He sat in her living room, wearing flared jeans and boots. He had grown a mustache. "You look fantastic," Artie told her. "I was afraid you might have cut your hair."

Tasha had washed her hair when she had learned Artie was coming. She had slipped on a blue mini-dress and dabbed on rose essence, but she wasn't feeling powerful. "Is it the nurse?"

Artie nodded. "She's a complete drag, she's nowhere near Jay's level. She's never heard of Nietzsche. She's never even heard of Big Brother and the Holding Company. She's one of those girls who make a point of letting you know she's a virgin."

Tasha's hand jerked up.

"Listen." He moved closer. "He's marrying the wrong person. That's why I've come all this way, don't you see, You're the right person. Jay still loves you. You can't let him fuck up his life like this. You've got to go out there and stop the wedding."

"Are you crazy? How could I do that?"

"All he'd have to do is see you."

"No."

"You still love him, don't you?"

"Please." She shut her eyes.

"Just answer me, do you love him?"

"Artie, that door has been closed for more than a year."

When Artie left, she had to drink another cognac. She picked up the phone, dialed Jay's number in Seattle, let it ring once, twice. She hung up. She was crying. Why had Artie pulled this stunt? Was he a messenger? What if she *was* the right person? She remembered the sweetness of that summer by the pool in the Hollywood Hills. She wrote a letter and tore it up. She wrote another letter and mailed it. "I should congratulate you, but the

truth is I'm very sorry. I suppose I've always had it in my mind
that some day we might be sharing life together."

Immediately there came a reply from Jay. "Margo doesn't have
your adventurous spirit, but she loves me and wants to have a
dozen kids. I've heard from Artie about your life in New York.
Could you be happy leaving that? If I thought you could . . ."

Tasha tore up the letter and flushed it down the toilet. "I had
to destroy the evidence so Mark wouldn't find it," she recalls.
"But I cried until it felt like my heart broke. I wanted to marry
Jay and live happily ever after and I knew I couldn't. But what
huge pain. The affair wasn't ending right. Part of me was
tempted to go back to California, fuck up Jay's marriage and
claim *my life*." She laughed softly. "I knew that was garbage.
But all I could remember at that moment was the love."

Mark's one-man exhibit opened on April Fool's Day of 1968
and was a sellout. "Natasha, Stone" had been set up in the courtyard so it could be viewed from the ground and the terrace,
while electronic music that evoked druids and forest rites played.
The piece was purchased by the Boston Museum of Fine Arts
and reviewed in *The New York Times* and *Art News*.

To celebrate, Mark took Tasha on a trip. They flew south to
Sanibel, an island in the Gulf of Mexico off the coast of Florida,
which he had heard was a shelling island, unfrequented by tourists. It was the first time they had been away from New York and
the freedom of not having to watch over their shoulders made
them feel like children sprung loose from school.

They went fishing with old-fashioned poles. They rented a cottage that had hurricane lamps and a stuffed alligator head over
the fireplace. They rode bikes through the bird sanctuary, a
mossy swampway alive with flamingos, roseate spoonbills and iridescent bluebirds. They gathered shells. The Gulf Stream carried
the shells up from the Caribbean, South America and Africa and,
as if by caprice, dumped them by the thousands on this finger of
sand. The shells glistened like pieces of bone and spilled jewels.
Mark said the place felt primordial.

The iridescence of the shells inspired him to paint water
colors, while Tasha sat under a banana tree doing needlepoint.

She had started making tapestries to keep her hands busy and help her stop smoking. Everywhere she went she carried a bag of yarn. She invented the design day by day, and at Sanibel, the sight of a horseshoe crab skuttling up a dirt road caused a fanciful brown shape to recur on her canvas.

At night, when the tide went out over a mile, Tasha and Mark made their way across the beach with high-powered flashlights. "We'd see the live shells walking around, making strange sucking and clicking noises. We really felt the lure of this fabulous place and started asking about buying land."

One night at Scotty's Pub, they were eating shrimp steamed in beer when a waitress named Charlie who had a bleached blond ponytail told them there were islands beyond Captiva where squatters' rights prevailed.

They were intrigued. They could build a wooden house. Mark could sculpt and Tasha could make crayfish bisque and work the shells into her tapestries. That night as they were sleeping, she shook Mark. "I just had a very strange dream. I was drowning in the ocean and a golden dog scooped me up and carried me to shore in a big white shell." Mark kissed her. "Let me hold you."

The next day the weather was super strange. No clouds, but the air was wet and muggy. They drove to the edge of Captiva to rent a motorboat so they could go see the outer islands. The man who rented them the boat had gray eyes and a face speckled like a turkey egg. As they pulled out, he said, "There's two ways to go, by the ocean or the bay. Go along the ocean because the bay side is dangerous. The water gets shallow and the boat can go aground."

Tasha said lightly, "If we're not back by three, come and look for us."

"Why should I?" he said. "I got your money and the boat's insured."

She did a double take, but he turned and walked down the dock. Mark headed the boat for the ocean. It was so warm and wet he took off his shirt. After they had been out no more than twenty minutes, the sky went dark. Lightning cracked, rain fell and waves rose up to six feet high. "Let's turn back!" Tasha said.

As Mark shifted the rudder, an eight-foot swell caught the edge of the boat and flipped it over. Tasha was struck on the neck and pulled down by a whirlpool under the boat. She was dazed but not panicked. The water felt good, she was always at ease in water. She observed, I didn't know I was going to die this way. I was worried about cancer or a heart attack. This was one I hadn't thought of. Suddenly she remembered her dream—drowning in the sea. Where was the golden dog?

Mark had her by the arms and was pulling her to her feet. The water was not deep so they were able to wade to a narrow shoal. They looked for sticks to build a fire but there was nothing on the sand but shells and fish skeletons. Tasha's mouth was full of salt. She threw up. They were digging to bury themselves in the sand for warmth when a fishing boat appeared with their little boat in tow.

When they stepped, shivering, onto the dock at Captiva, the boatman said, "Did the motor get wet?"

Tasha said, "We were almost killed, and yes, your motor got wet."

Mark put her to bed under a nest of quilts. "Do you remember the dream I had?" she said. Mark pressed his palms together and touched them to his lips. "Your dream was a warning. We should have listened to it."

When they returned to New York, Mark asked Roberta for a legal separation. She refused, and continued pretending nothing was wrong. Mark decided to go out with Tasha openly. "I can't stand the juggling any longer. I want Roberta to be free and I want to be free, I want to marry you."

Tasha didn't believe him and besides, she couldn't conceive of marrying Mark. "We could never have children, and in twenty years I'd be alone." But it was not just the age difference, there was his willfulness. "One of the worst running battles we had was over a raincoat my mother sent me. It was made of pink corduroy and Mark hated it. He said it was cheap-looking, but the more he complained, the more tightly I held to it. One night he ripped it with a knife and I was furious. I thought he was hung up on appearances, but I gave in and we bought what he wanted

me to have, a two-hundred-dollar raincoat from Bergdorf-Good-
man. We always bought what Mark wanted me to have. I
thought the things he chose for me were matronly, and he
thought the clothes I picked out were studenty."

Among the outfits he selected for her was a fawn-colored
suede suit by Givenchy. She was wearing it one Sunday on Fifth
Avenue when she ran into Candy and Bobby Moss. She had
heard that they were married but hadn't seen them since Berkeley.

Candy was to remember years later, "Bobby and I had just
flown in from London, we were suffering from jet lag and felt
like hicks. When I saw Tasha, what startled me was that she
didn't look as beautiful as I'd remembered. She didn't have that
glow, but she was dressed magnificently in a powder-blue suede
suit and she was walking with a distinguished-looking older
man. We talked for a minute and she said crisply, 'Would you
excuse us, we have an appointment?' I remember being amazed.
We were living in two different worlds."

Tasha says, "I felt like we were in two different worlds but
with Mark I always felt in a different world from everyone else."

Her childhood friend, Beth Warren, was getting married to a
medical student, Harvey Bernay, and it was to attend her wedding that Tasha went to Los Angeles in the summer of '68. She
immediately asked Harvey to fix her up. She was sure she could
find someone more suited to her than Mark. Because she was
staying with Beth, she was immersed in a couples' world of dinner parties and baby showers. Everyone she knew in California
was getting married: both her brothers, Jim Lieberson, even
Steven Silver had decided to settle down with a girl who was a
concert violinist. They all looked at Tasha with patronizing concern, and she herself began to feel "I had missed the boat. Other
boats were leaving and I was missing them too."

She went out with doctors and eager young lawyers working
on the McCarthy campaign but nothing clicked. Mark sent her
hysterical letters saying his life was a shambles and she had to
do something. He was having a show in Paris in October and
wanted her to come. She wanted him to go alone and rejoin her
in New York.

"Either you come to Europe or it's over between us," he wrote. Then came a telegram: "Don't expect letter from me in near future. Much too upset to write."

In the middle of the night she was awakened by another cable. "May kill self. No blame."

She called him at the studio. "What the hell is going on? Are you trying to do me in?"

Mark said he couldn't face going to Paris with Roberta. "Are you willing to take our affair a step further or not?" he asked. She was not, she said. "Then come with me just for the trip."

The day before Tasha and Mark left for Paris, they had a fight during which she slammed the bathroom door in his face and gave him a black eye.

They landed at Orly at 7 A.M. and took a cab to the flat where Mark had spent a good part of every year for the last two decades. Tasha was overwhelmed. The flat was in a quiet, cobblestoned neighborhood dappled by sunlight filtered through chestnut trees. His studio had a solid wall of windows. "Everywhere I looked there were beautiful things to see: a carved sandalwood chest; silver miniatures from India; Bunraku Japanese puppet heads and a Noh mask of a red fox." Mark led her up a flight of stairs and showed her the bedroom where he had built a leaded-glass skylight. Three steps above the bedroom was a sunroom which he had collaged with posters torn off old kiosks and which opened onto a terrace from which they could see the Eiffel Tower. "There was a tranquillity and a coziness about the place that immediately made me want to hang up my clothes."

Mark walked from room to room, gathering up Roberta's papers, art supplies and bottles of pills and stuffing them into paper sacks. Then he lit incense. They went to sleep because of the time change and upon waking, made love and went out to Conti where they ate mousse of salmon, roast partridge and straw potatoes. Tasha was enchanted. It had been four years since she had last been in Europe and she had forgotten the sparkling quality of the light and the musty smell of the Métro and the sound of French people chattering which reminded her of birds twittering. Mark took her to his favorite cafés and to see old detective movies at the Cinémathèque.

Within days, however, word passed among his friends that Mark had dumped Roberta for a girl half his age. His closest friends in Paris were Bob and Carmen Sloan, two artists who held potluck dinners every Sunday at which one was likely to find James Baldwin or William Buckley or Marietta Tree or Jonas Salk or Daniel Barenboim and Jacqueline Dupre eating spaghetti and arguing about the May Revolution with a noisy crowd of expatriate Americans and Parisian artists and intellectuals.

Mark had practically lived with the Sloans when he was in Paris, but Carmen called and said she felt loyal to Roberta and wouldn't have Tasha in her house. Tasha told Mark, "You go and see them. They're your friends and they don't have to be mine."

The scenario was repeated until Tasha learned that Iris Lawson, her mother's friend, was in town. Iris knew the Sloans and started to work on Carmen. "How can you treat her this way? You don't even know her. You've had lots of people in your house who are far more immoral than her."

So after two weeks, Tasha was allowed to go to the Sloans. The women who knew Roberta looked at this twenty-five-year-old girl with turquoise eyes and blond hair sweeping to her waist and at every opportunity, turned their backs and marooned her. Only the men would talk to her. She wanted to hear about the May Revolution but most people said they were fed up. A few students she met from Beaux Arts still believed the popular chant:

> *Ce n'est*
> *qu'un début,*
> *Continuons le*
> *Combat!*

Mark's opening was a noisy success and afterward, he and Tasha retreated into an idyllic routine. By day they lounged in bed under the skylight, took walks through the produce markets and drove around Paris looking for buildings that were being torn down. If they spotted an interesting old door or stone carving, they set the alarm for 4 A.M., snuck back, absconded with the door and carried it up six flights to the roof where Mark was building a star corral, a three-sided structure made of old doors with a bench in the center. They would sit there at night with glasses of Calvados and watch meteor showers.

It was a rare time for Tasha because she was content "being hedonistic." In New York, whenever she left town for a day she took a brief case, books, Xeroxed material and a goal she wanted to accomplish. She had the whizzing air of a hummingbird; if you met her by chance on the street or in a store, she spoke quickly with her eyes glancing in the direction she was going and her feet inching toward the door.

It was only when she was away from New York that she could stay put and enjoy simple things. Reading. Cooking. Listening to music. Having a good cup of coffee. She and Mark felt a resurgence of passion. "We were away from the distractions and the sadness that was to envelop us on our re-entry."

The trip to Paris, it turned out, was more than just a trip. All their friends in New York knew that Tasha had gone to Paris while Roberta had stayed home. The charade was over. Tasha was angry at Mark and more angry at herself for letting him manipulate her into doing what she hadn't wanted to do: make a commitment.

The next three years in her life became a dark journey, in which she sank and sank into regions below the reach of sunlight, warmth or air. "Twenty-four hours a day I was not happy. I didn't like New York, I didn't like my job, I didn't like Mark. My head was full of grotesqueries. I was sitting on the edge of my chair, watching for the door to open a crack so I could make a dash for it and then not moving, not being able to make the dash when the crack did appear."

She quit her job at Hilda Carson's because it was too complicated working in the gallery where Mark exhibited. She became a private art dealer with a friend, Roger Masson. Tasha was tired of graphics anyway. "It had become a repeat performance, and I thought it might be interesting to switch to expensive paintings."

She and Roger rented a one-room apartment on East Eighty-third, painted the walls chocolate brown and filled it with sparkling glass and chrome furniture. But they had no capital, so they had to hustle other dealers to give them works on consignment. They might find a collector who was willing to let go of a Degas pastel for $4,000, and then they would search for someone to buy it for $6,000.

Most days Tasha felt miserable in the dark brown office so removed from the flow of life. She sold whatever pieces she could get, but she felt she was playing a low game: outsmarting people and manipulating them into paying higher prices than they wanted.

One evening as she was walking down Madison, feeling disappointed with life and her wasted potential, she stopped at a newsstand and bought a copy of *Vogue*. A picture caught her eye: a picture of Candice Bergen with her hair in the glamorous mane popularized by Baby Jane Holzer. The hair swept up, crested and fell to the shoulder in a perfect bell curve. The caption said, "hair coiffed by Christian." Tasha stopped in a phone booth, called up Christian and made an appointment. She had not had her hair cut since she was nine, but she was tired of looking like a Berkeley waif. She was selling $100,000 paintings and wanted to look grown-up.

She took the copy of *Vogue* with her to Christian, who cut twenty inches off her hair. Other customers sucked in their breaths as the strands of blond hair fell to the floor. Tasha did not watch; she was reading *Harper's* magazine and had come upon an article by an old roommate. What do you know, she thought, my old friend Sara. I wonder what she's like now. Probably tough as nails. Christian brushed her hair into a shoulder-length mane. "It was nice," she remembers, "but I did not look like Candice Bergen."

Tasha now appeared to the world as she saw herself in photographs: "a common-looking girl who seems from her expression to be very uncomfortable." The light in her face was submerged, and because she had gained weight from taking birth control pills, she looked bottom-heavy in low-cut jeans.

Mark was delighted with her hair cut off, because she at-

tracted less attention. He was worried that she might run off
with someone younger.

Roberta, by now, had agreed to a divorce, so Tasha stayed
with Mark most nights at his studio. She had no idea what she
wanted from her life but he knew exactly what he wanted from
his: to sculpt, be recognized, live surrounded by beauty and
have friendships with deep and distinguished people. She was
swept along his current. "I believed in his work and we shared a
purposefulness about it. I became his apprentice, secretary and
assistant."

Often they would stay up all night working. Mark would wear
plaster-stained pants and move about silently while Tasha
cleaned his tools or sanded wood. "Between midnight and four
A.M., the studio was like a church. Mark worked in a trance, letting the images rise from his subconscious. He never started out
with a preconceived idea so what I witnessed was the act of discovery." At dawn they would change clothes to go out for breakfast, then walk home and sleep until noon.

What she dreaded about their life was the social circuit of
openings and formal parties and dinners with Beautiful People.
When she was seated at a table between Mrs. William Paley and
Danny Kaye and across from Sen. Jacob Javits, she told herself,
the next time we go out I'm going to read *Harper's* or *Newsweek*
so I'll have something interesting to say.

She had a siege of insomnia and violent nightmares all
through the winter of '69. "It was as if I were six years old again,
afraid of the dark and death and time passing. The only good
night's rest I could have was if Mark stayed up all night working. Then I was protected, the goblins wouldn't attack, the demons would keep behind the trees if he was on deck."

She dreamed about Kenny Livingston, her boy friend from
high school. In the dead of February, she dreamed that she was
sleeping with Mark in his bed at the studio. He had left the door
ajar. She heard a noise and sat up. A grinning man with brilliant
red hair and blue eyes tiptoed in through the open door. She
shook Mark. "You've got to get that character out of here. He's
not right." Mark mumbled, "Okay," and turned back to sleep.
The red-haired creature tiptoed closer, lifting his knees high in

the air with wild delight. "Mark," she whispered, "he's a psycho-path!"

At her words, the red creature pulled out a gun and shot her dead. She fell back. Air hissed out of her as if she were a tire that had been slashed. When she awoke, she was sleeping in the very spot where she had died in the dream.

Mark was in therapy with a Jungian analyst, Dr. Von Pieters, whom he told about Tasha's dream. The doctor said he wanted to see her to learn whether the red-haired psychopath was an aspect of Mark's unconscious or hers. The red-haired man was an archetype for the devil, and Mark, in the dream, had left the door open.

When Tasha went to see the doctor, he told her it was highly unusual for someone to die in a dream. "Most of the time, people wake up at the instant they're about to die. What we can surmise is that part of you wants to die. It's an ego death, so your soul can evolve to the next level."

"Words like soul turn me off. I don't believe in God."

"You don't have to," he said. "Our objective is to put you in touch with your instincts. You're all bottled up in your brain."

Tasha began seeing Dr. Von Pieters twice a week. He suggested that she stay in her own apartment several nights and sculpt, write or paint.

She bought a bucket of terra-cotta clay to start with. "I'd dig a chunk out of the bucket," she recalls, "pat it a few times and see an ugly creature, almost as if it were in the clay." She sculpted monsters, dwarves, dinosaurs, trolls, vultures, winged apes and hunchbacks, and after every session she felt a subtle relief. "Before long my house was full of hideous things that I wanted to destroy but Mark wouldn't let me. He rescued them, sent them to be fired and had them stored because he thought they contained power."

On the nights she stayed alone, Mark called three times to check that she was there and not out with someone else. She was pulling away from him sexually. She had stopped having orgasms and almost never took the initiative as she had in the first years.

17. Black Panthers, 1969. (© 1969 Stephen Shames)

18. People's Park, Berkeley, 1969. Police take over the playground that students and street people had built from a muddy parking lot owned by the university. (© 1969 Stephen Shames)

19. Susie watched Jeff tearing at the chain link fence installed around People's Park. (Hank Lebo, Jeroboam, Inc.)

20. The National Guard was called to impose order in Berkeley after People's Park. Above, a mass arrest on campus. (Dick Corten)

21. Woodstock, 1969. Santana and crowd of half a million. I had a stage pass and was afraid, at first, to wander out in the crowd because of the density, the stench, the noise. (© Jim Marshall)

22. Woodstock proved to be a festival of joy. Despite rain and mud, garbage and food shortages, not one act of violence was committed. (© Jim Marshall)

23. Woodstock, bathing in the lake. (Baron Wolman)

As her interest diminished, his grew. "How often do you want it?" he asked.

She sighed. "Two or three times a week?"

"I guess I'll have to live with that."

She found herself counting: "We've already done it twice since Sunday . . ." After they made love she felt used, like a wastebasket. Mark didn't want her, he wanted a woman and she happened to be there.

One night at a party, she told Mark she wanted to go home. He was drinking Bourbon and talking with a heavily mascaraed South American lady sculptor. He walked Tasha downstairs and put her in a cab. "I'll be home in a little while."

Tasha let herself in the studio but couldn't sleep. Somebody might break in. *Three A.M.* She dreamed that Mark was removing all her things from the studio and locking her out. *Four A.M.* She heard drunken quarreling outside. *Six A.M.* She felt the bed beside her. Empty. *Seven A.M.* She got up to walk her dog. *Ten A.M.* Mark stumbled in hung over.

"Where did you sleep? With that bitch lady sculptor?"

"We were just talking."

"The hell you were."

"Dammit!" He spun around and threw a jar of acid wash at the wall. "I can't help it. You don't want it."

She was shaking. "I was so scared," she whispered.

He was shaking also, from lack of sleep and too much Bourbon. They crawled into bed and clutched at each other. "I need you, don't leave me," she wanted to say, but when she opened her mouth, no sound came out.

19. SARA

Anywhere I wandered in the fall of '68, Michael's voice was in the air. In boutiques, taxis and homes, the radio would be tuned to his station and I would hear him announce: "The Beatles. Let's stick with 'em. Here's 'Hey, Jude.'"

I would look about proudly and say, "That's my husband."

After the fight in Los Angeles, we had decided that we would both start therapy and try to stay together. Michael's voice was the new young sound and he was hot because "he communicates," the managers of the station decided. He was auditioned to be the voice of airlines and cola companies. He made pilots for television and his novel was being published. The phone rang constantly with new offers and I was thrilled and jealous and depressed.

My career was in the doldrums. The city of New York was falling apart with garbage strikes, school strikes and police scandals and every week I filed dozens of stories that were read by nobody I knew. I wanted to be connected to the city where I was living.

"I'll never make it in New York," I mourned to Michael. "Yes you will," he kept saying. "You're too good not to."

I decided the moment had arrived for me to apply for a job on

The New York Times. It was the High Court of journalism, the spot I had been aiming for from the moment I had set eyes on New York. I put together a portfolio and two of the *Times'* star reporters offered to sponsor me. We discussed strategy; what I should wear and say. They warned it would not be easy because one of the most powerful figures at the *Times* hated women, but I had been the exception before and could do it again. I went for interviews with four editors, each of whom occupied a slightly higher rung. The fourth editor asked me to write him a letter stating what I would report on if given "the best of all worlds."

I spent weeks on the letter and felt it was masterful. On the day of the interview, I wore a subdued, beige mini-dress, brown stockings and Papagallo shoes. I walked crisply to the editor's desk, prepared to receive his warm praise. He waved me to a chair. "Miss Davidson, yes." He squinted as if trying to place me.

"Did you receive my letter?"

He poked at the papers on his desk. "Um. I seem to have misplaced it."

My smile faded. "I can send you a copy."

"No, don't bother. It'll turn up sooner or later. Well. We like to think that each new reporter brings something unique to the *Times*. We confess to being strongly attracted to writers with a compulsion to pursue verbal accuracy. We also admire wit, irony and a style that is sophisticated, never conned or starry-eyed. What do you think you might contribute?"

I wound myself up and gave him the pitch: he needed a young reporter, someone who had rapport with students and hippies, but someone who could cover a broad range of stories. . . .

As I spoke, he drew back his head like a turtle. His myopic eyes narrowed in a smile. Was he warming to me or scoffing? I went home to wait for word, and after three weeks, received a call from an under under assistant. "A decision has been reached on your case," he told me. "The decision is unfavorable."

Looking back from a distance of eight years, it is difficult to believe the totality of the despair into which I sank after that call. It was not simply a rejection. The High Court had passed judgment: I was a fraud.

For the first time ever I was unable to work. There were

squeezing pains in my chest and stomach. I tried to knock myself out with Valium but after four hours, my eyes snapped open and I was shaking, even before I could remember what had happened. When Michael left for work in the morning, I stayed in bed. I was frightened of everything: the plants growing; the mail arriving—there might be a death sentence. When the doorbell rang I cried out, "Who is it."

"Florist."

A box of red roses with this card: "Marrying you was the most brilliant decision made in my life. I will love you forever. Michael."

I read it and cried more, I didn't deserve it. Hideous pictures filled my head. Michael dying or losing his job; me losing my legs. I had fistfights with memories, trying to hold them down, but some slipped through and made me cry out while standing at the bathroom sink.

For weeks I did not work; I told the *Globe* I was sick. I wandered through the gleaming aisles of Bloomingdale's, buying glasses, towels and bath rugs. I spent hours in bookstores turning pages. One afternoon, flipping through a pamphlet called "Free People," I thought I saw a picture of Susie Berman. I stared at the photograph. It had to be Susie. She was sitting in a sea of rubble, wearing a button that said, "In revolution one wins or dies." Her arm was raised and the finger pointed at the camera as if to say, "You." I saw in her eyes an authority I would not have wanted to question. In her lap she was holding a baby boy. So Susie had a child! I knew it was her child. I began to weep. I had no baby. I had no authority, my existence was futile. All I could think was, I should have stayed in Berkeley. I've missed out on everything.

That night as I lay beside Michael in the green room I sighed. "Woe is me."

"Woe is *not* you," he said, and in spite of myself, I laughed.

Michael had found a psychiatrist, Dr. Pearl, whom he asked to recommend someone for me. I called the number and a Dr. Collins replied, "I kin see you on Friday at two forty-five."

"He's from the South," I told Michael. "He won't understand me. Why can't I have a Jewish shrink like everyone else?"

"Just give him a try."

After the appointment on Friday, I walked, brooding, out on the street, looked up to hail a cab and there was Michael. He had canceled his appointments to be there waiting. I melted when I saw his black eyes staring out of our beat-up Volkswagen.

He took me in his arms. "How was Collins?"

"I liked him. He's strange-looking, he has a beefy face and he smokes nonstop. But he made me feel calmer. Oddly enough, his drawl relaxes me."

"That's wonderful," Michael said. "And I have good news. I ran into a friend, a writer I haven't seen in years. I told him about you. He's invited us to dinner."

The friend was Richard Schickel, who, at Michael's prompting, took an interest in my work and sent me to see his friend Robert Kotlowitz, the managing editor of *Harper's* magazine. *Harper's* was on everyone's lips in those days because the young editor, Willie Morris, gave his writers rein to experiment, to use the language as it's spoken. *Harper's* would print "fuck," which no other slick magazine would do.

"What would you like to try for us?" Kotlowitz asked.

"How about a profile of a young rock group?" This was before anyone knew much about rock bands.

Kotlowitz nodded. "Good idea. You'll have to do it on spec, of course."

Of course. I would do the research on the weekends and write it on my vacation time from the *Globe*. This could be the chance I had been waiting for. Once I was out of his office, though, I started worrying: I had been too brash, too cocky, he didn't like me or if he did I had fooled him, fooled Schickel, and now I would have to fool a group of seven boys I had never met who called themselves Rhinoceros.

The first Saturday in February, I drove through a snowstorm to Lake Mahopac, New York, where Rhinoceros was living in a Victorian house called the Gray Manse. The house looked like a relic from Sleepy Hollow. There were couches with fringes and tassels, stuffed elk, candelabra. Ear-splitting music was rising from the cellar and rattling all the windows. I called "Hello." No answer. The music stopped and I heard an eerie creaking. I spun around and saw John Finley, a gap-toothed blond who was the lead singer, riding down the staircase in a moving chair.

"Hi." He yawned. "I just woke up." It was 6 P.M. "Do you want some breakfast?"

John poured himself a bowl of Granola, then led me to the dark basement where the band was rehearsing. The band's first single, "Apricot Brandy," had just hit the charts with a red bullet. The word had been put out: Rhinoceros would be the next Super Group. Danny Weis, the lead guitarist, started around the basement pulling after him the red umbilical cord by which he was tied to the amplifier. He stopped in front of each player and caught his eye, matching up with him until they were all playing in sync, bobbing their heads and snapping their skinny torsos and juking and flexing and pulling on the strings and pitching together until the air was steaming with this communion.

At midnight they stopped for dinner. Three girls, groupies, floated down the stairs in a cloud of feathers and powdery perfume. No one in the band paid them any attention. The boys sat around the kitchen eating peanut butter and honey with spoons, drinking milk out of quart containers and smoking joints. The groupies retired to the second-floor bathroom and I did not see them again that night. But the place smelled of sex. Michael Fonfara, the organist, was saying that when he plays "Apricot Brandy," "I feel like I'm balling a chick. The beat does it to me."

Danny jumped to his feet. "Lots of times I've come on stage, just from the music, and it's unbelievable."

"No shit!"

"Sure man. I know certain lines on the guitar that, if I'm interested in a chick, I can look straight at her and do it to her. It's like a slap in the crotch."

Danny was twenty, the most erotic and exotic of the group. He had ice-blue eyes and long yellow hair that was layered, teased, permanent-waved and sprayed until it stood out and crackled like cat's fur.

Danny asked me, "Do you have to keep writing in that notebook? It's making me uptight."

"I think you'll get used to it," I said.

He shrugged and left the room.

It was snowing so hard I had to stay overnight. Alan Gerber, the pianist, doubled up with John and I slept in his bed on his pink satin sheets, while the sweet smell of marijuana trickled under the door. I was so aroused on those slippery sheets that I longed for someone, anyone, even the fat road manager, to steal in bedside me. I woke up at noon, still aroused, dressed and started down the stairs just as Danny was sprinting up. After we had passed he yelled, "Cunnilingus everyone."

"Cunnilingus!"

All the way home I fidgeted on the car seat, intent on catching Michael before he left for his show. When he saw the state I was in, he put earphones on my head and made love to me while Led Zeppelin played "She's Just a Woman." He was late now and had to run, but he threw a twenty-dollar bill at me and said, mock tough, "Thanks for the good time."

Michael's gusto about sex had set off fantasies I would have stifled before as perverse. He was constantly pushing me further —to take off our clothes and bathe with strangers at Esalen; to go see blue movies and nude plays: *Hair; Oh! Calcutta!; Che!; I Am Curious (Yellow)*. But he made me promise I wouldn't sleep with anyone else. "It's important to me. I want us to trust each other. I'd be mortified if you betrayed that trust."

For three weekends, I traveled with Rhinoceros to gigs in Philadelphia, Boston and Schenectady. I could stay up all night and sleep all day, wear see-through shirts, dance, smoke dope and take mescaline and it was okay because it was homework. On each car ride I sat with a different member to interview him. The youngest was the bass player, who was seventeen and so thin—110 pounds on a 6'2" frame—that he looked like a *Vogue* model photographed through a distorting lens. He wore black velvet pants, a Greta Garbo slouch hat, a satin shirt open to the waist and a turquoise cross bumping against his concave chest. As I listened to his story I felt prim and naïve. Glue sniffing at eleven. Acid at thirteen. Groupies at fifteen. "I picked up this chick Ruby Tuesday," he said, leaning over and dropping his voice. "She gave me two downers and said she was coming to bed a little later? The next thing I knew, I woke up and found I was tied with scarves to the corners of the bed. She was hitting me with a belt, just enough to sting, and in between she was, um, you know, doing me." I stopped writing in my notebook.

"Weren't you furious?"

He smiled. "No. I flashed on it. Thought I'd take the trip. The next night I whipped her, like, really hard, and she seemed to dig it." Michael and John in the front seat started laughing. Michael said, "A lot of chicks we meet are into whipping." He lit a joint. "Groupies love to be treated like dirt."

That evening as I slipped into bed at the Howard Johnson motel, there was a knock on the door. It was the seventeen-year-old bass player, wondering if, um, you know, like, well . . . I had to laugh. This had happened with all the members of the band and always directly after I interviewed them. It was easy to pass up the seventeen-year-old but most of the time I found it maddening.

I consoled myself that it was better for the story to preserve my objectivity. The band had become accustomed to my presence by now and even Danny ignored the note taking. I saw them squabble over nothing and ruin sets. They were the kind of fights teen-agers have, the fights Michael and I had, the fights that caused almost every rock group to split up in the early years.

I saw their humiliations: restaurant owners kicked them out because of their hair; truck drivers whistled and yelled, "Isn't *she* cute!"

And I saw the moments they called "magic." At the Boston Arena, an old roller rink where the kids were restless and the sound system was bad, Rhinoceros played a set that brought fifteen thousand to their feet. In waves, people rose up, bounced and writhed until there was a howling rush for the stage. The band was in ecstasy. When the set was over, the boys ran off the stage.

"Oh fuck, that was so good!"

"We killed 'em!"

They flopped into their cars and as they drove away, it seemed that all of Boston—everyone on the streets—had been touched by the magic. The kids they passed were still bouncing and howling, waving their fingers at each other in the peace sign. A black man had climbed on a car in Copley Square. "Stay high," he was shouting into the night. "Stay high!"

On April 14 Michael handed me the phone in the early afternoon. "It's Kotlowitz," he said. He watched my face and when I flashed him an O.K. sign, he leaped in the air. "Ya-hooo!"

"What on earth?" Kotlowitz asked.

"Oh nothing, Michael's just excited about something."

Harper's was buying the story for six hundred dollars. They were printing every word, down to "cunnilingus everyone." And they wanted me to start another article on commission, no more speculation.

I took the first assignment they suggested—the selling of Jacqueline Susann—because I had to prove I could do it again. Rhinoceros wasn't just a fluke. During the days I worked for the *Globe* and at night for *Harper's*. By June I was exhausted and came down with a cold the night before Michael and I left for Europe, a vacation I had been planning for months. Michael gave me Pyribenzamine, which he took for his sinuses. "It'll knock out your cold overnight," he said. "The only thing is, it makes you drowsy." I swallowed five tablets in the next twenty-four hours and by the time we arrived at Cap Ferrat, where his father had rented a villa, I was wheezing. Instead of feeling drowsy, I felt as if I'd taken speed.

The house had a red tile roof and a marble swimming pool surrounded by pines and bougainvillaea. Our room had a canopy bed draped with yellow velvet and a window looking out on the Mediterranean. A French chef who had been engaged with the house asked what we wanted for dinner. He rode his bicycle to the market and that night, set the table with a *salade niçoise* so beautiful we took photographs of it, *blanquette de veau, pommes frites* and lemon soufflé. I could not taste anything and by the time we got in bed, I was shaking so badly I thought I would never sleep again. Michael gave me two Nembutol. "This'll surely knock you out." But it didn't.

I concluded, too late, that so many barbiturates had accumulated in my system that they were backfiring and producing the opposite effect. I stopped taking all medicine and waited a day. Still no sleep. A doctor in Monte Carlo prescribed hypnotic suppositories. I now had a fever, and Michael wasn't well. His lip was bleeding. He had diarrhea and was peeing every ten minutes. "Mr. Excretion," I called him.

We had paid a thousand dollars to cross the Atlantic and here we were, spending our vacation in bed.

"List your symptoms, in order of severity," Michael said. Then he listed his. We laughed hysterically. "Let's face it," he said, enunciating as if he were on the radio: "We don't tra-vel well."

On the third day, Phillip came into our room which was littered with Kleenex and medicine and bandages, and said he had planned a wonderful evening. We would drive to Eze, a perched village in the Alps, where there was a two-star restaurant and if we went early, we could walk through the ruins . . .

"Dad," Michael said, "I couldn't walk through Hamburger Heaven tonight."

When we were well again it was time to leave for Greece, but Michael wanted to go back to New York. I did not realize how frightened he was until we were strapped in our seats on the plane to Athens. His black eyes darted around the cabin. "This is farther from the green room than I've ever been."

It was on that plane ride that I discovered Michael was not the man I thought I had married. He had traveled before, but reluctantly. Years later, Michael would tell me that although he had had "no desire to go to foreign ports," he had agreed to go to Greece "because I thought it was outrageous not to want to see the world. I thought, if I don't go, my wife will leave me. She'll see me for the lunatic I am. So I went. And I was angry."

When we landed in Athens, Michael wanted to leave instantly. I had to bully and cajole to get him on the helicopter for Mykonos, where we had arranged to meet my sister who was hitchhiking through Europe.

The sight of Terry's twenty-two-year-old face, happy and tanned, at the Mykonos airport, seemed to reassure him. We checked into the best hotel on the island, the Leto, which had whitewashed rooms and birds singing in latticework cages. He unpacked his pillow, six record albums which he couldn't play

but carried so he could see the familiar covers, a quart of Black
Label and a short-wave radio. The maid brought him ice and
after he had fixed a drink, he seemed, at last, to calm down.

That night in bed, Michael kissed me good night. "Who loves
you?" he whispered. It was a familiar routine but I did not respond. "Sara," he said urgently, "don't you know I love you?"

Yes, I said, annoyed.

Michael would not go to Delos to see Apollo's Temple. He
would not go waterskiing or sailing when we were invited. He
walked every day to the nearest beach where he sat himself
down in the same spot with his radio, the *International Herald
Tribune* and drinks.

We lay beside each other and barely spoke. I imagined
Michael was thinking about the Phillies. I was thinking about
what was wrong with Michael and whether I was in the right
place, married to such a man. It was occurring to me that I could
not "grow" with him. I stated the case: Michael wasn't open to
new people or groups.

He loathed any kind of learning situation, while I was a habit-
ual lessons taker.

He liked repetition, I liked discovery.

He loved Sinatra, I loved Jagger.

He drank whiskey, I smoked dope.

And yet, there was his humor, his capacity to be startled and
excited. And yet, I wanted a mate who could explore with me,
the way my sister Terry did. She and I took the boat to Delos
one day while Michael stayed behind on the beach. When I returned to our room, Michael was sitting by the window.

"I'm going home tomorrow," he announced.

"But . . . I thought you were beginning to like it here."

He cleared his throat. "I want to be in New York to see the
moon landing on television. This is a stupendous event, Sara, the
first human footstep on the moon. I don't want to be tucked
away in Greece. I want to be in touch with Walter Cronkite."

We had paid for the room for another four days. Michael said,
"You can stay if you want to. Keep the room, or maybe you
could go and see the other islands."

All during dinner, Michael attempted to persuade me that I

should stay in Greece and because he was pushing, I resisted. I wasn't ready to go back to New York, but I didn't want to stay alone either. In the morning, I left him asleep in our room and took a walk through the town. Mykonos was a maze of winding streets so narrow no cars could pass on them. Everything was whitewashed—the ground, the walls, the archways over the streets—and the sunlight ricocheted off the white surfaces. I made a turn, another turn, and suddenly I was lost. I saw white everywhere: white alleys, white doors. A pelican emerged from an archway and flip-flopped past me. I began to stop women dressed in black. "Leto?" I asked.

They pointed with their fingers.

"Leto?"

"Leto?"

I walked where they pointed, circling through alleys that all looked the same until I was breathless. When I came out by the harbor, Michael was standing on the balcony of the hotel, holding a hand to his forehead in a posture of anxious searching.

"Where've you been?" he called.

I climbed the stairs. I sucked in my breath. "I'm going home with you."

"Darling!" He rushed over and pulled me against him, looking happier than I had seen him since New York.

Woodstock Aquarian Exposition

Kids of America Do Their Thing

The first rock 'n' roll festival. "Three days of peace and music," the brochures had promised. "Crafts, food, acres to roam on." But the promoters had not known what would happen: that kids would journey to the Catskills until they were half a million, jammed in a crater on Max Yasgur's farm.

Roads were blocked for a radius of sixty miles. Gas stations ran out of gas, water pipes broke and portable toilets collapsed. A state of emergency was declared.

I sat through most of the festival in the performers' tent backstage, frightened to walk out into the crater. When I did, the bodies were packed so densely and the smell!—rotting fruit, urine, sweat, incense—I thought I would faint and be trampled. It was not until the second night that I was exhausted and stoned enough to enjoy the show: Janis Joplin at 3 A.M., Sly and the Family Stone at 4 ("Higher, higher"), the Who at 5 ("Un-fucking believable!"), and the Jefferson Airplane to welcome the sun.

When I came home, I wrote a story for the *Globe* about the miracle of Woodstock Nation. Despite the rain and mud, food shortages and overcrowding, there had been no violence, not one injury inflicted on anyone by another human being. "Young peo-ple have demonstrated that they truly desire peace and the com-munal experience," I wrote.

The story was my final article for the *Globe* before I left to go free-lance. In the fall, after the issue of *Harper's* with "Rhinoc-eros" hit the stands, I received a call from an editor at *McCall's*. "We'd like you to write a profile of Judy Collins and we'd like to pay you two thousand dollars." I nearly dropped the phone. My agent called next. "You're my hottest new client."

With each piece I had to prove myself again. I enjoyed gather-ing research but when it came time to write, my mood turned black and everything had to stop. I grumbled about having to cook dinner for Michael. I refused to go out or entertain. I had no interest in sex. I was snappy and churlish. I looked so tortured that people were uncomfortable being in the same room with me. Other writers I knew took speed to concentrate, but I took tranquilizers to calm me down. Sometimes I sat at my desk for twelve, fourteen hours, refusing to let myself eat or sleep until sheer fatigue forced me to crack through a block.

"Why do I put myself through this?" I asked Dr. Collins. He wanted me to lie on the couch and free-associate, and increased our sessions to four times a week. "It's as if I'm determined to make myself suffer."

"If that were true," he said, "why would you want to do that?" I said what came to me: "I'm bad."

My career, like Michael's, was now in flower, but I could not stop long enough to enjoy it. I had to be published by every magazine and have an article out every month or I would fade. When an editor at *Life* asked me to write a piece, I suggested, without reflecting on the consequences, "women's liberation."

Of all the movements that had their origins in the sixties, this one was to have the most profound effect, yet in the beginning, it appeared to be a joke—the notion of equality pushed to absurdity. "I think we're going to have to treat this movement seriously," I told the editor, who raised his eyebrows skeptically. "Could be."

I decided to go to Boston where much of the early theoretical work had been done. I called Phyllis Levine, who had been one of my closest friends when I was living in Cambridge. She insisted I stay in her house, but when I arrived, this woman, whom I remembered for her crinkly eyes and earthy laugh, looked nervous. She explained that a new collective was forming, Bread and Roses, and at their last meeting, they had fought for an hour about whether to co-operate with the writer for *Life*.

"But it's me, Phyllis."

"It's the bourgeois capitalist press."

"Look, you can't stop the press from writing about this movement. Isn't it better that I be the one? Doesn't it make sense to try to get your ideas across in the most favorable light?"

Phyllis pulled at her fuzzy brown hair. "I don't know, a ripoff is a ripoff." She gave me a stack of literature to read and went off to a class on "Women and Their Bodies."

I sat on the floor of her dark, drafty flat in Cambridge and opened "No More Fun and Games," a pamphlet published by Cell 16. I was unprepared for what I read.

"We take a stand against the nuclear family . . ."

"We advise single women to remain single . . ."

"Avoid pregnancy . . ."

"Leave your husbands and children . . ."

"Stop buying cosmetics . . ."

"Abstain from sexual relationships. If genital tensions persist, you can masturbate."

The most shocking tract was by Betsy Warrior, titled, "Man as an Obsolete Life Form." Betsy wrote: "All men should be killed, to preserve the rest of humankind. . . . Sperm banks and test-tube babies can take over Man's last function, his only function that has positive effects for the human race." Betsy said that if women balk at killing men, they can round men up and confine them to zoos.

With low dread, I picked up the phone to set up interviews with these women.

"I don't want to be used as an object by *Life* magazine," one girl said.

"Fuck off," said another.

"Go back where you came from or get yourself a gun."

I had stomach cramps by the time I went to meet Roxanne Dunbar, the head of Cell 16, at a karate class. I sat in a folding chair by the wall, watching a dozen women kick and snarl. Suddenly the instructor, Jayne West, shouted, "Bricks!" The women spun and raced toward me. My heart almost stopped. What the hell were they going to do to me? Bricks? I looked down and saw that I was sitting beside a pile of bricks. Each woman grabbed one, tore back to the center of the room and started pounding the brick with her fists.

After class, Roxanne said she was having second thoughts about talking to me. "What's in it for us?" she asked in a whispery voice that did not match her appearance: severe black hair chopped off in a straight line. "Would you donate your writer's salary to Cell 16?"

"I can't do that," I said, "it's my livelihood. But the interview will be read by eight million people."

She smiled primly and shut the door in my face.

Phyllis, by this point, was feeling sorry for me and pleaded my case before Bread and Roses. She told them I had written "good articles about the Movement" and could be trusted. "She's a woman, for fuck's sake. We're supposed to be women supporting other women."

So Bread and Roses sent four members for an interview, and they were as stable as a house of cards. They gave me their names but when I wrote them down, they changed their minds and ripped the page out of my notebook.

They searched me and my purse for a tape recorder. They asked me to tell them my life history, which I did, straightforwardly, until it came to Michael. I was embarrassed to tell them I needed a husband, embarrassed to say I was proud of Michael's fame, and frightened to talk about our problems because problems meant the marriage was oppressive and should be trashed. What I did tell the women seemed to satisfy them, for they consented to answer my questions.

At the end, one of the girls, Martha, said casually, "You're going to let us check this article before it's printed, right?"

"No."

The four women froze. They were incredulous. I was incredulous.

"Those are the conventions of journalism," I said. "You don't submit articles to people for censorship."

"Don't give us bullshit about conventions," Martha said. "The first rule of a revolutionary is not to talk to the press."

"If you broke your rule, that doesn't mean I have to break mine. If I interviewed President Nixon, would you want me to let him read the article and censor it?"

Phyllis burst into tears. "You lied," she screamed. Martha stepped toward me and I saw there were beads of sweat on her upper lip. "We're struggling to work collectively and you're still defining yourself by competition. You don't give a shit about the truth. You're not doing shit for the revolution. You're just using us to advance your career!"

Phyllis told me to get out of her house at once. I scrambled for my suitcase, drove to a motel and caught the first morning flight to New York. I felt wounded, enraged; I could not comprehend ending a friendship over political differences. I vowed to have nothing further to do with radical groups, but I was haunted by the accusations. Why wasn't I working for the revolution? It was true that writing the article would advance my career. Why was I seeking personal gain?

I wept with joy when I saw Michael at the airport. I was thrilled to be back in our cheery home, back in the green room where I could cuddle with Michael and get stoned while he programmed his show. After a week, I wrote the article for *Life* in a positive tone. My disenchantment had been with radical groups but not with the principles of feminism.

One evening, after a small dinner party in our house, a friend of Michael's said that of all the women he knew, I seemed the most liberated. "You have a career, you travel by yourself and Michael encourages it."

"Yes," I said, as I stacked the dirty dishes, "but we have an unequal division of labor in the house."

"Darling," Michael said in mock exasperation. "Every time you go off on a story, I never know what I'll get back. After you wrote 'Rhinoceros,' you wanted an electric guitar. After you met Judy Collins and she dragged you to an encounter group, you wouldn't let me blink without asking, 'What are you *feeling?*' Now it's women's lib. Holy shit! Is there no limit?"

Everyone at the table was doubled up laughing. "Why don't you write an article about the color white? That can't cause me any trouble," Michael said. "The worst that can happen is you'll paint the house white. That's not so bad. *Please* consider it."

20. SUSIE

Let me say, at the risk of seeming ridiculous, that the
true revolutionary is guided by great feelings of love.

Che

For a very brief time in the winter of '69, Susie and Jeff felt a
sense of hope. They were confronting what needed to be con-
fronted. They had defined the trouble between them as sexual,
and now Susie could have orgasms. But only with the vibrator.
Jeff tried using his fingers and she tried hers, but after ten minutes they gave up because "there was this thing in the drawer. It
was foolproof," Susie says. "In seconds, there I am—heaven." But
the batteries wore out and Jeff moped that he was being
replaced by a machine.

When the rainy season started, Jeff caught the flu. Being sick
made him weepy. "Tell me you love me. Tell me I'll get better."
Susie hated taking care of him, she had a baby to take care of.
She hated cooking him soup. She hated his tennis sneakers. She
hated the way he blew his nose. She hated his smelly under-
shirts. Hate hate hate. As she walked to the drugstore to buy
cough medicine, she wanted to step in front of cars.

When Jeff was better, she packed up Sam and took a plane to
Los Angeles to visit her parents. She left the house in a state of
chaos. It was a beautiful house on Virginia Street that she had
worked hard fixing. She had refinished the floors and restored the

beveled mirrors, but Jeff threw his clothes on the floor and left newspapers and rotting food all over.

It was a relief to be back in her childhood room on Beverwil with the neat white woodwork and Bates bedspreads. Her mother took care of Sam, and Susie spent her days by herself, learning how to weave. Toward the end of the week, Jeff called. She let him talk with Sam, then took the phone in her room and closed the door.

"What are you up to?" he asked.

"Nothing much. Weaving a blanket. What's happening with you?"

"Same old shit. The Third World Strike is still on but it's fucked. I've been rapping with my lawyers and I think we've got a strategy. We're gonna argue that opposing the draft is legal because the war is illegal. That way we'll force the jury to rule on the war and the First Amendment. I'm excited—we'll be using the court as a platform, the way the Chicago Seven are doing."

"What if the jury doesn't buy it?" Susie said.

"I could get three years in the federal pen."

"Are you uptight?"

"Not about jail."

"What then?"

"I don't know, Susie. I've never been real in touch with what's bedeviling me. Maybe it's the devil."

Silence.

"I went to see Jimi Hendrix," Jeff said.

"Oh yeah? Who'd you go with?"

"Jack. We picked up these two chicks and got ripped. But it was a bummer. Both the chicks dug Jack and he was into having a group scene but the chicks wouldn't go for it. So we all went home to our separate beds."

"Too bad."

"I've been thinking a lot about where I go from here. I'm thinking it's going to be, 'Jeff Berman, professional revolutionary,' and that feels pretty comfortable except I have the feeling I'll never be much of a lover. Not a sexual performer but a lover. Like Jack. He understood all the stuff these chicks were saying, stuff that sounded like bullshit to me."

"What kind of stuff?" Susie said.

"Oh, like 'finding your center.' Maybe it wasn't bullshit but it went right by me."

Susie sighed.

"I miss you. God, I miss Sam something awful. The other morning I woke up freaked because I had this feeling I'd lost you for good. I couldn't convince myself that I'd ever been able to tell you how much I love you."

When Susie hung up, she lay down on her bed, the same bed on which as a girl of eight, she had dreamed of having magic powers so she could heal the world. As she closed her eyes, she felt as if she were floating along a tunnel, at the end of which was a faint light. The light was far away. She floated closer, until she could make out a figure in the light. It was a woman holding a child. And she thought: I could be with Sam alone.

The thought completely startled her; she set it aside to reflect on. When she flew back to Berkeley, Jeff met her at the airport and before they were home they were screaming at each other.

So began their rounds in and out of the house on Virginia Street. Jeff would split, stay with friends a few days and come back, then they would fight again and Susie would split and return, all the while they traded Sam back and forth. With Jeff gone, Susie became close with Roxanne, who was splitting up with her husband, Bob. All the couples in the encounter group were splitting up. One evening while Bob took care of the kids, Roxanne came to Susie's to get ready for an affair. They went through Susie's closet and dressed Roxanne, brushed her hair and rubbed musk oil between her breasts because Susie had read in *Vogue* that French women do that. Susie waited up for Roxanne to come back. Roxanne could not spend the night with her lover because he had a wife from whom he was not quite separated.

When Roxanne returned at midnight, the two of them put on long nightgowns, got in bed together, drank cocoa and ate cookies. They were laughing and being silly, hugging and giggling and Susie was struck: this is what love is. This is what fun is. This is feeling connected and that's what you want with a man.

Within minutes, Jeff walked in the front door. He got in bed with the girls and then Roxanne went to sleep on the couch. Susie was so aroused that she threw herself on top of Jeff and started making love to him. He responded not at all. Susie opened her eyes. "What's the matter? You always wanted me to come on to you. You never saw me before when I was turned on. Now I am." Jeff rolled over on his side. "I just came home to see you. Not to ball."

Jeff's trial began in March and his picture was in the paper every day. As Susie sat in the courtroom, she had fantasies that he would be convicted and go to jail. Then she could be free for a few years; she could do what she needed to do and he would come back. But she was ashamed. There had to be another way.

When spring arrived, she bought seeds for a garden but couldn't plant them. She wanted to get away from the house. Her friend Maureen helped her get a job at a bar in the Haight-Ashbury, the Can-Do Club. It was Susie's first job since she was nineteen. She and Maureen served beer behind the bar and they were careful about venturing out into the room because things could get rough. In the front of the club were tables where hippies sat. Then there was a dance floor and behind it was the ghetto: down-home, funky dudes and ladies with straightened hair; bejeweled players sniffing coke and junkies shooting up in the bathroom. Creedence Clearwater sang on the juke box, "Rolling on the river, rolling on the river." Susie wore a miniskirt that barely covered her ass, black tights, high boots and long, long hair. She looked and felt sexy. She watched blacks dancing and tried to imitate them. "Born on the bayou!" She danced behind the bar or if things were quiet, she'd dash out to the floor, dance one and duck back.

She loved earning money and making tips. She was constantly being offered dope and getting invited to parties. She brought black men home with her and told them about women's liberation and how the situation of women was like that of blacks. The men listened but all they wanted to do was fuck and all Susie wanted to do was fuck.

After two months, though, she was sick of the scene. Men hitting on her every minute. She found that sex with blacks was usually brutal and she didn't like it. They were into ramming it without foreplay or cuddling. The regulars in the bar were obnoxious. She hated them. She was angry at men, angry at the goddamned male-dominated society and furious at Jeff for teaching her wrong. He had attacked hypocrisy everywhere but at home. He couldn't talk about his feelings. He couldn't deal with pain. He was always telling stories, playing with the energy and ranting about capitalist society. But he couldn't face himself, Susie, their life or his problems. And he had fucked her up sexually, pushing her all the time.

The first thing she did with the money she earned was to go to a dermatologist who cut out the tattoo. It left a scar but she could handle a scar, it didn't embarrass her like an ugly red and green flower on her chest. One night at the bar Jeff dropped by and they got drunk. When they drove home she told him she'd had the tattoo removed.

"Let me see," he asked.

She opened her blouse and triumphantly showed him the wound. He had done it to her. "It hurts like hell," she said.

She had joined a new women's group in San Francisco, the Red Witches. They modeled themselves after Cell 16 in Boston, and had a rule that only half their members could be married. Susie knew most of the rhetoric was bravado. The women were shaky and needed each other to build "healthy egos." When they talked about their marriages, Susie came to a conclusion: "I didn't know who I was and I married Jeff to avoid having to figure it out." With the group, she was learning that she could think on her own, she didn't need Jeff. She could learn to do everything: write and give speeches, fix cars, build a house, shoot a gun.

The women started a Sunday Ladies Rifle Society as part of their program to learn to feel strong. The first gun meeting was held at Susie's house. The women arrived with eight .22 rifles which they cleaned and took apart on the hardwood floor. Sam and two other kids crawled around over the bullets. "I hated guns and killing but I'd never seen a gun, let alone held one," Susie says. "I did it for the experience, to understand the men's trip. I saw what it felt like to have an arsenal on your floor. I saw what it was to load and cock a rifle, pull the trigger and have it go crack! The sense of power was phenomenal."

The Witches talked about moving to Martinez, getting jobs with the phone company and organizing women clerical workers to be the vanguard of the revolution. But Susie wasn't ready to tell other women what to do. How could she when she was so confused? In a way she was afraid of the whole women's movement because very early she ran it through and saw the consequences: pain, broken relationships, broken families and hard times, a lot of women alone who might not be able to survive on their own with children, no money and no day-care centers. Susie says, "If women had to stay in bad marriages because they were too scared, I understood that. I wasn't gonna put them down."

Jeff's case went to the jury in April. After only six hours, a verdict was returned. Susie clutched Sam in her lap. "Ouch!" he said and wriggled to the floor. "Shhhh, let's listen to the judge."

". . . not guilty."

Susie was stunned. The jury had voted for Jeff and against the war. She heard chairs scudding, voices cheering, "Power to the People!" All their friends and the lawyers were hugging. "We won!"

As if her reaction had been delayed, Susie bolted to her feet. She ran up to Jeff and kissed him. Flashbulbs popped. She smiled and raised her fist but she was acting.

Jeff said he had mixed feelings about the verdict because it meant the system worked. He had been knocking the system as totally fucked, and now it would look like you could believe in the American people and the American judicial process.

If Susie was let down, it was because the verdict dropped her and Jeff right back in the quagmire. The week after the trial, she was taking a nap when Jeff came in and sat on the bed.

"I thought you were staying at Jack's," she said.

"We can't go on like this."

She rubbed her eyes. Jeff put his hand on her thigh and she wanted to cringe.

"You know, I still feel a lot of tenderness for you. My family is so important." Susie looked at him: he was wearing a green fatigue jacket and his head drooped forward over his nobby shoulders.

"I don't know what the fuck love is," he said, "but maybe we can cut through the shit. Maybe we can discover the positive things. I wish I knew what they were so I could tell them to you over and out."

No. There. "No." She said it. "I don't want to struggle anymore. I'm tired of the shit. Can't you see? It's over. I have to get away. I've got to get out of this town because as long as I stay here, I'll never be anything but 'Jeff Berman's wife.' "

"Where will you go?"

"I don't know."

"What about Sam?"

"I'll take him with me."

"You can't take my son . . ."

"Oh can't I?"

Jeff leaped up. "Goddammit, you've got me by the short hairs. I feel powerless."

Good, she thought. See how it feels for a change.

Jeff moved out of the house and into a commune called Maggie's Farm. Susie started making preparations to drive across the country with Sam in the summer. In April she heard that the street people who hung around Telegraph were building a park in a muddy, garbage-filled lot owned by the university.

Something was up. She put Sam in a stroller and walked over to check it out. She saw dozens of people digging and laying sod. The land had not been turned in hundreds of years and had an oily blue sheen when cut. Someone handed Susie a spade. She put Sam in a sandbox that had just been built and went to work. It was back-breaking, cutting through the rocks, but lemonade and joints were passed. Everyone sang. No idle hands. "So this is how the Chinese build walls."

At sundown a rock band arrived with a generator. Two suckling pigs were roasted and everyone ate and got stoned. To Susie it was anarchy in the best sense of the word. There were no leaders. Whoever had an idea for something took charge. A flagpole was erected and a sign nailed to it: "People's Park. Power to the People."

Even though Susie was about to leave Berkeley, she could not help but join the effort. The spirit was infectious. In weeks, the once-muddy lot was abloom with flowers, trees, slides, swings, teeter-totters, a Maypole, a dance platform festooned with prayer flags, a barbecue pit and a set of giant wooden letters spelling KNOW that Sam loved to crawl through. The street people were working like madmen for the first time in their lives. A boy named Cloud told Susie, "I've been drifting and bumming since I was sixteen. I hated every job and either quit or was fired. But this is different. There's no boss. We're building our own desires." Looking at his bare tanned chest made Susie want to ball.

For three weeks, Susie hit the park every day. Even straight ladies, university wives, were bringing their kids, but there were rumblings of trouble. The university owned the land and announced plans to build a soccer field on it. The street people set up a "bulldozer alarm." Fuck private property. Nobody wanted a soccer field. The street people had turned some useless land into a park everyone could enjoy. They printed leaflets that warned the university, "You ripped off the land from the Costanoan Indians a long time ago. Your land title is covered with blood. If you want it back you'll have to fight for it again. We are the people!"

For the first time, Susie was in a struggle by herself. She was out of the planning circle and part of the masses. She knew what Jeff believed and what he'd taught her to think, but she didn't know what she believed on her own. She wanted to see where she fit, but it was confusing because Jeff was now leading the struggle.

One day, she was working on a wading pool when Jeff climbed onto the dance platform to speak. He was with a girl named Leslie and pulled her up after him, the way he had always pulled Susie up. How could he get with someone else so fast? She watched him surreptitiously; he was sneaking looks at her. Should she leave? Sam was sitting between her legs. "There's my daddy!" At that second, Susie looked up and saw a strange young man with a camera focused on her. She raised her arm. "Please, no." But the shutter had been tripped. A short time later, she saw the photograph of her in a booklet called "Free People."

"Free," my ass.

On May 15 Susie was jarred awake at four in the morning by a call from Cloud. "The police are at the park. They're putting up a Cyclone fence. Get over there. Call everyone you know." Susie heard kids running through the streets banging drums and ringing bells. She put Sam in a backpack and hurried to the park. It was 5 A.M. but already there was a crowd, peering through the hard gray light in disbelief. Police with gas masks and shotguns were lolling on the swings. Construction men were installing a fence, trampling over flowers everyone had worked so hard to plant. Susie saw Jeff tearing at the chain link fence with his hands, screaming "Pigs! Fascists!"

Somebody whispered, "Berman's on a death trip. His wife just split. He's got nothing to lose."

Susie shivered and turned away. "Emergency alert—noon on campus. Spread the word." She had to get rid of Sam. She didn't want to dump him with a strange baby-sitter but she couldn't miss the action and it was no place for children.

By 11 A.M., Telegraph Avenue had been cordoned off to traffic. Susie saw police with telescopic rifles stationed on the roofs of bookstores. Thousands of kids were streaming to the campus. Angry and tense. Troops massing for battle. She had a premonition. At Sather Gate, she stopped a professor she knew and told him, "Somebody's gonna get killed today."

The rally lasted an hour. The crowd milled and buzzed. Dan Siegel, the ASUC president, was last to speak. "The entire South Campus area has been closed so Chancellor Heyns can build us a soccer field. He doesn't want anyone to doubt who's boss of this university. Well." Siegel paused. "One alternative might be to go to the park now."

From the air came the cry: "Let's go to the park!" Three thousand people turned and took off. "We want the park!" As they passed the Bank of America they kicked in doors and hurled rocks through the windows. Susie moved with the group. She spotted Tom Hayden, ran up to him and yelled, "Tom, you've got to stop this. People will get killed." Tom was carrying a medic's bag and had his pockets filled with rocks. He was punching his fists jubilantly and shouting, "The park belongs to the people!" He brushed Susie aside. "This is what the people want. If it's too hot for you, get out of the kitchen."

She saw another friend, Michael Lerner. "Somebody's got to do something, Mike. This is a mob." Michael cupped his hands and started yelling, "Okay, everybody keep cool."

When they reached the Cyclone fence the police were jittery. Rocks were thrown. Insults. Then shots—real bird shot! Susie ran for two blocks and stopped. She teamed up with three people and began edging back. The closer they got to the park, the heavier the fighting. Smoke. Gunshots. A girl was screaming, "Jerry, they shot Jerry!" Young people were running in all directions with blood streaming down their faces. A radio truck was cruising the streets: "This event is being broadcast live on KPFA."

Word was passed, go to the campus, a safe area. A crowd massed on Sproul plaza but it was a trap. The cops blocked them in and a helicopter flew low spraying C.S. gas that made them vomit.

The crowd ran in all directions. Susie fled with strangers, then she was alone. Everybody's your friend. But no Jeff.

In her house that night she sat by herself, listening to the radio. "I felt very naïve for someone who'd been through all I had. I must have said, 'We need a revolution,' hundreds of times but I'd never conceived of this. It was war, only they had guns and we had rocks."

The National Guard was called in, and for nine days battles raged in the streets. On the first day, James Rector, a twenty-five-year-old who had been standing on a rooftop, was shot in the stomach and died. Hundreds more were hospitalized. Bands of young people fought the pigs with Mace, bats—whatever they could improvise. Helicopters whirred overhead. Tanks rumbled along Shattuck. Graffiti on the walls announced, "Welcome to Prague."

A mass march was scheduled for Memorial Day to draw as much support as possible to Berkeley. There would be memorial services for James Rector and a party at People's Park Two, which had been built on a strip of public land after the loss of People's Park One.

Susie went to planning meetings but the hassles gave her a headache. The heavies wanted to keep fighting. The moderates wanted a celebration. Young people were arriving from all over the country and pitching tents on People's Park Two. Susie woke up on Memorial Day not knowing whether to take her helmet for battle or to take Sam because it would be a party. A freak named Super Joel invited her to ride on a flatbed truck with rock musicians. Okay, she thought, I'll bring Sam.

They rode around Berkeley singing and waving. It was a brilliant sunny day and the streets were awash with shocking-pink rhododendrons and yellow acacia. Susie saw everyone, an insane cross section: heavy dudes with chains and their faces greased for battle; mothers-for-peace wheeling strollers; schoolgirls; Hell's Angels; old ladies with walking canes; bohemians wearing ponchos; merchants from Shattuck; professors down from the hills; and black people up from the flats.

It was the family of Berkeley, united on this day in the rightest cause ever. In the air were kites and Frisbees. Dope dealers carried sacks of joints which they tossed like flowers to the crowd. But there was a rawness to the jubilation. Tanks and helicopters were on alert and any second, the pigs could go crazy.

An enormous swell—more than thirty thousand—gathered at People's Park Two. When Jeff took the microphone, Susie clenched her fists. Let him say the right thing. Shit, had nothing changed?

Jeff found the words to cool the crowd. "The university will give us back our park. We've seen enough bloodshed. Look at the strength of us. We can build anew, even in the face of guns. We can turn the South campus into a free territory for revolution. Let thousands of parks bloom!"

Susie decided it was time to get away. Working by herself, she built a crib for Sam in the back of her Volkswagen. Two days before she was to leave, Cloud came by and said he would join her somewhere on the road.

She set off on the morning of the Fourth of July, Independence Day. She was getting it on! She put Sam in back in his pajamas at 4 A.M. so she could drive a few hours before he woke up. They stopped for breakfast and drove another hour. She had names of people to call everywhere, and in Nevada City, friends of friends let her stay in their cabin. She called Cloud. Was he coming? Did he really love her? He showed up the next morning. Susie recalls, "What a jerk. It didn't take a day for me to see how obnoxious he was. He did nothing, said nothing. I couldn't wait to be rid of him."

She drove across the Rockies, picking up hitchhikers and sleeping with them in the woods, steering the car across steep passes, admiring the views, all the while passing toys and animal crackers back to Sam. In Aspen her car broke down. Fuck! The problem was beyond what she'd learned in her auto mechanics collective. She walked into a garage and told them she didn't want them to fix her car, she wanted them to teach her how to fix it. They were about to kick her out when a young freak who worked there looked at Susie's legs and long hair and told her he'd teach her in his spare time.

In New Mexico she visited the Hog Farm Commune. Wherever she went she recognized her brothers and sisters. "They looked like I did, had long hair and spoke my language." She stopped at Drop City, New Buffalo and the Reality Construction Company where she found the tribe naked on the roof making adobe bricks with their feet. She was getting concerned about Sam. He was seeing her with so many different men. So many bizarre scenes. She herself had never seen twenty people naked in the open. One of the women in the tribe, Debbie, had a son named Crow, the same age as Sam. When Susie climbed on the roof to make bricks, she left Sam with Crow in the dirt.

"Mommy!" Sam yelled.

"What?"

"Come down."

"I'm going to work for a while. You play with Crow."

Sam started to scream. Susie watched him. Debbie said, "Let

him cry. He's got to dig that you're not gonna be at his beck and call."

"But he's only two and a half," Susie said.

One of the men said, "If he gets away with this crap he'll cling to your skirts forever."

Sam wailed so hard he turned red and started choking. Susie scrambled down the ladder and took him to the car where she rocked him until he fell asleep.

Susie felt most comfortable with the people at Reality because they were the most political commune. They had guns for self-defense and community organizing projects. One of the men, Russ, asked Susie to be his old lady. She moved into his tepee and had fantasies of becoming a country woman, but after a few weeks, she knew she couldn't stay. She was too insecure. Did they like her? Was she contributing enough? Was she handling Sam all right? They kept pressing her to let him run wild. At meetings she wondered if she had a right to talk. Was she a passer-through? Were they sick of passers-through?

Susie recalls, "I was paying attention to the mistake I'd made with Jeff by not evolving on my own. Maybe I belong in a commune, I thought. It was a good idea, but I wasn't there yet and I wasn't going to skip any stages. I was back to twenty years old as it was."

Jeff tracked her down and phoned her in Gallup, New Mexico. He wanted to see Sam. "It's outrageous to take him so far away. You owe it to me, and Sam, to bring him back to California."

"What about L.A.? I don't want to go back to Berkeley."

Jeff sighed. "Oh shit."

Susie arrived at her parents' house in Beverly Hills with Sam, a black hippie who wore nothing but an aviator suit and fur-lined slippers with turned-up toes and a young German student who had escorted her on a motorcycle from the Grand Canyon. Her mother fed them all and took Susie aside. "Have you lost your head?" she said with tears in her eyes.

Susie hugged her. "Don't worry. I know what I'm doing."

V. BUSY BEING FREE

1969–1971

There's a man who sent her a letter and he's waiting
    for his reply,
He has asked her of her travels since the day
    they said goodby,
He writes: "I wish you were beside me,
    we can make it if we try . . ."
But she's off somewhere being free.

Joni Mitchell, "Cactus Tree"

21. SARA

The front wheels drop and the car falls slowly down a muddy ravine and squishes to a stop. Thick night fog, raining hard. I get out and sink to my ankles. No flashlight. No waterproof gear. Utter blackness except for the car's dulled lights under the mud. I climb back in, but because of the forty-five-degree angle, I'm pitched forward against the dashboard. Turn on the radio. Only 8 P.M., a long wait until daylight. Am I anywhere near Wheeler Ranch? I honk the horn. Cows bellow back from what seems very close range. I imagine angry ranchers with shotguns. To-morrow is Sunday—eight miles back to town and nothing will be open. Is there an AAA out here? Oh God, I'll pay anybody any-thing if they'll just get me out of this!

"Back to the land"—that was the call of 1970. Step off the train of history and live in a tribe, find Eden.

I had dreaded the arrival of 1970 as some people dread turn-ing thirty, or fifty. Skirt lengths were falling and the Beatles were splitting up, but I refused to let myself believe that the turning of the decade would mean the end of it all. I vowed I would never wear a calf-length skirt. If I could not wear minis I would wear only pants, men's pants.

In January I accepted an assignment from *Harper's* to write about "rural communes like the Manson family." I was curious, as Susie Berman had been curious, to see if living in a tribe in the woods was something I should do. It was difficult, though, sitting in New York, to gather information about such communes. I could not call ahead and test their receptivity to the bourgeois capitalist press. In communes where "voluntary primitivism" was practiced, there were no phones.

I asked everyone I knew for leads. I was introduced to a doctor in Brooklyn who showed me slides of a mesa in New Mexico where his son was settling. "Be sure to take a sleeping bag and food," the doctor said. He gave me a pamphlet, "Open Land," which told about a place in California, Wheeler Ranch, where land was free—anyone could settle there and no one could be asked to leave. "We learn from the wind, the trees, the brooks, the animals."

I had never lived anywhere but a city and had not touched a sleeping bag since Girl Scout camp. I went to buy equipment in a surplus store and by fortuitous accident, stumbled into members of the Hog Farm, who had fed the hordes at Woodstock and were living in a bus parked on the Bowery. A boy called Sky, whose clothes were tie-dyed from his cap to his sneakers, invited me inside. I asked him for names of people at communes but he was vague. We smoked a joint, drank wine and I no longer cared. It was 6 P.M. and outside the bus it was rush hour, horns honking and derelicts hustling the drivers trapped in their cars. Inside the bus it was another world. Dark —the curtains were drawn and the ceiling was painted black with iridescent stars. Warm—the bus had been gutted and in place of stiff seats there were couches, a heater, soft lights and a stereo playing "White Bird."

A taxi driver banged on the bus. "Come on in." He stuck his head inside. "Oh yeah, I seen dis in *Alice's Restaurant*." He gave a goony laugh. "It ain't much but it's home, right?"

"It's a lot, brother," Sky yelled, "and it's more than home."

I stayed for dinner on the bus and thought how colorless and lonely my apartment seemed. I decided that when I had a baby of either sex, I wanted to name it Sky.

Michael liked the name but he didn't like the idea of any project that involved sleeping bags. He agreed, reluctantly, to come to California with me in February because I assured him there would be luxury and sun in the desert resort, Palm Springs. We stayed at the Tennis Club where bungalows cost fifty dollars a night and two men fought over a specific lounge chair when a whole row of them sat unused. To my surprise, Michael was enchanted with the desert. The dry heat cleared his sinuses, and he did not feel cut off from the world as he had felt in Greece. For a week we played tennis and baked by the pool, then Michael flew home and I went up to San Francisco.

I tried to locate Rob Kagan in Berkeley, thinking he would have connections to communes. When I dialed his number, I was told, "Rob's on his land in Humboldt County." There was no phone, of course. "Is he still doing his artwork?" I asked. Silence. "Rob would say that he's living, and that's his art."

After a dozen more phone calls, I had acquired directions to Wheeler Ranch and a warning: some of the communards were armed with guns. "I don't blame them," a radical lawyer said testily. "The media killed the Haight. This is the last stand."

I stalled around Berkeley and took two Librium before I set out in my rented car. I thought about how fearless I had been at twenty-two, able to walk up to strangers and blithely ask for anything.

California looks so weird, I thought. The narcotic pastels of the stucco houses. The smell of charbroiled hamburgers cooking. I stopped in a diner and on the back of the check was this message: "We think you are a nice person. We hope something good happens to you today." The clouds were low and the San Rafael Bridge seemed to climb straight into the clouds and disappear. As I headed for the sky, the tranquilizers took over and radio KABL was playing "Shangri-La."

I made several wrong turns and at sunset, a storm came up. Rather than turn back and have to start again, I continued along winding unmarked roads. I reached a crossing, which proved to be the town I was looking for. I stopped in a bar. "How do I get to Wheeler Ranch?"

Heads turned. People froze, drinks in hand. I made up a story.

"My sister's run away and I think she might be there." The faces softened. A woman with milky eyes said, "Honey, there isn't any sign. You just go up the road six miles and there's a gate. Then you have to drive a ways to git to it."

After six miles, I found the gate, opened it and drove through splashing mud until I reached a fork. I picked the left road, drove in a circle and came back to the fork, tried the right road and bumped against two logs. I got out in the downpour and heaved the logs aside. Nothing could stop me now. Another fork. To the left the road was impassable—deep ruts and rocks. To the right was a barbed-wire fence. Enough. Rain slamming on the roof. Pitch-black. Can't see, try to turn the car around, give it more gas . . . then the wheels slipped out and I fell with the car.

I wriggled into my sleeping bag for warmth. The night was interminable, the sun would never rise. At about 5 A.M. I heard rustling noises and pressed my face to the window. Dark forms—horses—pawed around the car. An hour later, the rain let up and I ventured outside. I found a path and a crude sign, "Wheeler's." I walked a mile, then another mile, through rolling green hills thinking, if I can just get out of here. I saw a house, no, it was a clump of dark trees. At last around a bend was a tent and a sign, "Welcome, God, love."

I pushed open the flap of the tent. Bells tinkled. A young man who had shaved his head except for a stripe of hair down the center, like a Mohican, was curled in a real bed on a dirt floor. He lifted his head and smiled. "Come in."

My hair was wild and my eyes red and twitching. "I tried to drive in last night, my car went over a ravine and I've been sleeping in it all night."

"Far out," he said.

"I was terrified."

The Mohican said, "Of what?"

"There were horses."

He laughed. "Far out."

My throat was raw. "Could we make some coffee?"

He looked at me sideways. "I don't have any." He handed me a clump of green weeds. "Here's some yerba buena. You can make tea." I stared at the weeds.

"Where're you from?" he asked.

"New York."

"Far out. Do you have any New York grass?"

I gave him two joints, hoping to enlist his help in digging out my car. He started down a path and motioned for me to follow. The path connected up with a network of trails that crisscrossed the 320-acre ranch. Every so often, we would come to a clearing with a wobbly tent or shack straight out of Dogpatch, wake up the people in their soggy sleeping bags and ask them to help push the car.

A plump blonde called Nancy said, "Don't waste your energy, get Bill Wheeler to pull you out with his jeep. What's your hurry now? Sunday's the best day here. You've got to stay for the steam bath and the feast."

I found Bill Wheeler on the main dirt road. He was big and barefoot, with deep-set blue eyes, a beard and flowing hair that were yellow as the sun. Despite my state of agitation, he smiled and reached out his arms as if I were the most beautiful sight to greet his eyes.

"Don't worry, I'll rescue your car," he said, still smiling when I told him my tale. "Let's go to my studio where it's quiet." Bill was living in a tent with his wife and their infant daughter, Raspberry, and was using the studio to paint canvases that looked to me like bad Jackson Pollocks.

"It's nice, for a change, to talk to somebody who isn't a hippie," Bill said. In New York, months later, when I appeared on a radio show, the host said, "Our guest, Sara Davidson, is a hippie." On both occasions I looked exactly the same, wearing green corduroy jeans, black boots, a white blouse and a string of blue beads from Greece. Bill said, "We have an open policy about the press, so feel free to write anything you want." Too late. I was catching the first plane back to New York.

I tagged after Bill, reminding him about my car, as he chopped wood and started a fire for the steam bath. "Open land requires a leap of faith," he said. "What's adventurous and sacred about open land is that it guarantees there will always be change, and change is life. Stagnation is death."

What happens if someone behaves violently? I asked. He

looked at me in earnest. "The vibrations of the land will take care of that person." Then he laughed. "Don't worry. God will provide."

With his jeep and a chain, Bill pulled out my car in seconds. As the wheels landed on secure road, I felt my tension drain away. I looked around. The sun had burned through the fog, highlighting streaks of wild flowers in a sea of kelly green. Black angus cows were grazing by the road. Maybe, I thought, I should stay for the feast.

I walked the three miles back to the ranch, which had taken on the aspect of a nineteenth-century tableau: women in pioneer skirts and shawls, men in lace-up boots and hillbilly pants tied with pieces of rope, all sitting on the grass playing banjos, guitars, lyres, wood flutes, dulcimers and accordions. Children who looked, male or female, like Tom Sawyer were scampering up and down the garden playing tag. In a field to the right were the community animals. As far as the eye could see there were no houses, no traffic, nothing but verdant hills and the ocean with whitecaps rising in the distance.

We lined up with paper plates before pots of brown rice, red beans and fruit salad. I felt as if I'd stumbled into a company picnic, only I didn't belong to the company. After we ate, Bill took me on a tour of the land. We passed a Maypole around which were dancing four naked teen-age girls. "Hippies are all horny," he said. "The sexual vibrations on the land are fantastic."

We came to a bluff overlooking the sea, turned and opened our lips to speak. We stopped, said nothing and kissed.

I pulled away.

"Why not?" Bill said.

"Why?" I asked.

He gave his farmboy smile.

"It feels good."

I laughed. I could think of no response. "My husband and I believe in fidelity?" I wasn't sure, these days, that it was true. I said, feebly, "I don't want to get pregnant." So we lay on the grass in the sun and did things that wouldn't result in my getting pregnant.

What being a hippie had meant to Susie Berman was freedom

to run naked and fuck, but what being a hippie represented to
me was freedom from the compulsion to work, to account for
one's time. At Wheeler Ranch, the days mulled together and no
one wore watches. I felt myself slowing. What did not appeal to
me was the mystical doomsday talk and the scary experimental
attitude toward children.

A girl I stayed with at Wheeler's, Rosie, was twenty-eight and
had borne children by three men. On the day she was showing
me how to bake bread, Harry, who lived in a tent down the
Ridge, was minding her infant son, Blue Jay. Harry came back
with Blue Jay at dusk.

"What a mellow day," he said. "I dropped mescaline and we
were lying in the garden and ya know what? Blue Jay started
playing with my dick and I sucked his cock."

Rosie dropped the bread dough. "Are you crazy? A baby can't
handle that."

"Naw, he dug it," Harry said.

"You swear to me on the Urantia book you'll never do that
again or I won't let you near Blue Jay."

"I can't swear anything," Harry said. "You're always telling
me, there's no right and wrong, no good and bad."

"Out of my house."

"All right," Harry yelled. "When Blue Jay grows up he'll decide for himself who he wants to hang out with."

But by this time Rosie was on the floor laughing.

I drove back to San Francisco the following day, stopping for
hitchhikers until there were nine people and two dogs stuffed inside. The car was so encrusted with mud that you could not tell
its color. All the way to the Golden Gate Bridge, my passengers
sang: "I shall be released!"

Michael's radio station held a party for advertisers the night I
returned from the West. The party was at the Crystal Room
which, like so many New York restaurants, served overpriced,
tasteless food in an atmosphere of cloying elegance. As Michael
made the rounds, drinking scotch, I sat at a table with salesmen
in shiny suits who told dirty jokes and flicked their cigar ashes on
the damask cloth. One of them asked if we could talk about "the

drug problem. Just how serious is it, Sara? You've been to these places where kids live together. That scares me. Where I come from, everyone is happily married." He swung his arm, to indicate his colleagues. "Will the family as we know it disappear?"

I tried, politely, to answer him, but suddenly he leaned over and whispered, "I wonder if you'd be a good sport, go along with me on a little practical joke?"

"What is it?"

"I made a bet with these guys that I could pick you up. Now if you'd just write something on a piece of paper here, pretend it's your phone number, and hand it to me . . ."

I stood up and went to find Michael. "I'm ready to leave whenever you are."

"We just got here."

"I'm sorry, darling. Let me catch a cab and you can stay as long as you want."

"Goddammit Sara."

"Why are you angry? You're always telling me at parties, 'I want to go home now.'"

He slammed his glass on the table, grabbed my arm and jostled me out the door.

We screamed at each other all the way downtown. I screamed about how crass the New York radio world was and how the waste and decadence of the Crystal Room made me sick. Michael screamed that just because I'd been living like an animal with a bunch of fucking grain eaters I thought I knew everything but I was full of shit. He dropped me outside the apartment and said he was going to spend the night at the office he had acquired recently, in which there was a bed and a hot plate.

I sat up all night plotting my escape. I took out our bank books and made calculations. First thing in the morning I would close the accounts, take the money and catch a plane for Brazil or Hungary and leave Michael a note telling him not to bother because there was no way on earth he could track me down.

In the morning he came home and we talked, sitting in the spots in the living room where we always sat for our morning-after talks. No matter what we had argued about, the resolution was the same. I would explain my position, he would explain his

and then I would set out to refute him point by point. Once I
started to argue I was bent on winning, but the more verbal am-
munition I summoned, the more frustrated Michael would become. He would call names, make wild statements, throw objects, until he was forced to apologize and I forgave him. But as
I held him in my arms I was troubled. How is it possible that I'm
always right? Michael said, as he invariably did in those moments, "Let's have children." For weeks afterward there was
peace.

He was earning, by the spring of 1970, more than enough for
us to live on and we had some hope that the marriage might last.
He panicked at the idea of moving from our apartment, so I
hired a designer to remodel the interior. We had couches made
to order from Haitian cotton dyed my favorite shade of purple.
We bought a white Parsons table and chairs imported from Den-
mark, chrome lamps and glass shelving which we filled with
plants and books, and when the room was completed, all spanking white and airy with highlights of purple and glass and
greenery, we sat in it for an entire Sunday, thrilled because it
was not only beautiful but felt exactly like us.

We rented a cottage in Westhampton to use as a weekend retreat. We dug clams in the bay and I cooked them in chowders.
The novel Michael had written during his unemployed years was
about to be published, and a photographer from *Newsweek*
drove out to photograph Michael walking on the beach.

I decided to stay in the country by myself for a few weeks and
write short stories. But it rained and the rain turned Dune Road
gray and sodden. I was frightened of the silence and the mildew.
I couldn't work. There was no one I could talk to. Our neighbors
were straight families or groupers—singles who blasted out on
the weekend with trunks full of beer and volleyballs. There was
nobody like Bill Wheeler, with whom I could smoke dope and
talk about organic gardening.

I remember driving out on the Long Island Expressway, passing miserable row houses and industrial smokestacks and being
struck with guilt that I was spending so much money on a beach
house for just two people who had another home as well.

I was tired of working, competing. What was the point? Every time I had an article published, I would receive a handful of admiring letters and a proposal of marriage from a twenty-year-old in Nigeria, and someone I had quoted would threaten to sue me and the cycle would begin again.

The week my article on "Open Land" appeared, Michael's father took us to dinner at 21. He was carrying a copy of *Harper's* and a copy of *Newsweek* that contained praise for Michael's novel. "I'm so proud," Phillip said. "The press you're getting is fantastic."

"Dad, it's the most amazing thing. The book's on display in the window of Doubleday's. For a first novel to get twenty rave reviews, and the whole column in the daily New York *Times*—it's unheard-of. Don't you think, Sara?"

"Absolutely."

Phillip asked the waiter, "How's the veal tonight?" Then to Michael, "What about the film rights, any news?"

"It looks like Warner Brothers is going to option it."

"Mar-velous." Phillip grabbed Michael by the neck and hugged him. "And you!" He turned to me and squeezed my hand so hard my wedding ring dug into my fingers. "A cover line in *Harper's!* Let's order champagne. This is a celebratory occasion. Oh, darlings, after this there'll be more articles, and more books, and more films!"

I smiled, but I was thinking, and then what?

The bombing of Cambodia. The killings at Kent State. In the night, throngs of students marched past our apartment chanting, "Ho ho, Ho Chi Minh, the NLF is going to win!" I wrote to my parents:

> I'm convinced we're at the brink of revolution—fighting in the streets. Virtually every college campus is now radicalized. President Nixon has instructed the Rand Corporation to make a study of what measures he should take if, in 1972, there is too much civil disorder to hold a national election. Many of our friends expect a military take-over. You can see it in fashion—repression is ahead. The freedom of mini-skirts is being yanked

away. Michael and I are planning what to do when
fighting starts. We will probably go to London.

I don't remember why we picked London as a haven, but one
factor may have been that Candy and Bobby Moss were living
there. After a year of living apart—Bobby in Boston, Candy in
London—Bobby had joined her and was writing his thesis while
she continued training as a psychoanalyst. By coincidence, they
came to New York for a visit at the height of the Moratorium.
They were staying with Bobby's parents in a penthouse on Fifth
Avenue.

I had not seen Candy in three years. I was longing to hear her
breathy sigh, to see her close-set brown eyes and hear her speak
in exaggerated voices that made me laugh, and had always made
me feel loved.

After hugging, we sat at some distance in the formal dining
room. We were alone in the penthouse, and our voices echoed.

"You look great, Sare," she said.

"Thanks. You look . . . like a lady." I was thinking she looked
matronly. Her hair was fastened in a bun and she was wearing a
blue suit that covered her knees. She said she did not wear mini-
skirts because she didn't want to encourage her patients to fixate
on her sexually. I remembered that she had never liked her legs.

"Are you getting used to London now?"

"Very much so. It feels like our home."

A buzzer rang, making both of us jump.

"It's the revolution!" Candy said with mock horror.

"We're in the wrong place," I said. We laughed, and in the relief of having cut through the strain, I began to cry.

"Sare, what is it?"

"I don't know." I tried to stop the tears; it was useless. "I feel
so hopeless. I've been in analysis a year and a half and I don't
feel the slightest bit better. I loathe myself, I hate my life. What
kills me is that from the outside, everything is flowering and I
should be happy. I have a husband who loves me, I'm twenty-
seven and I can write for any publication I want. I've fulfilled all
the ambitions I had when I started, and I wake up every morning thrashing and moaning 'no.'"

She put a finger to her temple. "There must be a reason you feel that way. What could it be?"

"Oh, Candy, I wish I could drop out and be a hippie but I can't. I don't believe in the system either. I'm not here and I'm not there."

Candy said, "You know, one of the things that's always delighted me about you is your capacity to become so involved in things without losing track of who you are. Okay, so you're not in either world, you're somewhere in the middle. That's better than getting sucked into movements mindlessly. You should have seen the girl Susie Berman sent to look us up in London. She was the first person I ever heard talk about 'women's liberation' and I thought she was deranged."

Candy stood and struck the pose of a soap-box orator, shaking her fist. "This girl said: 'You have the right to *demand* thirteen orgasms every time you make love.'"

Candy looked so funny I laughed.

"But Candy," I protested, "you were a leftist before Susie knew what it meant. You lived across the ocean from Bobby because of your work when we thought that was crazy. You read *The Doors of Perception* when I'd never heard of 'mind expansion.'"

Candy shook her head. "I never took LSD. I think LSD, even grass can ruin your mind, destroy your ego and bring on psychosis. And I don't feel, anymore, that if you get masses of people chanting for peace you can change the world, because the other side can get just as big a crowd and chant just as loudly."

Is Candy lost to me? I thought. How could we have swung so far apart in our thinking?

She went on. "Knowing which side you're on doesn't answer everything. It doesn't explain why you have trouble loving yourself or others. . . ."

I shrugged and looked away, but before things got sticky Bobby came in with his friends from Princeton and the penthouse filled with joking and the sounds of Simon and Garfunkel. We piled into Bobby's car to have dinner in Chinatown and see *Bob and Carol and Ted and Alice*. I called Michael and asked him to join us but he refused, he wanted to have drinks with the program director.

I was resigned, by this time, to the fact that Michael had a tight circle of friends and was not open to mine. I was not much interested in his tight circle either. The men talked business and sports and the wives talked Bloomingdale's. Michael and I had become accustomed to going out separately.

We did not seem to make love more than once a week, if that. I began to ask, "How come we don't make love very often?"

He was indignant. "No woman has ever complained. I'm one of the most highly sexed men on the earth."

"But weeks go by . . ."

"That's because of our schedules. I could make love every morning of my life but you're a wreck in the morning and at night I'm too tired."

We made appointments for the afternoons. He drove downtown and I interrupted my work but as soon as we were in bed, I would bring up subjects like the housework. I wanted him to cook some of the time or do the dishes and he consented, angrily, to wash the dishes once a week but that was it. By the time we negotiated the pact, it was late and we didn't get around to making love.

At Westhampton, I waited all weekend. If I wore my new black bikini, would that do it? I studied myself in the mirror. My breasts—had they fallen? I walked, wearing the new bikini, past Michael but he did not look up from the New York *Post*.

On Sunday he spent the afternoon watching baseball games. I sat on the sundeck, fuming that he would make time for the Phillies but not for me. I could tell from his "Ya-hoos" that the Phillies were winning. ". . . catches the ball . . . and the Phillies sweep the three-game series!" I heard the television switch off. Michael's footsteps on the deck. He knelt beside me. "What do you say we make a little love now, hmm? Come inside and take off your clothes."

I could not remember the last time Michael had removed my clothes or I his. We undressed separately, lay down and reached for each other, crisscrossing arms. What had been, in the early years, uncontrolled and scary had turned to rote performing of steps that followed in a predictable order to a predictable end. Frequently there would be a point, as there was this Sunday, when I knew I was not going to come no matter how long we continued. I would flex and moan. When Michael got up to take a shower, I would flip over and use my fingers, furtively, listening for the water to stop running, hurrying to get over in the next sixty seconds before he would be back in the room.

"How about Renée's Casa Basso for dinner?" Michael said, drying himself with a beach towel.

"Great." Was my face all flushed? "I'm really hungry, could we eat a little earlier tonight?"

"Sure."

We agreed to go at nine, but at nine, Michael said, "I want another drink. Fifteen more minutes and we'll go."

Four drinks later, at ten, the restaurant was closing and Michael had a fight with the captain who refused to let us in. I had to coo to him in the car, telling him I loved him and he was my darling bunny or he would fight with everyone and we would never eat. The only place we found open was a bar that served sandwiches. In the booth beside us, a man was ordering "one more drink." We could not see his face but his voice roared over the booth. There was shuffling. A woman's voice said, "I'm going to go home and do the packing."

"Is something wrong? You're lookin' at me like you're aggravated with me. What's a matter, we had a beautiful weekend and now you have to go spoil it."

"What are you talking about?" the woman said. "I'm happy."

"Well, you looked at me like you were accusin' me of somethin'."

Pause.

"Don't walk away from me, lady!"

"Well, don't start up with me. You're paranoid or somethin'. I didn't do anything."

Silence.

The man's voice, shakily: "Tell me you love me."

The woman's voice: "I love you."

Michael looked away. "I wish you hadn't heard that," he said.

24. I went home and wrote about the miracle of Woodstock Nation.
(© Jim Marshall)

25. Radical couple, 1969. (Alan Copeland/Photon West)

26. Mick Jagger returns to the stage in 1969, promising to give a free concert for The People of Altamont. (Photo by David Fenton)

27. Altamont. Susie had to be there, but The People fought and shoved.
Hell's Angels beat members of the crowd with pool cues. (© Bill Owens)

28. Back to the land. A couple at Wheeler Ranch in northern California.
(© Bob Fitch)

29. Women's Liberation Day, New York, 1970. (© Bettye Lane)

30. Pir Vilayat Khan at Chamonix, France. Tasha felt "a huge amount of negativity tumbled out of me and what replaced it was a sense of the eternal, a sense of the marvelous journey I was on." (Photo by Daniel Entin)

31. Baba Ram Dass. (Rameshwar Dass, Hanuman's Mirror Works)

32. (Bonnie M. Freer)

22. SUSIE

In December of 1969, Mick Jagger and the Stones were going to pay their respects to The People with a free concert in San Francisco. Free! The People and the Stones, the flowers and the dream would come together in the cradle of the counterculture.

Jagger was ballsy. He was tough. Raise his fist and ten thousand fists would hit the air. Never mind the Berkeley deadheads who griped about the politics of "Street Fighting Man." Pick up on "Let It Bleed."

And pick up on Jagger: you could watch him strutting and sucking on his harmonica and know that any raunchy, dirty, off-the-wall thing you ever wanted to do or have done to you, he would do.

Jagger had not been on stage since 1967, the year the Big Three—Dylan, the Beatles and the Stones—had stopped touring. Now the Stones were coming back to America, charging the highest goddamn prices ever charged for rock 'n' roll. But at the end of the tour, the Stones would play for free.

Susie had to be there. Jeff did too. Why not go together? Susie caught a plane to San Francisco with Sam and when Jeff picked them up, he showed her two stage passes.

"Far out."

They left their son at Jeff's commune and drove to the Altamont Raceway the night before the concert. Smart thinking. They had beaten the crowds and could spread their sleeping bags on the dry brown grass near the stage. Bonfires crackled through the night. Joints were passed and tapes of "Abbey Road" were played. At sunrise, Susie and Jeff swallowed tabs of mescaline. They were feeling all happy and immobile when at 7 A.M., the gates were opened.

Down came The People, trampling over Susie and Jeff and scattering their belongings. In minutes, there was no room to move. Hell's Angels who had been hired to guard the stage gunned their bikes through the crowd, causing bodies to fishtail away.

Fuck this shit. Jeff and Susie pushed their way around the track and because of the stage passes, were able to crawl over the sound equipment until they were in the first row. There was nothing between Susie and the stage but a rope. Behind her, all she saw were people and they were ugly: shoving, popping pills, throwing full beer cans. More packed in until there were 300,000—the largest gathering in California history.

When Santana started playing, the crowd licked forward like flames. Those in front were the most ravenous and shoved the hardest. Susie was smashed against the rope and couldn't move. Because of the drug, her teeth were chattering. She watched the faces around her blow up like balloons. *The masses she loved were capable of killing her.*

She screamed, "Jeff! I'm suffocating. I'm gonna die. Help get me out of here." He called to one of the Angels who grabbed Susie by the armpits and lifted her out. She lowered her head and fought her way uphill against the crowd until she was on a fire road and there was space to sit down. She leaned against the tire of a hippie bus. She nodded out. When she awoke, she saw people having picnics and kids playing in the dirt.

"How ya doin', babe?"

She looked up and saw Jeff. "How did you find me."

"Lucky."

They sat together and watched the sun set, but they could

hardly hear the music. Now that Susie was feeling better, she wanted to go back in close and see Mick Jagger.

By the time they had worked their way to the stage, it was dark and the Stones were playing "Midnight Rambler." Beer cans and pool cues flew through the air. Hell's Angels kept diving like hornets into the crowd. Susie was shocked to see how small Jagger was. He looked thin. Scared. In spite of his outrageous costume: black pants with silver studs down the side, a devil's cape, an Uncle Sam's hat and a horseshoe figure—the sign of Leo—on his chest. He kept halting the music to stammer, "Brothers and sisters . . . why are we fighting?" As he sang "Under My Thumb," there was a sickening commotion. Knives flashed in the blue spotlight. That did it. Susie and Jeff headed home, as if returning from a war. It was not until the following day that they learned an eighteen-year-old black man had been stabbed to death in that commotion. Gloom descended on Berkeley. "Aquarius Wept." This was the new culture rising? Lord help us.

Susie stayed with Jeff at Maggie's Farm, the commune where he was living with five other people and three children. At dinner she was silent. "I felt real uncomfortable. I thought he was living his life righter than me. He was part of a collective and I had no world of my own."

After they had put Sam to sleep, Jeff lit a fire in his room. "There's something I want to tell you," he said.

"Ummm." She was thinking about collectives.

"When you were pregnant, I never treated you as if having a baby were extraordinary. I went right on with my life and expected you to go on with yours." A log split apart. "I'm sorry."

Susie nodded.

"Do you think there's any way we could get back together? Take a trip or something?"

"Why?"

"So we can be a family again. We could go anywhere you wanted."

"And what would happen," Susie asked, "when it came time to go to bed?"

Jeff flinched.

"I'm sorry." She folded her arms. "Our marriage was wrong from A to Z. It wasn't good for either of us. I've got my own struggle now, but when I'm around you, it's as if nothing has changed. I've got to be on my own."

She returned to Los Angeles and rented a bungalow for ninety dollars in an old part of Hollywood. She painted the living room red and Sam's room green. "I didn't have a style. Deciding what to wear was the big decision of the day. I didn't even know what I wanted to eat. I was feeding Sam hot dogs. I went to a health food store but I didn't know what all the grains were for."

Russ, the farm man she had met in New Mexico who had asked her to be his country lady, called and said he was coming to Los Angeles. Would he be her new love? When he arrived, Russ taught her how to cook brown rice and plant vegetables. But she wouldn't let him unpack. "I kept him in a suitcase," she says, and she wouldn't let him fix anything, he had to teach her. She was relentless. She wanted to be completely independent but it was confusing because it meant twice as much work. Big fucking deal, she thought when she took out the garbage cans. You've eliminated role differences but now you have to do all of them.

Russ good-naturedly put up with it. He always smelled nice and took his time making love. For hours they would lie in bed, talking and singing "Someday Soon," and he would slowly undress her. Once as he was swaying above her, he looked in her eyes with unaffected sweetness. "Hey lady, I love you." She felt a spinning in her head, a tingling all through her. "It wasn't like the orgasms I'd been giving myself with the vibrator but it was astounding." She thought about it for days and began to wonder if she had not been focusing on the wrong thing. "It wasn't just a penis, it was the context of the love-making. It hit me that to have orgasms with a man, I would have to deal with profound issues like surrendering, trusting and letting go."

It frightened her to let a man see her out of control. She liked Russ but she didn't want him there anymore. She wanted to be alone so she could read, write, masturbate, smoke dope, paint pictures, have men over. She kicked Russ out.

Through a former professor, she found a job on a sex research project at UCLA interviewing lesbians about their lives. Her mother took care of Sam while she drove to far-flung communities she had never heard of: Sunland, Glendora, Tarzana. She began to have dreams about making love with women. She was angry at men, she was surrounded by gay women, she wanted a female kind of love with tenderness.

What impressed her about the gay women she met was that they had known early in life that they were going to have to take care of themselves. At thirteen, they had thought about issues that Susie was only getting to at twenty-seven.

Like work.

The very word obsessed her. Meaningful work, helping work. She made a list of careers: painter—no, doesn't help me help others; sociologist; carpenter; paramedic; dope dealer; newscaster; radical psychiatrist. She applied to UCLA to get her master's in political science. She applied to the Kinsey Institute to become a sex researcher. She started a journal to become a writer.

"I'm jealous of women who have work," she wrote with a red Pentel. "I want to go see the world. Be somebody." She lettered signs and posted them in her room: "Forget about orgasms and just dig it!" She made lists of her lovers, her acid trips and her goals. On page 29 she wrote in green ink:

What I want to do and why:
1. Learn to cook well. Independent of women's role shit, it's something I'd enjoy. It entails giving to people.

There were no other numbers.

What annoyed Susie was that every time she wrote or thought something, she instinctively asked herself, what would Jeff think? She could not concentrate long enough to finish a list or read a book. She was rushing off to work, making dinner, mending clothes, fixing her car, typing reports, going out by herself and picking up freaks on the street.

And Sam. There was always a buzzing in her head about Sam:

what was he doing, did he have his warm jacket? Because of Sam she couldn't run off to Mexico. Because of Sam she had to stay in touch with Jeff—through tense phone calls and hostile notes.

Jeff was lecturing at U.C. Santa Barbara, and at Christmas, Susie drove there with Sam so Jeff could take him for the holidays. She parked the car and took Sam's arm as they walked to the office of the Third World Liberation Front. Sam was straining like a puppy on a leash. They opened the door.

"Hi, Daddy!" Sam cried. Jeff scooped him up and swung him in the air. "Holy shit, Sam. You're growing so fast, you're gonna be as big as Muhammad Ali." Sam shrieked and giggled as they dropped to the floor and wrestled. It was minutes before Jeff spoke to Susie. "How was the trip up?"

"Okay," she said. She was hungry. Should she ask to have lunch, the three of them?

"I'm late for a meeting," Jeff said. "Let me walk you out."

They exchanged slips of paper with phone numbers, then Susie kissed Sam, got in the car and drove away.

When she reached the freeway exit for Hollywood, she had an impulse to turn the car around and drive back to Santa Barbara. What the fuck was that about? She unlocked the door of her house. She didn't like the empty sound—her footsteps on the floor. She squatted on her heels by the phone. She picked up the receiver, but after a moment, placed it back in its cradle. Who could she call? The girls she knew from high school? She had cut all those ties years ago. Her parents? She couldn't talk to her father. He didn't laugh, he didn't cry, he watched television all weekend. Her mother was okay when they went shopping or did stuff with Sam, but alone? Forget it. Her brothers? She wrinkled her nose. They had turned out so straight, so dull.

It was occurring to her that she might have been naïve in telling Jeff things were over from A to Z. "I had thought you would walk out the door and be reborn. You would leave one relationship and immediately start another. There were millions of men out there waiting for you." Bullshit. She was free—no responsibilities, no ties—and she did not know what to do.

On Christmas eve, she wandered in an all-night supermarket,

watching burned-out ladies with matted hair and smeared lipstick, talking to themselves as they picked over oranges. She imagined that she herself would go down, wallow in garbage and lie in the street strung out on heroin. She wanted to hit bottom. Then she could piece herself back from scratch.

What stopped her from going to the depths was Sam. When he returned from Santa Barbara, she had dinners to fix and play group meetings to attend. She had to stay sane, and to that end, she began to connect herself up once again with people on the Left.

She drove out to Venice to work with the Vietnam Veterans Against the War. She felt at home in the storefront with the old, familiar posters, the longhairs and the ringing phones. A guy she knew vaguely from Berkeley, Rubin, asked her to go for a walk on the beach. It was a foggy day, the first of March, and as they sat watching gulls, Rubin confided in her that he was a Weatherman.

"No shit," Susie said. "What's that like?"

Rubin said they had one goal: to lead white kids into armed revolution. They were living in affinity groups with people they trusted. No one could be married. No personal loyalties could interfere with the needs of the group.

"Are you happy?" Susie asked.

"We don't talk about being happy. We talk about being strong." He gave her a sideways look. "Hasn't it occurred to you that it's time to take your destiny into your own hands? Our collective could use strong women."

"I don't know, I have a son . . ."

"That could be worked out."

Susie frowned. "Whenever I visualize holding a gun and killing somebody . . . I can't get my head around to that."

Rubin said, "Violence exists in this country. Violence is as American as cherry pie, like Rap Brown said. So it's not as if you have a choice. When the revolution comes, and it's a minimum of six months, maximum six years . . ."

"What the fuck are you talking about! The revolution isn't words, it's blood, real blood, death, hiding people, families being split up, secret passages in your house, orphans, cripples . . ."

Rubin cut her off. "What do you want to do? Reform the system? The ruling class won't give up its power without an armed confrontation. You of all people should know that. Revolutionary violence is the only way."

She stood up. "I'm not convinced every other way has been tried."

They parted coldly. Susie went home and pulled the blinds. Why had Rubin dumped this on her? He didn't even know her. If it was really that heavy, he couldn't afford to take chances. What if the FBI came around? She wrote in her journal, "I am living in a historical time of great chaos."

The next Friday, a town house in New York being used by Weatherman as a bomb factory exploded and two Weatherpeople were killed. The survivors went underground and were placed on the FBI's Ten Most Wanted list. Susie became convinced there were men watching her house, but if Weatherpeople needed help she couldn't turn them out. She had her phone unlisted and thought about changing her name. If Jeff got involved in this, she and Sam would be sitting ducks. She told Sam to come sleep in her bed.

"Why, Mom?"

"Things are gettin' heavy."

"Should I put on my helmet?"

She laughed and hugged him. "No, I just want you close to me."

The following week, Jack Fried, who had been one of Jeff's closest buddies since the days of FSM, came down from Berkeley and told her not to worry, Jeff was more sympathetic to RYM II than Weatherman.

"How is he?" She tried to sound casual.

"Bummed out. Doing penance for fucking you over."

Jack told her everyone in Berkeley was going crazy. His own wife, Lynn, had left him to join a gay collective and had taken the kids with her. "In the last six months, every knock on the door has been someone in anguish. Can you imagine the chutzpah? Trying to change the world when our personal lives are such a mess? Look at me. I'm twenty-nine years old and I'm living in a flophouse on Shattuck that has piss-stained carpets and foul odors."

He and Susie laughed until tears ran from their eyes. Sam woke up and wandered out in his pajamas. "What's going on, Mom?" She carried him back to bed. "Oh, nothing. Jack and I are talking about the good old days."

Jack said, "You remember the early sixties?"

Susie: "Sure I remember. I thought I'd never grow old. Life was one big joke."

Jack: "We knew what politics was then. It was marches, elections. Now politics means who you fuck, what you eat, how you cure a cold. No theory is big enough to encompass that broad a notion of politics. That's why the New Left is dying. Okay, we know we can't unlock the problems of this country without doing something about sex, the body, the blacks, the schools, ecology. But what is the priority?"

He halted, then flashed: "It's a gestalt of priorities!"

Susie did something she'd never done before. She asked, "What does that mean?"

Jack laughed. "I don't know what it means."

"Do whatever you feel like?"

"Right on." Jack howled. "Man, we didn't know what we were up against. We thought if we really wanted a revolution, all we had to do was explain it and people would say, oh yeah, right, let's go. Well guess what, it's going to be harder than we thought."

Susie stopped laughing and was pensive. "So now we're mature. We're resigned that it's gonna be a long struggle, a long process. Maybe it won't even happen in our lifetimes."

Jack said, "In a way it's a relief. You know? After all these years of proving we won't take shit from anyone. Maybe we can just be ordinary people."

They finished a bottle of hearty burgundy and walked, hand in hand, to the bed. Susie scrunched up her face. "It feels like we're two old people, doesn't it?"

"Yeah."

They made love, cozily, desiring not to see stars but merely to be warm. "You know something?" Susie said.

"What."

"I think I might like being ordinary."

23. TASHA

"I'm going to California by myself," Tasha told Mark in June of 1970. "I don't want you to phone me or send disruptive letters. I want no communication for six weeks, so I can resolve it in my heart: yes or no."

She moved into her mother's house in the Hollywood Hills. (Only five minutes from where Susie was living. They had to have crossed tracks all summer—Susie in her Volkswagen with the kiddie seat, Tasha in her mother's Jaguar—but they did not see one another.) Within a week, Tasha was offered a job running a gallery on La Cienega, but the job meant a two-year commitment and she couldn't do it. "I didn't know if I was leaving New York or leaving Mark, and working in the art world was part of my whole nausea."

She had stopped dealing art the year before to write a children's book. She had followed school kids through the Metropolitan Museum and found that what caught them was the story behind the painting. "They loved to hear the myths, so I conceived of writing a series of books: the creation of the world in myth and art; the underworld—fabulous creatures in myth and art. I didn't talk to publishers first because I didn't want to be discouraged." She ordered the photographs at her own expense but before they had arrived she was sick of the project.

She planned to finish the book in Los Angeles, but instead she lay in her bikini on the grass in the back yard reading Joan Didion. The sun made her lazy. She watched her skin turn golden and her hair bleach out to the color it had been when she was seventeen. She lost the taste for eating and her weight dropped to ninety-five pounds. She hardly went out, except to see her old friends Beth and Harvey Bernay, who were living in Westwood with their two young sons. Harvey was now the chief resident in psychiatry at UCLA. "Hey," she said, "don't you know any nice young doctors for me?"

Harvey laughed. "I wish I did."

He was barbecuing hot dogs one night and Beth and Tasha were making potato salad when the phone rang. Harvey answered it. His eyes flicked to Tasha. He stood with the receiver to his ear, not talking. At length he said, sounding embarrassed, "Of course," and took the phone in another room.

When he rejoined the women, he looked perplexed. "That was Mark."

"My Mark?" Tasha said.

"Yes."

"What did he want?"

"He said he was worried about you. He wanted to know whether, if something happened to him, Beth and I would look after you. He said there was one other person he was calling with this message. He wants to make sure there are people who'll care for you if he's not around."

Tasha's face turned red. "It's a ploy. He's the all-time king of the manipulators."

Beth said, "Maybe he *is* worried?"

Harvey looked dubious. "What I heard was, 'I'm cracking up under the strain of waiting for Tasha to make some decisions about us.' But instead, he turned it into this Wagnerian gesture. 'Look what I'm doing for Tasha.'"

Tasha said, "He's performing for the camera. He's always aware of how it plays. He's completely self-absorbed and impossible." Her face puckered. "And really precious."

Oh God, what was she going to do about Mark? They had had a good two months in Paris that spring but things were always good in Paris. They took walks through the quarter and sat in cafés, talking deeply, and Tasha was struck once again by the awesomeness of Mark's drive to create. It thrilled her to watch his pieces take form. Everything she herself did in Paris was charged with creativity: the needlepoint pillows she sewed; the terra-cotta figures she sculpted; the children's stories she wrote in the studio while he sketched and hammered through the night.

But after the good spring in Paris, they had had a wretched two months in New York, living from crisis to crisis: sculpture being lost, the ceiling falling in and Mark making too many plans and promises. Because of the chaos, Tasha could not work on her book. She tried painting water colors and made a composition in lapis blue which she called "The Magic Mountain." It was the first of her pieces that she liked, and she asked Mark to hang it in the studio. Weeks passed. Every time she reminded him he had an excuse for not hanging it. Instead he came home one day and presented her with three fur coats that Ben Kahn had traded him for sculpture: a mink, a seal and a Persian lamb. She couldn't look at Mark. I'm going to escape, she thought, I'll go to Italy, to Assisi.

When she saw Dr. Von Pieters, she said, "I don't think I would be with Mark if my father were alive."

The doctor said, "You're with him because you have work to do and you should stay with him until you understand what that is."

"I know what it is. Because of the way my father died I can't bear to be around a man who isn't fulfilling himself. Unfortunately, Mark does it at the expense of others. He's the opposite of my father. Steven Silver was the same way. We spent a lot of time on Steven, now we spend a lot of time on Mark and I don't ever get down to the business of myself."

Dr. Von Pieters tapped his pencil on a bronze miniature of Krishna. "I suspect you have a great deal to learn yet. I don't think you're finished."

Of course he didn't.

She had exactly eleven days in Los Angeles before a telegram arrived from Mark. "New factors arising. Must know if you're coming back."

That evening, her mother showed her a copy of the *Village Voice* in which there was a photograph of Mark at a party in South Hampton. Tasha squinted at the picture. He was laughing, and he seemed to have his arm—could it be—around a girl, a blond waif type in a caftan. Tasha called up a friend in New York who had worked with her at Hilda Carson's. Yes, the friend said, Mark had been "all over town with the girl." Tasha panicked. She was losing something dear. She called Mark, who said he was beginning to care for this new young woman so if Tasha wasn't coming back . . .

The next day she met Mark at the L.A. airport. He had vomited all the way across country and had 101° fever. Tasha rushed him to her doctor's, then to her mother's house and put him to bed.

Several nights later they were asleep in Tasha's room when Mark woke her from a dream of sea monsters and coral that grew in terrifying bursts like Jack's beanstalk. "It's either yes or no," he said. She brushed the coral from her sleep-fogged eyes. All she knew was pain, with him or without him. Yes, she said, because she couldn't say no and she couldn't say I don't know forever. In the morning they caught a plane back to New York. She gave up her apartment and moved into his studio.

Rachel Eisen was her one true friend in New York. Rachel was an actress and a dancer who was forty but seemed, from her velvety skin and rich, dark hair, closer to twenty-five. Her body was pleasingly rounded and she had a throaty, voluptuous laugh which could make Tasha, even in her darkest moods, burst into her tinkling laugh. Rachel lived with her husband, Greg, a sculptor, in a mews house in the Village. Tasha would often spend the afternoon there, reading, dying yarn for needlepoint or baking carrot cake with Rachel and drinking strong coffee. But some of the things Greg and Rachel did were strange. They threw yarrow sticks to divine the future and they listened to tapes by some weirdo called Rum Dass or Rum Baba. Whenever they started in on the weird stuff, Tasha would gather up her yarns and head home.

In the fall of 1970, when Tasha returned, beaten, to New York, she found Greg and Rachel were on a new kick, natural medicine. They were taking a class in healing and nudged Tasha, "Come with us, what have you got to lose?"

When Tasha arrived at the windowless loft in the East Village, she was told to take off her shoes. Inside, she saw dozens of people sitting on the floor. At the front of the room was a giant. He must have been seven feet tall, he must have weighed three hundred pounds. He had kind eyes and merry pink cheeks and Tasha immediately wanted to hug him. "That's Hans," Rachel whispered reverently. "He lived in India for eight years." Hans was talking to the group about meditation. "There are many techniques: counting one's breathing, repeating a prayer, staring at a candle flame or just sitting and trying to empty the mind of all thoughts until it becomes like a hollow reed."

The boy next to Tasha asked loudly, "Why do that?"

Hans said, "To find inner peace. Let's meditate together. If you start to think about the laundry or your husband or anything other than what's happening right here, tell your mind gently, 'not now.' Close your eyes. Focus your attention on your heart. Think of your heart as a golden sun, melting away all the dark clouds around it. Feel the warm, healing energy move out from the heart to your shoulders. Breathe deeply. As you breathe out, let the energy travel down your arms to your hands and your fingers."

Tasha felt her fingers grow prickly. The people in the room took off their rings and watches. They paired up and Hans showed them how to massage the pressure points on the soles of the feet. They took off their glasses to work on the eyes. They took off their shirts, by which time Tasha was so absorbed in feeling the knots in muscles and the energy meridians that she wasn't worrying about her small breasts. As she dressed herself later she thought, Mark would faint if he knew I'd taken off my clothes and been manipulated by strangers.

She began to attend the classes and on Sundays, she got up at five in the morning to drive to Big Indian, a yoga ashram in Woodstock, where Hans gave workshops in massage. "I loved Big Indian. People were living in the country, meditating together, putting their feet in the stream together. There was so much exuberance and joy in that community. A new breath of air was blowing in my life, and I started to have this . . . curiosity."

The people she met talked about cuckoo things like kundalini, an invisible force that was supposed to lie sleeping, coiled like a snake at the base of the spine, but which you could rouse by contorting your body and panting. It was crazy, but massage wasn't crazy, it was a powerful form of medicine "because you were stimulating the organs, the blood stream and the nerves."

In her afternoon visits to Rachel and Greg's, she began to look through all the weird books and examine the pictures of gurus and saints. The most prominent place above the altar was given to Pir Vilayat Khan, a Sufi master. Tasha picked up his photograph.

"What's a Sufi anyway?"

Rachel stretched herself out like a cat. "It's hard to describe. Basically, the Sufis are people who yearn to achieve union with God, and they do it through means of ecstasy. Their practices are dancing, whirling, chanting. But the practices aren't as important as their passion for union."

Union with God? Come on.

Rachel told Tasha that Pir Vilayat was coming to New York in April to give a meditation seminar. "I think you ought to go. He'll teach you how to meditate in a way that will bring you concrete results."

Tasha was dubious but she figured, I might as well see this guy. She learned she would have to go by herself; Greg and Rachel were escorting Pir Vilayat.

"What the hell do you wear to a meditation?" she asked Rachel. They laughed. Rachel said, "Anything that's comfortable." Tasha decided on a leotard and a denim skirt, but on the morning of the seminar she stalled around until it was so late she had to take a cab and tell the driver to hurry, which meant running red lights and bouncing over potholes. I probably won't know anyone, she thought. Except, it's possible Sara Davidson might be there.

She had read an article of Sara's in *Harper's*, "The Rush for Instant Salvation." She had thought of writing her a note but chickened out. Sara wouldn't want to see her. She probably knew a million people and ran around with literary types.

It was raining when Tasha arrived at the Prince George Hotel. She hurried through the lobby and into the elevator. She turned and looked up. "Sara! I knew you'd be here."

Too strange—the two of them stepping in the elevator at the same moment.

"Tasha, you look beautiful," Sara was saying.

"How come you've never called me in all these years?" Tasha asked.

"I wanted to, but I was afraid. I thought you'd be angry about the table."

"What table?"

"Don't you remember? In our apartment. The black coffee table. It belonged to all of us and I gave it away and you were furious."

Tasha thought, was Sara dreaming?

Later, as Tasha sat on the floor and tried to meditate, up floated pictures from Berkeley: the A. E. Phi house, the cottage on Blake Street, the Terrace, Steven Silver, Sandra Jason, no! The pictures would suck her down and she was just coming up.

Pir Vilayat said in a cool, ripply voice, "We want to awaken from our very limited consciousness, from the emotions of our everyday life. Imagine that you are floating in the aurora borealis. Feel the freedom of those limitless spaces. . . ."

After the seminar, Tasha walked all the way home, three miles up Madison, watching the light change and fade and being awe-struck at the beauty in every face. "I thought the Sufi world was my world and I could relax. Meeting Sara, my long-lost friend, at that moment was a fabulous sign. I was out of the danger zone."

When she joined Mark at the studio, he was pleased and apprehensive. He wanted to go to Sufi meetings with her but when he did, Tasha found she couldn't meditate with him in the room. "His vibrations overwhelmed me."

One night, she and Mark massaged one another and sat on the bed looking into each other's eyes. Tasha felt a shiver of aversion. Mark was cold. She blinked; now his face looked innocent, hopeful.

She listened to the air drawing in and hissing out as their chests rose and fell, rose and fell. Mark slid closer. They were breathing in unison, keenly aware of every inch of space between them. Their faces were flushed. They opened to each other, poured into each other, melted, pulsed and swayed together, came together and slept pressed wetly.

Tasha dreamed that she was on a rock high in the Alps when over the crest came Pir Vilayat Khan. They made love as if they were twirling through space, weightless. She wasn't using birth control but she was in ecstasy; whether or not she became pregnant was in God's hands.

She had many dreams of Pir Vilayat as the summer came on. He was holding a retreat in Chamonix, in the French Alps, in August. Rachel and Greg were planning to go but Tasha didn't want to leave her natural medicine class and besides, Mark was taking her to Italy in August. "In my dreams, though, I was being called to Chamonix." Three days before Greg and Rachel were to leave, she sat Mark down and told him she was going. She ran out to buy a sleeping bag and get shots, packed and caught the plane for Geneva with Rachel and Greg.

From Geneva, they took a bus to Chamonix, rode a teleferic up the mountain and climbed another hour on foot until they were far above the clouds. Tasha did not see a sign of human life. Only mountain peaks, mist and jade-green fir trees. "We were extremely close to the sky," she recalls. The silence was so profound that her breathing thundered. Suddenly they came to the top of a saddle and in a meadow below, saw two hundred people in a vast circle dancing with their arms linked and singing with all the stops out: "Al-lah! Al-lah!"

Greg and Rachel threw down their gear and ran toward the circle where they were pulled into the dance. Tasha felt deserted. She wandered through the Sufi camp by herself, "trying to look as if I had it together," and worrying about the weather. She learned it had been raining every day, but she and Rachel had expected August heat so they had brought mostly halters and shorts. That night, Tasha put on every piece of clothing in her suitcase and was to live and sleep in those layers for three weeks.

The first dinner she ate in the Stone House called the Vacherie
consisted of beets and raw carrots. Rachel and Greg sat with Pir
Vilayat. Tasha sat at a table of strangers. "I learned instantly
that you couldn't do the New York party routine. If you asked
people, 'Where are you from and what do you do?' they said,
'I'm here and I'm doing this.' If you asked their name they had
Sufi names like Nur, Wali Ali and Salik."

She had to sleep on a narrow board in a white tent that
leaked. "It was bitter cold and I was homesick." In the morning,
the sun broke through and they ate breakfast of hot millet and
tea on wooden tables. Pir Vilayat appeared and from that point,
Tasha was swept into the rhythm of the camp.

Every day they meditated; sang; meditated; cooked and did
laundry; took planetary walks to tune into the energy of Jupiter
and Venus; meditated; bathed in an ice-cold waterfall; danced
and sang and retired to sleep. She grew close to people about
whom she knew nothing except that they had worked together in
the kitchen or danced on the Jupiter walk and shared a moment
of bliss, when all was love. In her meditations she floated into regions where she lost track of time and her thoughts bled to noth-
ingness like waves dispersing on sand.

"What happened in Chamonix," Tasha says, "was that it felt as
if I'd sprung a leak. What was leaking out most rapidly was my
fear of time and death. Such a huge amount of negativity just
tumbled out of me and what was replacing it was a sense of the
eternal, a sense of the marvelous journey I was on."

One night in the kitchen, she opened the oven and it exploded.
Flames covered her body. People slapped at her and when the
flames were out, they examined her and saw she hadn't been
burned. "I thought I'd lost my face. Rachel fished out a little mirror so I could see I was okay and I realized, for two weeks I
haven't looked in a mirror. For two weeks I haven't given a
thought to what I look like."

The day before she left Chamonix, the entire group climbed in
silence up slopes covered with wild flowers and solitary sheep.
The air was so pure that just breathing made her high. They
meditated all day, walked back in silence, ate a simple meal and
dropped into welcome sleep. Many of the people were now pre-

paring to go off on three-day retreats where they would meditate by themselves and have meals brought to them. Tasha wanted to go on a retreat but she had arranged to meet Mark in Paris.

"It was a heavy moment when the teleferic hit the bottom of the hill," she recalls. "Rachel and I went into a café and ate omelets, which was weird because it was so noisy and such an effort to get the waiter's eye and choose what you wanted from the menu." They rented a car and drove to Paris, singing and chanting "Al-lah!"

Before she had left camp, Tasha had gone to see Pir Vilayat for a personal meeting. He was living in a cave in the side of the mountain, where she found him perched on a flat gray rock. She sat down facing him.

After a time he spoke, telling her he saw in her a great well of disappointment. "All your suffering is due to emotions," he said. "You become enslaved to your emotions and feel completely at their mercy. This is what holds you back from making great strides."

Tasha nodded. Was he through? Should she leave? She thought, I want to ask him if I have the potential to overcome this.

At the moment the words ticked in her head, Pir Vilayat smiled and said, "You do."

24. SARA

Over the Christmas holidays in 1970, when Tasha was first hearing of the Sufis, my sister Terry, who had just turned twenty-four, came to visit and threw our house into a turmoil. She had become a disciple of a Hindu swami and insisted on getting up at 4 A.M. to take a cold bath, ring gongs, read the Bhagavad Gita and fix odd meals like squash with pumpkin seeds. She made hostile remarks about Michael and I being animal killers, and in the midst of one of her harangues I was so frustrated I slapped her, as I had not done since I was six.

Not only had I lost my closeness with Candy over ideological differences, I was now losing my sister. When she left, I decided to write an article about seekers of salvation, to expose their delusions and hopefully knock some sense into Terry's head. I also knew the piece would be perfect for *Harper's*. The more bizarre the people were, the more shocking and controversial the article could be. And seekers were bizarre.

I went to see Peter Max, who greeted me wearing an alpha-wave headset. His right eye was bleeding, he said, "because I just spent three days in the desert on an enlightenment intensive. At the height of it, my eye opened up and wept. I discovered who I am and what life is about." Great, I thought, writing it all down.

The enlightenment intensive had been run by the Institute of Ability, founded by a California couple, Charles and Ava Berner. I read their literature and found it preposterous. Their religion was called Abilitism and its premise was that every human being is a God and has "infinite ability."

When Charles Berner visited New York, he told me that during his intensives, half the participants become enlightened "wham—like that." This I had to see. I asked if the intensive would benefit someone who couldn't conceive of being a God. Charles said yes. "We don't ask you to accept our ideas. Our masters never say one word about what you are or are not. But it's funny, everyone always comes up with the same thing in different words. No one has ever come up with, 'I'm a sack of mud,' or the *Communist Manifesto*. They could, but they never have."

I packed my sleeping bag and boarded a bus with twenty-two seekers for a retreat lodge in the wilds of Pennsylvania. The lodge was a quaint, pink salt box, containing a meeting room, a fireplace and a funny little stage. One man took off his clothes and walked out in the snow. Others sat motionless in pairs, staring bug-eyed into each other's faces. No behavior was regarded with any surprise. We slept head to toe in our bags on the floor and at 5 A.M., a girl, one of the "monitors," circled the room droning, "Start waking up, start waking up."

Ava Berner, who was leading the intensive, gave us our instructions. For the next three days we were to think and talk about nothing except the question, who am I? "Don't eat or sleep unless we say so. No smoking, no sex, no drugs, no phone calls or writing." But an exception was made for me—I could take notes during rest periods.

We were to choose a different partner every hour and alternate talking and listening for five-minute intervals. We would look into each other's eyes and one partner would ask, who are you? Ava said, "When it's your turn to talk, just say whatever comes. Then a bell will ring and you'll ask your partner, who are you? Listen but *don't* respond, don't judge and don't give advice. Just be there for him."

In the first five minutes, I said everything there was to say about who I was. I knew life was absurd and haphazard, and I was the sum of my characteristics and experience. Around me people were saying, "I am the sun!"

"I'm a mother and I need to be less hard on my kids."

"I am a baked potato."

The hour was unendurable. When the final bell rang it was only 7 A.M. I realized I had made a dreadful mistake. I would have fled instantly had there been transportation. How could I endure three days of this crap? I couldn't stand most of the people. Ruth reminded me of my third-grade teacher. Melvin was repulsive, with beady eyes, a hook nose and bad breath. Monique was clearly psychotic. She sat in a catatonic lotus pose with her eyes rolling up in their sockets and she whispered, "When I am near people I feel I am in the presence of a snake."

We were given little food and not until midnight were we allowed to sleep. "Let your body go now," the monitor said, "but *you* keep holding the question."

I sat up in the night. One of the monitors was walking by the windows in a long yellow dress, giving instructions. "Let your body rise and fall, the mind never sleeps. . . ." Angrily, I pulled a blanket over my head. Wouldn't they even let us sleep in peace? Twice more I woke up and the girl was still talking. In the morning I asked Ava why a monitor had to patrol all night. She raised her eyebrows. "No one was patrolling." The others concurred. The monitors had slept together in a separate room. Ava said, "It was probably someone walking around in her astral body. These phenomena happen all the time."

The only thing that kept me going that day was the determination to memorize what people were saying so I could write it down during the breaks. The sessions were endless: more eyes; more bad breath; more prattling; but gradually the talk was changing. At some point, each of my partners would express the same thoughts: I'm afraid of dying, I want to love and be loved, I don't want to be hurt. Everyone was vulnerable, everyone had pain and after listening, I could not help but feel compassion, even for beady-eyed Melvin.

On the third night, while everyone slept, I again saw people walking around the room. I woke up with paralyzing aches in my neck. By mid-morning I was convinced I wouldn't live through this. I started crying and said I had to call my husband, but I couldn't reach Michael at our apartment or his office or the station. He was dead. I leaned against the pay phone, shaking, and one of the monitors, Dan, said I should sit and be his partner.

"I don't want to be your partner, I want to go home!" Dan put his hands on my shoulders, walked me to the center of the room, found a cushion and pushed me down. Then he sat facing me. I continued to cry. He had an Asian face with sloping green eyes and when I looked at him through tears, the room dissolved. We were spinning in a circle and only our eyes in the center were still. We moved our lips but only whispers came out. He took my hands in his and somehow I felt his warmth and concern flow into me.

After that hour I no longer cared what happened. I floated numbly, I stopped watching the clock and I almost began to enjoy the sessions. After lunch, I was working with Ruth, feeling close and affectionate with her and remembering with amusement that I had despised her on sight, when I thought: If I can feel love for every person here, what's wrong with . . . me? When in all my life, I asked myself, have I ever set out to hurt someone? Never. I was no different from the others. And yet, all these years I'd been terrified I would be stoned to death if people saw through the façade. If they saw my bad black soul. But it wasn't black, there was nothing inside me to hide.

During the next hour, my partner, Min, a Chinese boy, said, "I never knew contacts between people could be so joyful. It blows my mind that you open yourself so totally to me. You don't tell me anything about your job, your family—you just show me your power. I can hold it in my hands. If I never see you again, you will always be close."

When the retreat ended and the bus delivered us to New York, I ran into Michael's arms. "It was a nightmare," I told him. "I never want to go near anything like it again." And yet, I felt so high I could have floated. Such a weight had been lifted. When I saw Dr. Collins the next day, I asked him, "How could I have believed all these years that I was bad? There was absolutely no basis." He laughed and for the first time in our relationship, got up from his chair, walked across the room and shook my hand. "Congratulations." I attributed this flip-over in my perception of myself not to "enlightenment" but to the analytic work we had been doing for three years. The retreat had merely been the catalyst.

In March, Michael and I went to Palm Springs. He had developed a passion for the desert resort, it was the only place he would go on vacation and he was establishing a routine. We stayed in the same cottage at the Tennis Club and had dinner the first and last nights at Don the Beachcomber's. Every morning Michael drove to the spa to weigh himself on a hospital scale, then stopped by Bookland for *Variety* and the New York papers, drank two gin and tonics by the pool before lunch, which was a hamburger on sourdough bread, then tennis, a massage and a jacuzzi bath in the late afternoon and three scotches in the evening.

We had a terrace on which we could sun-bathe nude and I felt lithe and tan and beautiful, but although Michael was continually hugging me, I never felt him look at me with desire.

"You don't find me attractive, do you? I'm too tall, my breasts aren't large enough?"

"Darling, don't be silly."

I went and sat beside him. "I don't see why . . . I mean, if the opportunity arose and you wanted to sleep with someone else . . ."

He smiled. "What you're saying is that *you* want to sleep with someone else."

"Well it's hard for me to believe you're not. You have an incredible sex drive, where's it all going?"

He threw ice from his glass into the sink. "I jerk off every morning. But I haven't even done that lately." He frowned. "I don't feel sexy."

"Is it because of the play?"

He nodded. After the success of his novel he had been asked to write a rock play, but the production had been on and off and with each setback, he retreated to the green room and mourned, "We're dead." Then came a phone call, a request for a rewrite, and he was up again. "We're not dead yet!"

In Palm Springs the deal looked dead. "I can't read the fucking script one more time. It's a piece of shit."

"It's not," I said. "It's the finest piece of writing you've done since I've known you. You've got to detach yourself from the business hassles."

"Mmmmm."

I stroked his arm. "Why don't we make love? It'll make you feel better." His body stiffened in defense. I stood up.

"Please, darling, I can't force it. When you're writing, lots of times you have no interest at all."

I conceded he was right.

"Be a little patient."

In April I flew to Davis, California, for a three-day Earth Rebirth Festival. A dozen gurus and thousands of their followers were gathering to demonstrate the "Aquarian Way of Life." It was a glorious, green spring weekend and I could wander through the lectures and dancing in the fields without being forced to participate. One speaker claimed to be a messenger from Venus. The Reverend Kirby Hensley from Modesto, who had pink skin and flyaway ears, ordained 116 people and one dog as ministers in his Universal Life Church. A woman representing the White Brotherhood taught people to breathe light through their skin. George Peters, the clown of the spiritual movement, said he gets people enlightened by locking them in black boxes for forty days. I sat on the grass, wearing a blue T-shirt and purple jeans, sunning myself and taking notes. I remember, at one point, looking into the eyes of an American swami as he mouthed platitudes and laughing to myself, what a schmuck.

In an orange tent, Charles Berner, Yogi Bhajan, Swami Satchidananda and the other stars of the mystic world were meeting to "experience each other." I walked to the tent but stopped a foot away. Standing there, checking names off a list, was the most beautiful young man I had seen on the spiritual circuit. He had dark hair and blue eyes, a combination which was due, I would learn, to a mixture of Mexican and Scottish blood. There were dimples in his cheeks and a cleft in his chin. He wore a muslin shirt and a shoulder bag with a bright yellow patch that said, "Have a happy day."

"Hello, I'm Noel," he said, "who're you?"

He kept his eyes on mine, as if we were partners at an enlightenment intensive, but it was clear that he viewed the proceedings with humor.

"You've heard of the smoke-filled room?" he said. "This is the incense-filled room. So unless you're a holy man, uh, holy person, I'm afraid you'll have to wait outside."

I told him Charles Berner had given me permission to attend. He bowed and stepped aside. Later in the day, Noel walked in the room and and sat down beside me on the floor. "Getting a good story?" I handed him my notebook and asked him to write down the names of the gurus. "I don't know them all, but I can find out," he said, and wrote down phrases to remind himself of who had been sitting next to whom:

> Miss Mystic
> Sallow
> Toupee
> Mrs. Light House
> Mr. Light House
> Potentate

I started laughing. Noel put his arm around me and said, conspiratorially, "How would you like to leave the white robes here and see what's happening outside?"

We walked across the field past dancers and drummers and settled ourselves under a eucalyptus tree. To my surprise, he filled a pipe with hash.

"You do drugs?"

"I'm an Aquarian," Noel said. "I synthesize everything."

"I thought you were with the Institute of Ability. Charles says they get high naturally."

Noel nodded. "I don't smoke around them." He handed me the pipe. We lay on our backs and watched sparhawks ride air currents. Noel said happily, "Life is perfect." I said I wasn't sure that was so. "Would you change places with anyone? Would you turn back the clock?" Maybe, I said. "Then you wouldn't be in this moment." He put my head in his lap and began massaging my tense shoulders. I was wondering where he was sleeping that night, where I would be sleeping, when a girl in a torn white sari ran up. "We're ready to split for L.A., Noel." He jumped to his feet. She giggled, "The car's really crowded."

"Yay!" he said and hugged her.

Then he hugged me good-by. It was a long embrace, seekers were constantly embracing but our bodies fit together and his hair smelled of sandalwood.

The next day on the plane to New York, I did not know what to do first: look out the window at the Grand Canyon, watch the movie, read books or listen to the stereo. I felt higher than I'd ever been and I had taken no drugs. Was it a contact high from three days around gurus? Noel was right, I thought, life *is* perfect.

I believed, in the spring of 1971, that I would never again feel so black, so hopeless, because I no longer had to conceal a hideous secret. I thought Dr. Collins should be paraded down Fifth Avenue in a sedan chair while the masses threw garlands. My life had been saved. But I asked the doctor, "Is this just the manic side of manic depression?"

"No," he said with a laugh. "I feel the way you're feeling most every day."

I had not taken tranquilizers in months, and when I wrote, I could put aside my work at the end of the day and go out. At a party of radio people, it was Michael who took me aside and said, "I want to go home now."

In our apartment he sat on the purple couch and sulked. "You look like you're fucking glowing, but it has nothing to do with me."

"What are you talking about?"

"I want to feel responsible, like I contribute to your happiness."

"But you do."

He took a Nembutal and went to sleep.

The next day, I was sitting in my study listening to Donovan sing "Happiness Runs" when the phone rang. It was Noel, calling from L.A., asking if I wanted to write about a World Enlightenment Festival they were planning for the summer. He babbled in a business voice and I blurted, "Noel, I really love you."

"That's great," he said, sounding uncomfortable. I switched back to business talk and he responded in kind.

When it came time to write the seekers article, which was to be titled, "The Rush for Instant Salvation," I was not in the same frame of mind I had been in when I started gathering research. I had found that I liked being around these gentle, spacy people who were working to develop attitudes of joy and love for others. But there was no way, high or not, that I could believe their theology. When the article went to press, one of the editors asked if I had resolved my ambivalence. "Yes," I said, "I think there's something valid in there, but I don't know what it is."

A few weeks later the doorbell rang. It was Noel, wearing a blue shirt that matched his eyes, white drawstring pants and no shoes. He had hitchhiked across the country. The World Enlightenment Festival had collapsed in a heap of screw-ups and he was drifting. We sat facing each other across the room. I could smell sandalwood, and Michael's voice, silken and sensual, wafted out of our JBL speakers. I listened to Michael and looked at Noel and felt the room light up and gray over. I jiggled my knees. Noel said that when he first saw me, he thought of black tulips. "It's a tall plant with straight, dark petals, like your hair." I laughed. "My hair is as curly as yours. It takes me three hours of work to straighten it." I took him in the bathroom, wet his hair and was showing him how to blow it dry when Michael walked in. Noel and I stammered and fumbled with the hair dryer. Noel left and Michael refused to talk about it, except to say he didn't want "that freak" in the house again.

I met Noel secretly for dinner at Cleopatra's, we walked along the Hudson and he told me his story. He was thirty-three, had married his high-school sweetheart, Karen, in Des Moines and worked as an advertising writer until he and Karen had taken LSD. After the visions, he had quit his job, sold all their belongings and moved to the East Village where he started making psychedelic light sculptures. He and Karen became tight with another couple, Francie and Stew. One night they switched mates, switched apartments and never moved back. Noel said he and Francie had burned each other out in six weeks, but Stew and Karen were still living together, somewhere in Arizona.

I kept looking over my shoulder, fearful that Michael might be driving down the West Side Highway. When Noel hugged me good night, he gave me a gift—a blue paperback that said on the cover *Remember Be Here Now*. It was written by Baba Ram Dass. "He used to be Richard Alpert," Noel said. "He's the dude who got kicked out of Harvard with Timothy Leary for experimenting with LSD."

That night I read the book at one sitting. Alpert's story matched mine: he was a "neurotic, Jewish overachiever" who had found at a young age that his achievements and success left him empty. He had gone to India in despair, found a guru and come back a yogi sadhu. I decided I would try to interview Ram Dass. He expressed himself with humor and intelligence—none of the singsong gibberish I had heard at Davis. If anyone could clear up my confusion about the spiritual scene, I thought, this man could.

Noel and I continued to meet in restaurants and talk about God and love and each time I told myself, this is the last. Then I went to see him at the Institute of Ability where he was staying in an attic painted yellow. "Very Leo," he said. The radio was on and Michael was playing "Sympathy for the Devil." Noel turned down the volume. "Excuse me," he said, "but I want to talk to your old lady."

We smoked a pipe of something he called "angel dust," which I later learned was a tranquilizer for horses. The drug made me feel all slithery and hot. Noel was standing at the window, talking on and on and there was such heat in my crotch . . . Jagger singing, "pleased to meet you, won't you guess my" . . . Noel walked in slow motion to the bed, stared in my eyes, then fell onto me and kissed me in a way I'd never kissed. His tongue slid all around my mouth, under my tongue, over my teeth, up across the roof of my mouth. "Your mouth is so open," he murmured.

"Sympathy for the Devil" bled into "Midnight Rambler." "What is it?" Noel asked. I told him I thought I should put in my diaphragm. He smiled. "I'm not bored with your mouth yet. Sometime in the next hour or so, we're going to take off our clothes and make what is absurdly referred to as 'love.' But there will be no embarrassment about going to the bathroom or fumbling with buttons. Just don't break the cord."

He touched me as if he had known me forever. The right places, the perfect progression. I came with his mouth on me and with him on top of me and under me and after he had come, I turned up the radio and heard Michael sign off. I dressed hurriedly and at my car, Noel said, feigning anxiety, "Are we ever gonna see each other again?"

"Soon," I said laughing, but I thought, it's out of my system.

I went to bed with his lemony-sandalwood smell on me and woke up longing for him. We made love every day while Michael was on the air. Each time, I felt miserably guilty afterward and resolved not to see Noel again. But the more we made love, the more I craved it. I was starved and the gates had been opened. I hated the deception and the sneaking but what could I do? I was married to a man who wouldn't fuck me.

In June the Institute of Ability folded and Noel planned to return to Los Angeles. "I don't feel badly about leaving you," he said. "I'm so full of you, and it was so unexpected." But I felt badly. I called him on a fake credit card at 11 A.M. in a corner bar, the Chateau Lounge. I cried into the pay phone and he lectured me about surrendering to God's will. A fat black woman put a dime in the jukebox, unleashing Gladys Knight and the Pips.

"Wow," Noel said. "I'm really rushing! You crying in the bar with Gladys Knight singing and me talking about your soul."

By evening I had rallied. My life was still saved, but Noel started slipping. He called and said he missed me. Couldn't I think of a way to get to L.A.?

I could. My sister Terry had just sold all her worldly goods and bought a one-way ticket to the South Seas. I told Michael this might be my last chance to see her in years. When the plane arrived I called him from the lobby as I always did when I flew anywhere. His voice was faint. He wanted to tell me something, he was frightened, but maybe over the phone . . .

What could it be?

"I've discovered, thinking about myself . . ."

Long silence.

"Darling," I said, "there's nothing you could say that would make me stop loving you."

"What I've discovered is that sex with you, the idea of making love with you, hasn't been turning me on. It has nothing to do with the way you look or anything like that. It's just, there's a switch that isn't working."

"But in the early years . . ."

"Truthfully," he said, "from the time we got married, making love to you has been . . . work.

"Sara? Please, Sara, believe me, it isn't you personally. I think it might have happened with any woman I had married. And I think it can be solved. If you'll be . . ." He stopped. "I'm scared."

I told him I was relieved. At least we knew what the trouble was. No more lame excuses about different schedules. It seemed to me that this was something we could handle.

Michael sighed. "Hurry back, I need you."

I sat in the phone booth, stunned. There was knocking on the glass. I turned and saw Noel, his arms filled with tulips.

Noel kept me stoned on angel dust for four days, about which I remember very little, except that we stayed in a condemned building in the valley next to a car wash with dozens of freaks floating in and out. I remember that there was a French couple, Nico and Zazie, and that Zazie wouldn't eat eggs because, she said, "zey supposed to be chicken, and if we eat zem, zey not become chicken." And I remember driving home from some beach, with Nico and Zazie fucking in the back seat. Zazie was sitting on Nico's lap and I was leaning over the front seat fondling her breasts and Noel had his hand between my legs, eighty miles an hour on the Ventura Freeway when the hood flew up and cracked the windshield. The others howled with laughter as Noel swerved off the road, but I was freaked. The next day I was bleeding from so much fucking and called Terry to come pick me up. I spent two days with her, recuperating, before I flew home to New York and to Michael.

Airports, whisper jets, baggage counters, rent-a-cars, long long corridors and accelerating roars. I have never flown so many miles in a year as I did in 1971. Six trips to California and in August, I flew to Argentina to write about the government of Gen. Alejandro Lanusse and to meet a branch of our family I had heard about since I was little.

One of the stories my grandfather liked to tell was how, when he left Hungary for California, his youngest brother sailed for Argentina. While I was growing up, I knew there was a family in Buenos Aires like ours, with two boys the same ages as my sister and I. For years the oldest boy and I exchanged letters. I daydreamed about what might have been: I would be an Argentinean girl, speaking Spanish, riding with gauchos, living at the edge of the earth in a place where I imagined there were parrots flying in the streets. I always thought that someday I would go to Argentina and meet this wing of our family.

Since Michael had no interest in traveling anywhere but Palm Springs, it was assumed that I would go alone. I planned the trip a year in advance. To cover some of the expenses, I arranged to write an article, but when the departure date arrived, the timing could not have been more absurd. I was no longer interested in whether Juan Perón would return from exile to Argentina and whether civil government would be restored. I landed at Ezeiza airport, Buenos Aires, wearing silver-studded jeans and carrying a shoulder bag filled with books on Eastern mysticism.

"Sah-rah?"

I turned and saw two small, middle-aged people, holding out their arms. They had Eastern European faces and wore gray coats, for in August it was winter in Buenos Aires. They drove me to their house in the suburbs; the house had lemon trees in the yard and was surrounded by a high metal fence. I took my place at the dinner table. Had it always been my place? I rec-

ognized the crocheted tablecloth, the Oriental carpets, the china
cabinet crowded with crystal and knickknacks. A maid served us
platters of beefsteak, mashed potatoes and vegetables. Our
glasses were filled with sweet wine.

The father, sitting at the head of the table, had the same blue
eyes as my grandfather, and with him I felt the same sense of
safety. He was a man who worked hard and spoke simply. He
had arrived in Argentina at sixteen, penniless, and over the
years he had become the proprietor of a small ranch and modest
factory. He and his wife, at the moment I met them, were supporting the military government of Lanusse. They were afraid
that if Perón returned to power, they might lose everything they
had worked for.

The oldest son was a philosophy professor at the National University; he was a socialist, married to a Communist, and had two
young children. Every day at one, he brought his family to his
parents' home for dinner. They did not discuss politics.

The youngest son was twenty-six and still living at home,
which he would continue to do until he married. "Don't you ever
want to be alone?" I asked. He raised his eyebrows. "I go in my
room and close the door. Then I'm alone." He made a gesture
with his lips as if to say, "So?"

I took it on myself to enlighten the sons about what was happening in the United States: the liberation of women, sexual
freedom, mind expansion, communal living, vegetarianism, but
as I talked, I saw them exchange disapproving glances. They
were quick to enlighten me that in Argentina, primitivism was
not voluntary. There was an acute housing shortage and meat
had become so scarce it was being rationed.

I set about interviewing politicians, workers and students, but
it occurred to me that I might capture the texture of the country
by writing about my family. I asked the parents if they would
mind. They were amused, flattered. I heard the mother tell a
friend, "Whatever I say—she writes down." After a week,
though, I became sick with anxiety. What was I doing? Coming
into their house as a relative, taking notes, leaving after two
weeks and publishing an article when there was every proba-
bility they would be hurt by some detail I wrote?

I called the oldest son and asked him to meet me in a coffee bar. He was the one I felt closest to, the only one with whom I could speak English. With the others I used my schoolbook Spanish. "Your parents have said it's okay to write about them, but I don't think they understand what I'm doing."

"They don't," he said, "but I do, and I take the responsibility."

He was most concerned that their identity not be revealed. "We have no problem, today, to give our political views, but in a few years, who knows what will be?" We agreed that I would change all names and send him a copy of the piece before it was published. Eventually I did, and he mailed it back with a few suggestions, signing his letter with love.

That letter was the last communication our family has ever had from the relatives in Argentina. Afterward, I sent a dozen letters which were not answered. I sent packages of jeans and books on feminism which were not acknowledged. The parents broke off a forty-year correspondence with my grandfather, with no explanation.

I became convinced something terrible had happened. I had taken no precautions. I had allowed Lanusse's press officer and members of the Peronistas—all of whom carried guns—to drive me home. I had left the parents' phone number with everyone I interviewed. They could have been traced. Were they dead? Did I cause it? I simply couldn't believe it, but what did the silence mean? To this day I do not know.

Michael called me in Buenos Aires and spent twelve dollars a minute to weep, "You're so godawful far away." But the night I returned, he sat me down and told me he wanted a separation. "I've found that I like living by myself. I like not having all my habits observed by you with condescension. Couldn't you find a man more suited to you, an explorer, a meditating man? I've read your journals. I know you're against me."

We sat in the living room, calmly discussing who would get the couches and the rya rugs, but I was in shock. We were down to the division of bank accounts when Michael said, "God, Sara, we've worked through so much together. The thought of starting over from scratch with someone else is just unthinkable."

"But we wouldn't start from scratch," I said, "we'd start from
the level we're at now." I took a stab. "Perhaps we can build
something better. Four years ago, it was incredible to me that
you understood my feelings, but I want more now. I want em-
pathy, sharing, just being . . . there." I snapped my fingers.

Michael said, "Maybe I don't want to be . . . there." He
snapped his fingers. "Maybe I still like to keep things"—he
placed his palm in front of his face—"hidden."

During the next few days, Michael talked about how, from his
earliest years, he had cultivated a terrain where no one, not even
his father, had been allowed. "I'm evasive and tricky, I play with
language and I always seem to be moving back a square or two
on the board."

He confessed his infidelities—some had been with friends of
mine—from the first months of our marriage. I was relieved,
again, to have the truth out. As painful as it was, it was better
than being fooled, but Michael said he didn't want to hear about
my activities. "I just hope," he said, "that you've found the sexual
pleasure I haven't provided you."

Several mornings later, I awoke and found this letter in my
typewriter:

> Dearest darling Sara,
> We are growing together. I'm frightened of you and
> longing for you all at once. I'm furious that you poke
> into private territory, and I pray you'll go in there and
> defy my rage because I'm worth it, every painful inch
> of it.
> I'm beginning to open out, and towards you. It is the
> first time in my life that I have allowed this to happen.
> Your tenacity and love have created the turning point.
> You mean everything to me.
>
>   Michael

25. SUSIE

Susie was lying in a coma. It was the winter of 1971, and she had returned from a trip to Death Valley with a fever and a cough. She had never been sick, so when the fever persisted, she went to have a physical. A TB skin test came back positive. Shit, what a nuisance. Bed rest and antibiotics were prescribed, but Susie didn't want to put chemicals in her body. She didn't want anyone to take care of her. She was proving she was strong.

She slept all day on her mattress on the floor, rousing herself to go pick up Sam, feed him and read him bedtime stories while coughing so hard she nearly blacked out. Even when she started to spit up blood she wouldn't ask for help. She thought her illness was like a bad flu.

It was her mother who, bringing Sam home from a movie, found Susie unconscious in the bathroom. When Susie came to, she was in a hospital. A team of doctors informed her there were cavities in her lung. It was the worst case of TB they had seen in years.

The next morning, the door to her room opened and in walked Roxanne. Susie burst into tears. "You came all this way . . . for me?"

"Sure, Berkeley's not so far."

Friends began calling from all across the country. Susie was astounded that so many people cared. For a week she floated in and out of a coma, crying and dreaming. She was a well of tears. She had lost her bearings and was alone in a fog, even when her room was filled with visitors.

After a month, she was taken in a wheel chair to her childhood room so her mother could nurse her. Jeff picked up Sam and from January to June, Susie did nothing but concentrate on getting well. Her world had shrunk to four walls and a lung. It was ten years from the time she had left home to go to college and she was back again, unmarried, with a child, having to be cared for like a child.

She lay in bed and thought about her life. She played out the years, looking at the steps, the turns, seeing how the pieces fit together. She analyzed her mistakes—how she hadn't seen this and misunderstood that. She reread Jeff's letters and began to believe he had loved her all along, she simply hadn't heard it. He had done the best he could.

Now that she had been separated from Sam so long, she understood how painful it was for Jeff to live apart from Sam. Before the illness, each time the day had approached for Sam to be traded, she had watched herself paying more attention to him so that the smallest bits of chatter would become infused with meaning. It was tricky, trading a child. She and Jeff had a tacit understanding that they would not speak badly of each other with Sam. "Oh, you're gonna go to your father's, won't that be fun," Susie would say, and Sam seemed to accept having two separate lives. He did not throw tantrums or play Jeff and Susie against each other. "Sam was incredibly loved and wanted wherever he went, and he always seemed happy." But she wondered if there could not be a better way. She began making notes for a letter to Jeff:

I want to apologize. I'm sorry I hurt you by running off in a blind rage. I'd denied my own desires for so long that when I left, I had to go like a house on fire. I'm able to feel for you now.

I want to relieve you of guilt. I'm not sorry I put you in my life, it was the right direction. I'm open to you, and although you might be closed to me now, who knows what the next months or years will bring? We've had a child together, lived five years on the earth together. I dream of a day when we can sit and remember the past without guilt.

She did not send the letter because whenever Jeff called, it was clear he was moving farther away. He was living with Leslie who was the opposite of Susie: low-key and quiet. Her parents had been Communists and with her, Jeff had joined the Party.

When Jeff brought Sam down to visit over Easter, he told Susie that he was quitting teaching. "I want to get a job in a cannery and live with the people. I've given up on students—they're middle-class trippers. If we're ever gonna make a revolution in this country, we've got to build a movement of the working class."

"You've really been through changes, huh?" Susie said. She was sitting up in bed, wearing a pink quilted robe; her hair was brushed back in a ponytail.

Jeff smiled from across the room. It was an easy, self-mocking smile that she had not seen in ages. "We were so arrogant," he said.

Susie: "We knew everything. Marx was an anachronism."

Jeff said, "It's been a transforming experience to rediscover communism, to find out that we do have a history of struggle in this country. The Old Left was nearly wiped out by World War II and McCarthyism. That's why the New Left seemed to spring from nowhere."

Susie tucked her legs beneath her. "It feels really good talking with you."

Jeff nodded.

"You know, I've been finding that almost everything I learned from you holds up. All the ideas are things I still believe in. And there was a lot I didn't hear. Like when you would talk about your family being important, I didn't understand—not until I got so sick—how important it is to create those bonds. During our marriage, didn't you . . ."

"Let's not get into that shit."

"Why not? There's so much that's unresolved."

"I don't want to talk about it. Maybe I would if I thought it bedeviled me, but it doesn't. It's not a part of my life any longer."

"You mean you never think about it?"

"I think we had a lot of good times. It's probably better we split up. We're too much alike."

He went to find Sam, then said good-by from the doorway. Susie cried and felt sheepish. In her journal she wrote, "He would rather forget. I don't want to go back with him, it's a relief he said no. Still, if it weren't for Leslie . . ."

Susie was at the hospital, waiting to have an X-ray, when she flipped through a copy of *Harper's Bazaar*. A feature caught her eye: "One Hundred Women in Touch with Our Time." A hundred women who had made it. Wait a minute, wasn't that an old roommate of hers? She read the caption: *"Sara Davidson, writer, New York, N.Y., deft 27-year-old evaluator of the current scene."* Susie felt a stab. She thought, is Sara one of the lucky ones who has both success and love? I wish I could go to New York.

In May she received a notice that her high school class was holding a ten-year reunion. She didn't look good, what would they think? Fuck that. She was the only single person to attend the event, a no-host cocktail party at the Beverly Hills Hotel. In high school they had felt grown-up and important when they had come there after the prom. The strange thing was that ten years later, no one but Susie saw it any differently. The women had their hair styled at the same salons and were dressed in midi-skirts and boots from Saks. Susie had thought of wearing jeans but decided she didn't need to make that kind of statement, so she chose a simple dress and pulled her long hair back in a barrette.

To her disappointment, people didn't mix freely but stuck to the pecking order set down in high school. They had all seen pic-

tures of Susie in the papers and thought she was a bra burner
and a bomb thrower. One girl said, gathering her nerve, "You
don't look any different." Susie laughed. "Neither do you." The
girl took Susie's arm and said, confidentially, "I heard you had
some bad luck."

Susie: "You mean my illness?"

"No, your divorce."

Susie shook her head. Bad? Leaving Jeff was the best thing
she'd done. She was a failure in these people's eyes but not in her
own. She was alive again. There was pain, yes, but it was better
than feeling blank.

> MY IDENTITY
> revolutionary
> hip
> Californian
> woman
> lover
> friend
> MOTHER

On June 30, 1971, Susie drove to the airport to pick up Sam.
All she could think of was rushing to the gate and scooping him
in her arms. What would he look like? What new words did he
know? She had missed him so much the last three months she
thought she would go crazy. She dreamed of him constantly. She
had come to terms with his existence, no more resentment of the
responsibility, she simply wanted him. Whatever she had to do
in life, he was included.

When the plane from San Francisco landed, she was first in
line at the gate. But no Sam! No Jeff! She almost fainted. It's just
like that bastard to fuck up. Then she started to worry. A car
crash? Accident? She heard herself paged. Jeff had missed the
plane, and Sam would be there in another hour.

So the home-coming was ruined. Susie paced around and
when she finally saw Sam she was in tears. "Mommy," he cried in
his gravelly, little old man's voice, and leaped in her arms.

"How's my baby, how's my boy?" She took him back to Grandma's where a pile of presents was waiting. The next day Jeff came by and he and Susie had a horrible scene. "Why do we assume he lives with you all the time? Why is all the burden of traveling on me?" Jeff shouted. Susie told him she had been flat on her back for six months and hadn't seen her son more than a day all that time. She had been living for this moment and how dare he try to take Sam away already.

Jeff stormed out. He called the next day to apologize. "You know, he never stopped talking about you. He never stopped asking when you would be well. I guess I'd always assumed that if he had his choice, he would want to live with me." Jeff's voice broke. "I'm sorry, it's just hard."

They agreed on a new plan: Susie would take him for the school year and Jeff would take him for the summer and they would switch off traveling. But Susie had other news to break. She had decided to go to Taos, to the Sangre de Cristo Mountains where the air was pure and she could rest and regain her strength. Through Russ, the farm man who had followed her to Los Angeles, she had met a woman named Gay who had a three-year-old son and a house in Taos which she wanted to share with another single mother.

Susie planned to stay in Taos three months, but by the end of the summer she was hooked. Gay's house was an old, pink adobe hacienda built in the square, squat style of the Southwest. Susie's room had a fireplace and a window looking out on a valley of silver-green sage. The ceiling was made of exposed pine beams and lattices of aspen. The floor was mud that had been soaked with ox blood to give it a hard red sheen. There were strings of bright red chilis hanging by the door and bowls of blue corn drying on the cupboards. Susie loved the kitchen because there seemed to be sealed in its mud walls the piquant smell of green chili and posole.

Every night Susie and Gay stopped whatever they were doing to climb on the roof and watch the sunset. Sam and Gay's son, Gilead, played tag while the women sat in silence, dangling their legs. Because the horizon was unbroken in all directions, there was an ocean of land and an ocean of sky. The sun turned fiery as it dropped below the mountains and sent up shoots of pink and red.

When the colors faded, the women went inside, lit oil lamps and cooked dinner on a wood-burning stove. Gay, a big-boned brunet who looked like she came from pioneer stock, taught Susie to cook things like popovers filled with cream cheese and green chili, zucchini from the garden and sopaipillas with fresh plum preserves. After dinner they built a cedarwood fire, put the boys to bed and brewed peyote tea.

Visitors were always dropping by, and Susie learned it was bad form to ask anyone what he did. Some were artisans or farmers but mostly they lived on welfare. Susie had been on welfare since Sam was born. People's energy went into hanging out, tripping and working on their relationships.

Whole days would be spent gossiping, or taking baths in the hot springs at Llano Quemada, or gathering piñon nuts or cleaning peyote buttons while listening to Indian chants. They endlessly analyzed people and love affairs. There was always a crisis —somebody running off with someone else's mate. Susie was the new girl in town, the ex old lady of a famous Berkeley radical and everyone was curious to meet her. The color had returned to her skin and she felt pretty again. Just breathing the air with its strong scent of sage and fresh wood made her high. But in the fall, as she sat in a meadow of aspens with leaves turning gold and scrub oaks turning scarlet, she felt uneasy. Why was she so lucky? Why was she sitting in these beautiful mountains when children were being burned alive in Vietnam? And why was she one of the only ones who cared about this stuff? No one else in Taos read the newspapers. You were supposed to be loose, smoke a joint, have a massage.

She knew she could lighten up a little, so she went gathering rose hips and wild mint and learned about composting and throwing the I Ching. Her style began to change. She wore overalls outside, and at home dressed herself in long skirts and antique shawls. She bought a mouton coat from the Salvation Army and filled her room with lace, funky lamp shades, quilts, old

Spanish and Indian fabrics and pottery. She made a list of what she wanted to accomplish in Taos:

> learn to play the drums
> drive a tractor
> sew a dress
> walk to town and back without having to rest
> tune up my car.

She gravitated to people who were most politically conscious and work-oriented. There was a doctor named Moe, a forty-eight-year-old refugee from New York who was starting a free clinic in town. Susie worked in the clinic three days a week and, by necessity, learned to diagnose hepatitis and VD and to prescribe remedies for flus. Moe was experimenting wth herbs and psychic healing. When a nineteen-year-old came in with a broken leg, Moe told him he could have a cast for eight weeks followed by physical rehabilitation, or he could wear an Ace bandage, keep the leg quiet and meditate on healing the break. The second way he wouldn't lose his muscle or skin tone. The boy chose the second, and Susie worked with him on sending mental energy to heal the leg.

One afternoon when she was admitting patients, she saw a young man who had bushy hair and wore a work shirt embroidered with a red fist. His name was George, and as he waited for the doctor he told Susie he had been an SDS organizer in New York, dropped out and come to Taos with his two sons. "What's bothering you?" she asked. He said he was tired all the time and it hurt to urinate. "You probably have hepatitis." She was right. Moe told George to stay in bed at least two weeks. Susie asked if he needed any help. He shook his head. "I'm covered. Catch ya later."

Susie found out where he lived and drove over to visit with a pot of stew. Moe told her she was crazy. If she got hepatitis on top of TB . . . She shrugged him off with a laugh. "Don't worry, I'll meditate on my liver."

George lived in a one-room adobe shack near the Rio Grande gorge. His kids slept in sleeping bags on the floor and George had built a sleeping loft for himself. He had enough energy to make love to Susie that night and twice the next morning. Her fantasies took wing. She and George were the same age. They had grown up in the Movement. Their kids would get along and they could fight the dragons of society together.

George rarely called her but she was liberated enough not to sit by the phone and wait. When she went to his place he was always glad to see her and eager to make love. Before long she was kind of half living there and Sam was sleeping on the floor with George's sons. But Susie began to feel anxious. Did he like her? Did he care? Did he want her there? George never said what he was feeling. They talked about the news and ecology rip-offs and listened to "Bitch" by the Rolling Stones.

"What do you think about me?" she asked him one night as he was reading *Revolution in the Revolution*.

"I can't say."

"Well, I mean, do you like me or what? I get the feeling that if I didn't come by, you'd never call me and I'd never see you."

"I told you, I don't want to be serious about anything. I don't want to be dependent on anyone and I don't want anyone to depend on me."

"But human beings *are* dependent, we're not islands."

He turned out the light and climbed in bed, leaving her sitting alone at the table.

From then on whenever they met on the street, Susie's heart would pound and she'd flirt and be bubbly and he would make an excuse to run off. What had happened? Am I so terrible nobody can love me? No, he was Jeff all over again. Those fuckers!

She wanted to slip George a note, telling him to meet her at the Gorge Bridge at 9 P.M. She would bash in his head, kick him in the balls. Then she found out he was sleeping with Gay.

"How could you," Susie screamed at Gay. "Men come and go, marriages come and go, women have to trust each other or we're doomed."

Gay said she couldn't help it, she had needs. "We still have to go to the bastards for sex."

"I wish I were homosexual," Susie said. "It would make things easier."

"No it wouldn't."

Susie said she wasn't going to compete with Gay. She would withdraw and Gay could have George to herself. Gay apologized and cried, and Susie forgave her and in the fragile closeness they felt afterward, they talked about their husbands. They drank enough peyote tea to get silly and on an impulse, tried on their wedding dresses. When Sam and Gilead came clomping home from play group, they found their mothers arm in arm in front of the mirror. Susie was wearing the simple white sheath from the House of Nine, and Gay was in a long white peau-de-soie gown with a train and an illusion veil. They were humming the wedding march, crying, or were they laughing or what?

George called one evening and told Susie he was moving to a bigger house. Would she help him? Sure, maybe afterward they could talk. She wanted to be friends.

On the way to the house they had to walk through an unlit barn. "Be careful," George said, "there are holes in the floor." Susie couldn't see and her arms were full of packages. "George, where am I walking?"

"Just keep going," he said. "We have to climb this ladder, cross a little ledge and then we're golden."

Keeee-wack! Susie fell off a beam, five feet down onto a pile of boards. George laughed as he pulled her up, but Susie couldn't walk. Her right leg was throbbing and the ankle began to swell. "I have to rest a minute," she said. She didn't want to be weak. George said, "This is a special night, you know. No one has been here with me yet. You're the first. I was hoping you could stay."

God, he was the lowest. He had set her up to fall, hurt herself and be helpless and she'd played right into it. She felt like a fool. And he was still fucking Gay. Gritting her teeth, she let him help her to the car and drive her to Moe's house. "Don't wait for me, I'll manage." She wouldn't give him the satisfaction.

She had a compound sprain, so she was back in bed again, analyzing and thinking about her life. She printed a sign and hung it on her wall: "No Expectations." She wrote in her journal, "I'm through with George. Goddammit, this sounds like a high school diary. I won't do it again—fall in love."

But she did. There was a one-eyed guitar player named Arizona and a wealthy turquoise trader who gave her jewelry and a twenty-year-old mountain climber and each time Susie had the future all planned. Then the fantasies collapsed and she was left hurt and clawing. She went back to using the vibrator but did it secretly and worried, "Can I only come with a machine?" Then the machine broke. Partly she was glad, because she was forced to learn to masturbate with her hand. Night after night she climbed in her double bed alone and hurried to sleep so she wouldn't feel the ache. It would be easy to fill the space in the bed but not the one inside.

That Christmas in Taos, 1971, was the first Christmas Susie had Sam with her. She and Gay made stockings, baked cookies and took the boys to the Jemez mountains to chop down a pine tree. One night they went caroling and another they blew eggs and hung them on the tree along with popcorn and piñon nuts and strings of gay red peppers. But Susie was depressed, pretending she wasn't. As she walked home Christmas Eve with Sam's special present, a two-wheeler bike she had been hiding in a friend's garage, she looked at all the lights in the adobe houses in Taos and envied the snug families inside. She knew that most of the people in the houses were miserable but she also knew she wanted a family, a home. A child is not a family, it's half a family.

On New Year's Eve, Gay and George asked her to go out with them but Susie stayed in with the boys. She threw the I Ching and came up with "The Wanderer." Sigh. She always ended up alone on New Year's Eve. Last year she had been in a hospital. And next year? Where will I be. Still alone?

VI. THE DAY THE MUSIC DIED

1971–1973

26. SARA

"Who wants a messy revolution where everyone ends up killing
everyone else? Sure I went to marches but it was for *them*. I was
afraid of being too straight."

I was in Berkeley, listening to a sixteen-year-old girl who had
organized a moratorium in her school when she was twelve, who
had taken acid at fourteen and slept with her boy friend when
she was fifteen and now, in the fall of 1971, she was telling me
that she was fed up. "I tried for two years to change things and
saw it was impossible. I have other things to worry about, like
getting into college."

What was I hearing? I had been sent to San Francisco by *Life*
magazine to bring back news from the next radical generation—
those in high school in 1971. For a decade, each succeeding class
had been more politically conscious and daring than the last.
Jokes were made that eventually there would be a revolution led
by infants, crying, don't trust anyone over ten.

When I talked with teen-agers in the Bay Area, though, I
found that what they wanted was not more change but security
and order. They were obsessed with getting into college and
making money. They were frightened of radicalism and worried
that there would not be enough wealth in the country for them

all. (We had laughed, I remembered, at job recruiters who came to the campus and talked about pensions. We had never feared poverty; we had feared conventionality.)

Bye Bye Miss American Pie. I drove from high school to high school, looking for teen-agers who had something on their minds other than money and security, but each interview verified the last. There came a moment, stopped at a signal on Telegraph, when I considered the awful possibility that we had been wrong. The New Age was not around the corner and I knew it a year before the proof came in: when half the voting population was under thirty and the majority, like their elders, voted for Richard Nixon over a peace candidate, George McGovern. On that day in Berkeley, I saw that I had assumed that the pace of change was going to accelerate unchecked for the rest of my lifetime, and I had been happy about this because I equated change with growth.

When I returned to New York with my report that kids were swinging back to caution and conservatism, Michael and his circle were jubilant. At a Christmas party, they grilled me for details. "Did you hear what Sara said? Isn't that a relief?" Michael stood up on a chair and declared, "Gentlemen! I knew if I sat in my green room long enough, drinking scotch whisky and watching the Phillies, that all this nonsense would pass."

"Hurray!" Everyone roared and raised his eggnog glass. Everyone but me.

There was a lull in the seas on Twenty-third Street as 1972 began. Michael sent me roses on my twenty-ninth birthday. In his dreams he saw us soaring in a helium balloon, laughing and waving at the cheering throngs below. We made love with more ease and spontaneity than we had in several years. We decided to stop using birth control. We decided to take a psychedelic—MDA—it would be the first trip for both of us. Michael's openness, the fact that he was willing to explore a new realm with me, made me hopeful for our future.

During our winter vacation in Palm Springs, we lapsed into easy ritual. In the morning, he would awaken first, drive to the Spa and on his return, come and sit on my bed, bringing me a glass of fresh-squeezed range juice and a plate of chocolate cake. We would play tennis, sun-bathe nude on the patio, then walk to the pool where he would gather me in his arms in the water and carry me around and around the shallow end.

"I'm dizzy," I laughed.

"No you're not, just relax." He put his face close to mine, then sang to me softly, "It was a very good year."

From the cold pool we went to the jacuzzi. "The pool is wonderful. Everything is perfect," Michael said. "Oh, Sara, this is what I want in life—to live in this beautiful desert."

By 11 P.M. he was in bed, holding his radio on his chest as the radio sputtered the news and the next day's weather. "Saaaa-ra," he would call. "Come in here." I would turn out the lights and slip into his arms.

We planned to take the MDA on our second-to-last day. We had been assured by a friend who had taken the drug many times that, unlike acid, "it never produces a bad trip." As the day approached, though, Michael grew jumpy. "I'll be thrown into an institution. I'll never be able to think straight again." Dr. Pearl, he said, had warned him the drug would trigger an irreversible psychotic breakdown.

"For God's sake, you weren't going to tell Dr. Pearl. You knew what he would say, he's hysterical on this subject."

Michael shrugged. "I told him."

So I took the drug, and Michael sat with me for a while but then he wanted to swim and lie in the sun and I told him to go ahead.

For the next six hours I lay on my back, stunned, amazed and euphoric. I could see my body from above and across the room. My mind spun and whirled, there was no holding on, the pictures and sounds flickered by as if someone were punching remote-control buttons. I heard singers and choruses in my head: James Taylor, "Love has brought me around," the Incredible String Band, "All will be one."

In the middle of the day Michael walked inside dripping with water in his black bathing suit. I saw him as a child, his limbs were transparent and his eyes incandescent with joy. He made love to me and although my nerves were disconnected, I felt us uniting at the roots. I stared at his face with complete accepting love. He had his own path to follow and that was perfect. All his tricks, his flamboyance, his playing and double dealing were his dance. It had begun long before I knew him and would continue regardless of what I thought or felt.

I saw, also, that I had never let myself blow up at him. So I whittled away, a little each day.

"Ho hum," I heard inside my head. It was a long buzzing sound, hooooo hummmmmm, like the signals that humpback whales send out when cruising the deep.

I laughed. Michael laughed back. He was the sun. I was the moon. My voyage was darker. Hooooo hum.

He was loving and playful as he passed in and out of the room. He said he wasn't frightened anymore and wanted to take a trip with me soon. But I learned, months later, that he had reported just the opposite to Dr. Pearl: the drug had made me crazed and, worse, I had wasted a spectacular day of sun.

When we returned to New York, a letter was waiting for me from Baba Ram Dass in India. I had written him, telling him about my interest in an article. His reply was that my letter "felt good," and when he was in New York we might "share a moment." In the meantime, I could keep in touch through Ronnie Richmond in Brooklyn. I called Ronnie Richmond, stammered about Ram Dass, he said something nonsensical and we started laughing. Ronnie told me he was thirty-four, a salesman of ladies' underwear, and had just been to India with his wife and two kids on his annual three-week vacation. He had been following Ram Dass since 1969, and was part of a meditation group led by Hilda Charlton, a grandmotherly woman who had been seeking God all her life.

The next Friday Ronnie came to my house. He played tapes of Ram Dass and talked about the process of "working on yourself," developing a witness in the mind that watches thoughts and feelings go by without judging. Ronnie reminded me of a toy lion. He had a mane of light brown hair, a floppy mustache, blue eyes and a pear-shaped body. His eyes dramatized whatever he was feeling—delight, shock. He spoke with a funky Brooklyn accent.

"The trip we're doing is bhakti yoga, and all it means is to see God in everyone and love everyone. That includes your husband." We laughed. I had told him about my problems with Michael, and Ronnie was having his own with his wife.

Although I was not sexually attracted to Ronnie, from our first phone call there was a chemistry between us. We drove around the city laughing and singing in his Volkswagen van with joss sticks burning and pictures of saints on the dashboard. We spoke on the phone almost every day and when we finished, I went zipping about the apartment, smiling to myself. It was insane. "What do you talk about?" Michael kept asking.

Ronnie took me to Hilda's meditation meeting in an apartment on Riverside Drive, where I found fifty people sitting in darkness, reciting affirmations: "I am God's perfect child, I am free." Hilda, a large, round-faced woman wearing a purple sari, sat beside the altar, on which there were pictures of Ram Dass, Christ, Satya Sai Baba, Maharaji, Pir Vilayat Khan and Hilda herself. My God, I thought, these people are serious.

They sang, played guitars and Indian instruments, Hilda led a meditation and when the lights came on, everyone was in each other's arms. I went to see Hilda to interview her, and meditated with her privately. "Close your eyes and imagine yourself rising in a balloon," she said. "If you have problems, think of them as sandbags. Write your problem on each sandbag, then cut it with a scissors and let it drop away."

I wrote on the sandbags:

> self loathing
> self pity
> fear of what people think of me
> fear that I'm unlovable
> just plain fear

I threw each sandbag overboard. "Feel yourself rising, rising to happiness, let go!" Hilda said. When I opened my eyes, I felt so lightheaded I could hardly walk. Ronnie shepherded me home in his van. "I hope you did that over the ocean," he said, "so nobody got hit by the sandbag full of your problems."

Before long I forgot that I had originally called Ronnie on business—to get to Ram Dass. I went to meditations every Friday night because it was more fun to sing and hug dental assistants than go to Sardi's and exchange gossip about deals. Michael thought my new friends were morons and I told him the people he spent time with were asleep.

"Ram Dass is a fag, I'd like to cut off his balls," Michael said one night.

"Don't you ever wonder," I asked, "why we go through all our dilemmas and challenges, just to die?" Michael turned on the TV set. "I want to watch the basketball game."

By some subtle process, we were reversing positions. In the early years, after our most volcanic arguments, Michael would snap back as if nothing had happened and I would be wracked with grief. These days, it was Michael who brooded.

"I feel like you're only happy when I'm completely beaten down. When I'm weak and emasculated, then you exult. You're an evil, destructive girl."

I sighed. "I think you feel weak because you can't level me anymore."

He narrowed his eyes. "Don't try me."

"Please, darling, let's not do this. Maybe you think I only need you when I'm miserable?"

"Possibly." He made a sour face. "I'm frightened of the direction you're moving in. Step by step you're marching away from me, my standards, my behavior. First it was communes, then drugs, now this." After a pause, "I've lost all sexual feeling again."

"What does Dr. Pearl say?" I asked.

"What does he know? What's he done for me?"

But Michael continued to see Dr. Pearl and I continued to go to meditations. A number of my friends, most of them writers, were taking the Arica training, a three-month program that cost $3,000 and promised to deliver aspirants into a state of permanent satori. Jacob Brackman, Ricky Johnston, Sally Kempton, Winnie Rosen, Rudy Wurlitzer, Artie Ross—all of them were taking it and giving me weekly reports. They were cracking their egos, they were cleaning their karma, they were getting Rolfed on acid, they were leaving for India and I was jealous.

I thought I was being left behind, and that compared to my friends, I was just flirting with mysticism. If I took Arica, I would have to quit analysis and give up Michael and I was not willing to do either.

The divergence between Michael and me was mirrored by the divergence between our analysts. They had been colleagues at Columbia and one had recommended the other, but in 1972, Dr. Pearl still believed that a person who turned to marijuana and mysticism was on the road to psychosis. My doctor, Dr. Collins, began to use words like "vibes" and "freak out," and found psychological equivalents for the spiritual techniques I was trying. He said the idea of a "witness" was like Freud's notion of the observing ego. He approved of looking at the self without judging.

When I spent time with my Arica friends or Ronnie, I felt nonjudgmental and loving, but with Michael, I swung between seeing him as God and wanting to knife him in the back. He was finishing a fourth rewrite of his play, and a new deal had been solidified. The day he finished, I bought steaks and ice cream for a celebratory dinner. I cooked his steak blood rare, fixed a salad with avocados and was dishing out the ice cream when he asked what had happened at the last meditation. I started to answer.

"Sara," he interrupted, "I married a fascinating cynical journalist and now I'm stuck with a religious fool. It's crazed!"

"If you want to carry on like that, it's okay, but I don't have to listen." I went in my room and opened a book. Michael walked to the doorway and said, "The next time I finish a major piece of work, maybe you'll find a way to show some enthusiasm."

"Poor thing," I said.

He slammed the door and left the house.

We started to look for a therapist who worked with couples.

I started to think I was pregnant. I was two weeks late and my breasts were so large that I could not lie comfortably on my stomach. Michael refused to believe it. "I'm sterile, you're barren."

Every time Michael spoke to me now, it was an attack and they grew fiercer until I broke. "You're on a campaign to upset me," I screamed. "A fetus won't survive all this crying and turmoil. I know what's happened. You've changed your mind about having a baby, just like you changed your mind about getting married. Well you should have worked it through before you impregnated me."

Dr. Collins called up Dr. Pearl to discuss the crisis, and when I next saw Dr. Collins he was distraught.

"Dr. Pearl has a *very* inaccurate picture of you," he said.

"What do you mean?"

"He's heard that you're having crowds of people to the house for séances and LSD orgies. He sees you as an unloving, ungiving person, and thinks you're afraid of having a child because it would interrupt your career."

"*I'm* afraid." I went home in a white-hot fury. Michael denied telling Dr. Pearl what Dr. Collins reported. Then the shrinks fought about who said what and who was schizophrenic, Michael or me. Michael disappeared for a night and called me to read a written statement:

"I admit that I've been obstinate and selfish. You're right about one thing—the possibility of pregnancy did make me agitated, because it solidifies a relationship that has contained unhappiness for me. Here are my complaints:

"—You constantly ridicule my interests and habits.

"—You're aloof and condescending to some of my friends.

"—You overpower me with words. I have to fight upstream, so I end up acting foolishly and then I'm forced to apologize.

"Sara, we're stuck in a mess."

In the middle of this I ran into Tasha Taylor in an elevator on the way to a meditation seminar. It seemed an omen that I was on the right track. On Sunday I scanned the newspaper ads for a one-bedroom apartment where I could live by myself. Then I turned to the ads for six-room apartments where Michael and I could live with the baby. I started talking openly about leaving Michael, and at the same time, I bought sheets and wineglasses from Bloomingdale's to replenish our stock. Was I mad?

"You're definitely pregnant," the gynecologist said. I took a cab home and collapsed in tears. I was frightened of having an abortion and frightened of bringing a baby into such chaos. Michael, unexpectedly, turned romantic. He sat all day gazing out the window, listening to Frank Sinatra sing the "Soliloquy" from *Carousel*.

"I desperately want this baby," Michael said. "I promise you I'll make things as peaceful as can be. I see you as my big chance in life, for change."

"It will have to be drastic. I want total commitment of all your resources, all our resources, to openness and change."

"You have it," he said. "I'll try anything. I'm even willing to consider moving from this apartment. Do you believe me?"

In May, *Esquire* magazine, which had commissioned me to write the article on Ram Dass, called and said they were anxious to have the piece and would send me to India. I cursed my luck. Reports filtering back were that Ram Dass had just left India headed for London, Scotland and eventually the States. His head was changing. He might not speak or give interviews. I tried to trace him, but it was like that infernal children's game where every clue to the treasure leads only to another clue. After three days of futile transatlantic calls, I gave up. I was not sure anymore why I was so compelled to reach this man.

On Friday, when Ronnie came to pick me up for meditation, I said, casually, "I bet he's in Boston right now." Ronnie went to the phone, dialed a number and handed me the receiver. Ram Dass answered the phone.

"Hi," he said, in that buoyant voice I recognized from the tapes. "Did you finish your article?"

"No, I haven't started it. I'd really like to see you."

"Well," he said, "I'm not living in time."

"I could get in my car right now and drive to Boston."

"You could, but you might get here and not find me."

I said that wouldn't bother me, but I had heard he wanted privacy and I didn't want to intrude.

There was a long silence, and Ram Dass said, "If you can find me, you can have me."

I was on the first shuttle flight the next morning. I had spent a sleepless night, deciding at 5 A.M. I could not go through with it and resolving at 6 A.M. that I would. At the airport I heard myself paged. Fuck! Something was wrong. But it was Michael, saying, "I just wanted to tell you I love you. I wanted to wish you well."

It was raining when the taxi dropped me at the townhouse in Boston where Ram Dass was staying with his father. I shouted through the intercom, "Is Ram Dass there?" I heard groans, shuffles. It was 9 A.M., a Saturday morning, and I had woken everyone up. Ram Dass opened the door wearing a white gauze shirt and pants and a jaunty plaid cap. He was taller than I had envisioned—6′2″. His face gave off a pink glow and his blue eyes were open so wide they seemed more vertical than horizontal.

"I took you at your word," I said.

He nodded, and led me to the study. "This is where I hang out." The room was filled with dark bookcases and a velvet convertible sofa on which the bedclothes were left as Ram Dass had just climbed out of them. I told him I had been asking myself why I had pursued him so single-pointedly and it became clear that I was to try to write something. He smiled. It was all so easy. "You have me. Go ahead."

I interviewed him for four hours, during which he talked about his experiences in India and his new understandings of the spiritual path. His guru had told him not to have ashrams or students, "but I find it useful for my own consciousness to work with individuals." I asked if he would do some work with me. "Not for *Esquire,* for me personally." He agreed, and we made an appointment for the following morning. As I left, I turned impulsively to hug him. He laughed with great sweetness, hugged me and patted my hair. Then he said abruptly, "My guru told me not to touch people."

SUNDAY, 10 A.M. Ram Dass was sitting in front of a brilliant bay window and stared in my eyes. Finally he spoke. "When I met my guru, it became apparent to me that he knew everything in my head. There is a Sikh saying that once you know God knows everything, you're free. Each of us has rooms in our head that we keep closed and guarded, as part of our social posture. That guarding is energy and it makes the things real. Freedom lies in knowing that everything you were protecting isn't who you really are."

He said he would look in my eyes as if they were a candle flame and say mantra to himself. "And that's our base camp, from which we work. There's nothing you can say to me that makes any difference. So I'll ask a simple question over and over: is there anything you can bring to mind that would be difficult, painful or embarrassing to share? Say whatever comes, don't judge it."

I said, "I feel so many emotions. Some things you say I believe, but others I don't, and I can't pretend . . ."

"You shouldn't."

"I hate you. There's another part of me that worships you in an infantile way. I'd like to hurt you, most of all I'd like to get you."

"Get to me?"

"Yeah, get you to break one of your vows. Like take off my clothes and take off yours and say, 'Let's see how holy you are.'"

Ram Dass: "Can you hear yourself saying all that? Okay, long as you stay here." He paused and asked the question again. "It isn't easy."

I said I was disgusted with myself.

Ram Dass: "That's judging, it's attachment to good and evil. You constantly judge yourself, are you good or bad, making it or failing. You identify with the judge, you think you *are* the judge, but the judge is just more stuff. Behind the judge, behind all that, we are neither good nor evil. We just are."

I was beginning to feel dizzy. I told Ram Dass I had spent most of my life convinced I was evil. "I never considered that I might be neither good nor evil, or some unstable combination of the two."

He laughed. "You're beautiful to work with. I'm beginning to feel a being in there." He asked again, "If there's anything you can bring to mind about you, me, any feeling, desire . . ."

I talked about my pregnancy and my battles with Michael. I started to cry. "At first I blamed Michael because I thought he was acting out . . ."

Ram Dass: "We can never blame another human being. The

more difficult your husband acts, the more he's helping you work on yourself."

"That's all very pretty, but the reality is I'm trapped."

Ram Dass: "The existential situation is this: there's you and there's your husband, and there's the entity growing in you, and there are your feelings, and there's the judge, and here we are. When you truly understand, you'll understand what I'm going to say, though you can't understand it now: it doesn't matter."

"Nothing matters?" I said sarcastically.

Ram Dass: "Watch that statement. It doesn't matter because either way you'll have work to do on yourself."

"But there are incredible . . ."

"Incredible's a judgmental word."

I stopped. "There's nothing I can say. You've stripped me."

"Oh, don't be silly. We haven't even begun yet."

"But if I'm not to judge, I don't know how to operate. You've taken away everything I use."

"You're still using things you can't even see yet."

I said I felt very uncomfortable.

"That's just another feeling, and they go by so fast. I'm uncomfortable, that's who I am. But you know that one thought away is total comfort, too. So how real could the uncomfort be?"

He was right. I suddenly felt at ease. When we finished an hour later, I told him I did not feel up or down so much as grounded, and strong. "You'll lose that," he said. "Cheap highs go fast."

I wandered around Boston for the rest of the day in a very unfamiliar frame of mind. Ordinarily, everything I saw or heard came into my awareness with a judgmental tag: that face is ugly; that color is nice; that man looks interesting; that scene is scary. But this afternoon everything was coming in directly, without the tags. The people on the street, the orange sunset over the harbor, the piped Muzak in the elevator, the smell of pancakes cooking—everything simply was what it was, and the play of patterns, rather than any single image, was breath-taking.

I flew home with thirteen hours of taped interviews, and my friend Ricky, who was breaking up with her boy friend, moved into our apartment and helped me transcribe. Ram Dass's voice echoed through the halls at all hours and Michael spent more and more time in his office. One evening I played him a segment where Ram Dass talks about anger being a mind moment and not real.

"Horse shit," Michael said. "My anger is totally real."

"You know," I said, "if I keep exploring these concepts and you insist it's horse shit, things might become very unrewarding."

Michael said, "I don't want to be locked in a wrestling match of change. I want to move at my own pace, not at your rocketlike speed."

"To me the pace seems agonizingly slow."

"Then there's no hope."

The next week I had an abortion. Michael moved into his office and told his friends he had been flooded out of his house by Ram Dass and Arica and Ricky. "I have to get my strength back," he said. "Sara and I are going to live separately for a while." I took off my wedding ring, to see how it felt. I worked on the article fourteen hours a day. The words poured out, sixty pages in two weeks, and I believed that everything I had written before was in preparation for this opus. I turned down an assignment from *The New York Times Magazine* to go to Cuba to interview Castro on his forty-fifth birthday. Michael said I was losing a major opportunity, but I knew what was most important to me.

When I finished the article, I dropped it at *Esquire,* went to Woodstock with Ronnie and spent three days feeling ecstatically relieved. Back in New York, though, I became edgy. After a week, *Esquire* called and asked me to come in. There were "problems." I wore a long lavender dress and a pink owl, Minerva, on a chain around my neck. "You look beautiful," the editor said, and I knew it was over. He fidgeted. "We can't publish the piece. Ram Dass comes off as silly and simplistic, and your willingness to embrace his ideas is incomprehensible." I said I had told him in advance that this would not be a hatchet job. He shook his head. "You'll thank us later for not printing it. It would destroy your credibility as a journalist."

I made my way across town to Michael's office and collapsed.

He took a week's vacation and we flew to Provincetown. I fetched him drinks, magazines, whatever he wanted. I was completely submissive. I lay in a lump by the ocean with my eyes open and did not see it. Michael had a wonderful time. When we returned to New York, I summoned the courage to read the Ram Dass piece again. I decided the editors of *Esquire* were wrong.

I asked my agent to send the article to other magazines, but the responses were similar: "Annoying." "Foolish." "We like Sara Davidson the journalist but we do not like Sara Davidson the convert." I thought my career might be finished.

From my new perspective, I saw that most pieces of journalism, certainly my most successful pieces, were based on an attitude of superiority and ridicule. If I wanted to honor the divinity in people, I could no longer treat them this way—coaxing them into spilling information I could use against them to make a good story.

I began to be discreet in talking about Ram Dass, for I noticed that at the mention of God, people would eye me as if I were losing my faculties. To reassure myself, I went through my books and made lists of artists and intellectuals who had experienced spiritual awakenings: Yeats, Eliot, Pascal, Whitman, Thoreau, Michelangelo, Einstein, Salinger. I realized there had been a gap in my education and resolved, for the moment, to read nothing but spiritual literature.

In July I wrote to a friend in London:

> I don't know what's going to happen now. I'm leaving to spend August traveling around the Southwest with my sister. In the fall, I may try to publish the Ram Dass material as a book. I may go to India. I may go to London. I may write a book about girls I knew in Berkeley.
>
> The crazy thing is that although mysticism has fucked up my whole life, I've never felt better.
>
> Lots of love and Om Shanti to ya,
> Sara

The summer proved to be one of the happiest of my life. I met Terry in Los Angeles, where she had returned after spending a year on Nuku Hiva in the Marquesas Islands. She had been the only white woman there, had lived in a grass hut, painted water colors and learned to dive for lobster and conch. She knew how to survive in the wilderness and could teach me. But where? I told her, "What I'd really like to do is spend the next month not making a single decision."

So Terry decided. We set out across the Mojave Desert, camped for two days, then checked into a motel so I could shower and sleep in a real bed. Before long we were sleeping out every night. We traveled from water hole to water hole: hot springs, rivers, lakes. Everywhere we met people who were meditating and doing yoga and reading dog-eared copies of *Be Here Now*. They sensed immediately that Terry and I were sisters. Nobody asked what we did or where we came from; everybody was in transit.

In Taos, where, although I did not know it, Susie had been lying in bed with a sprained leg, thinking about her life, I stopped in a pay phone and called Michael. He shouted over the beeper phone from the station in New York:

"You say I'm not a seeker, but I am in my own way."

"I know that," I said. "I accept your path, whatever you have to do." Through the glass I watched the sun setting over the prairie, black-gold.

"But how can we have a relationship when you think I'm blind and retarded?"

"I don't. I love you."

"You keep saying . . ."

"I don't say that anymore."

He shouted while the Rolling Stones played in the background and a beep sounded every sixty seconds. I hung up in tears.

"What is it?" Terry asked but before I could answer she was crying in sympathy.

We headed North past Taos, and a hitchhiker led us to a little-known stretch of the Rio Grande, where the river cuts through a gorge so the banks are protected by walls of rock. Hidden in nooks were orange tents and campsites. The hitchhiker, a former newscaster named Grady, showed us the trail to a hot springs, where three people were sitting nude in a pool formed by rocks.

We took off our clothes, soaked in the hot springs, then dove in the icy river and swam to the other bank. We walked in the sun down grassy trails, where there were golden tiger butterflies, wild mint and sunflowers. There was no need to ever wear clothes, Grady said, because few tourists found the place. We set up our tent by a fresh-water spring at a bend in the river and stayed for three weeks.

I let my hair go natural, which was an enormous step. For almost ten years, I had thought my long straight hair was my best feature. I would decline invitations to go out if my hair was not clean and I did not have three hours to wash and straighten it. When I let it go curly and wild, to my surprise, no one in the canyon seemed to notice except Terry, who teased me that I looked like Tiny Tim.

Before long, I had hooked up with a twenty-two-year-old named Clark, who had grown up in the mountains, had studied yoga since he was twelve and was voracious for sex. He made me promise I would not eat meat. He chided me if I drank Coca-Cola or ate a Hershey bar, and when I was shaving my legs in the stream, he said, "Doesn't that seem unnecessary?"

Shit. I had started shaving my legs in the first place because of pressure from boys in junior high. I was not going to stop now because of Clark.

Terry and I became regulars in the river community, which included T.J., who had been an aerospace engineer and played the flute all day; William, a statuesque, lethargic scion of an old Virginia family and his girl friend Apple, who had the most luscious body I had seen; Grady, who once wanted to be Walter Cronkite and now wanted to be an enlightened being; and Joe, a forty-year-old therapist from New York.

At night we sat in the hot springs together and chanted peyote songs, "Hee-yah, hee-yah." We massaged each other and picked wild berries. We drove in a caravan to the open prairie and lay on the ground watching shooting stars.

For several days, Terry and I observed silence. I found that most of the words I had the impulse to say were unnecessary and some were not even true. In the absence of speaking, the mind races noisily and throws up pieces of garbage from the deep: memories, old dreams, fragments of song. It was like having the head cleaned out.

One morning, William and Apple stopped by our tent. "You all got your program set for the day?" William asked. We laughed. Clark said, "We could climb into the Indian cave dwellings at Puye." William unzipped a leather pouch. "We could smoke this Jamaican grass." We smoked the grass and did not leave the river. In the afternoon we flopped naked onto rubber rafts and rode them through gentle rapids until we reached the ruins of a stagecoach crossing, the old Santa Fe Trail.

Michael and New York were as far away as the moon. "Why am I going back," I said aloud. "Back to a stuffy apartment in a slum to hassle with cab drivers and fight with my husband?" Clark was massaging the vertebrae in my back.

"When you're ready to leave it you'll leave," he said.

On Sunday we went to open house at Lama, a spiritual commune which had published *Be Here Now*. Hundreds of people arrived in pickups and vans from all over the West. During the meditation, I kept my eyes open awhile to check out the men. Was this how it would be if I were single again? Constantly aware of how people were linked, sexually oriented?

The next day I came back from a walk and found Clark and Terry making out in the tent. Clark asked, later, if I was angry "because I tried to seduce your sister," and Terry said it was natural that both of us would be attracted to the same men. I wanted Clark to choose, but he wanted to go back and forth and Terry decided to try celibacy.

I called Michael from a gas station at Arroyo Hondo. He related news about books and shows. "When people ask about us, I'm saying this is a nonchaotic separation."

I laughed.

"When are you coming back?" he asked.

"I'm not sure."

"I want to meet you at the airport."

"I bought you a turquoise ring."

"What day, Sara?"

"Please don't pressure me."

"I want to plan . . ."

"Soon."

The first week in September, rain sprinkled the river. William and Apple departed for Virginia, and Terry caught a bus for Los Angeles. I slept on the grass and when rain fell, pulled a tarp over me. Suddenly Clark roused me. "I want you to see the night." I fell back asleep and when I opened my eyes, an arc of sun was glistening at the rim of the gorge. A decision came to me. I smiled. It was not a decision I had been looking for but it was, definitely, a decision. I was not going to see Dr. Collins anymore.

27. SUSIE

Somewhere there were answers. Connectedness. Home. Her people. A place she belonged.

Susie had been in Taos a year and had not found it there, so when the one-eyed guitar player named Arizona came around selling hot airline tickets, she scraped together a hundred dollars and bought one. She wasn't tied anywhere because of a man or a job. She had always had a dream of traveling around the world, checking out all the countries, and if she could do it by herself for almost no money, shit, wouldn't that be something?

Arizona showed her how to write the ticket: San Francisco–Paris–Saigon–San Francisco. After each flight, he told her, she should take her ticket to an airline company and have it re-written. Paris–Saigon could be changed to Paris–New Delhi–Saigon. If anything went wrong, by the time the mistake was caught she would be in another country with a different ticket.

In the spring of '72, she drove Sam to San Francisco where he was to stay with Jeff. Then she outfitted herself. She bought a conservative blue dress and a proper suitcase so as not to attract attention at airports. Inside the suitcase she packed jeans, T-shirts and a sleeping bag she had liberated from the Alpine Hut. She told her mother she was going around the world with a friend who had inherited a whole bunch of money. "There's a part of my mother that can't deal with my life. She knew the story was fishy but she couldn't begin to fathom this."

On the day of the flight she was so nervous she couldn't stop talking. Roxanne drove her to the airport and they smoked a joint in the ladies' room until ten minutes before the plane was to leave. Susie hurried to the counter with her Samsonite bag. The agent stamped her ticket and waved her through. Fifteen minutes later she was in the air. Far fuckin' out! It worked. She flew over the pole to Paris where she stayed with friends of friends—radicals who had fought on the barricades in '68 with Danny the Red.

From Paris she flew to Geneva, Rome, Jerusalem, Ankara, Kabul and New Delhi. "It was blowing my mind that I was pulling it off." She no longer trembled at the airline ticket counter. She flew by whim, tacking and zigzagging, but always in her mind, her objective was Vietnam.

So she came, in the rainy month of June, to be standing in Cholon, the Chinese quarter, staring at a tear-stained map. She had been on the edge of tears since arriving in Saigon. She had cried on the plane when she had looked down and seen the lush fields, the slow-moving water buffalo, the bright flowering trees. How could anyone drop napalm on such extraordinary beauty?

(*Ho ho, Ho Chi Minh, the NLF is going to win.*)

She had cried at the wide white avenues of Saigon, the bicycles, the women in ao dais, the peasants in coolie hats, the tea shops, the orphans (*Hey hey, LBJ*) and the scarred flesh and missing limbs (*How many kids did you kill today?*) and the soldiers. Everywhere there were soldiers and photographers who dressed like soldiers and had to have a goddamned war going on as an excuse to be loving, to be comrades.

She was enraged. (*Right on, take Saigon!*) She put on a bright red T-shirt that said "Grateful Dead" just to show the motherfuckers and she walked across the river to Cholon.

"Well if it ain't Jane Fonda come to entertain the troops."

Susie didn't turn her head.

"Fuckin' A. Look at that ass, like to entertain myself good with that."

Susie stopped, deliberately, and unfolded her map. The soldiers overtook her. One grazed her arm. "Y'all lost? Like some help?"

"No. Fuck you." But when she looked up, she started. He was a child. No older than seventeen. Her anger dissolved and she felt the tears forming. These ignorant, unconscious children were going to die and she saw it in their jumpy eyes—they had no notion why.

Susie could not have stayed in Vietnam but for meeting Nguyen. They had seen one another at a tea shop near the university. Nguyen and his friends had been amused. They had never seen a girl who wore a T-shirt so bright it hurt the eyes and who talked so fast. "There are people in America and I'm one of them who are *tremendously* upset about this war and we're working in our country to try and stop it."

"Do all American women talk as much as you?" they had asked. She was pretty, with her almost Asian eyes and sparrowlike limbs. She did not look twenty-nine, as she said, she looked sixteen, like Nguyen's youngest sister.

But why was she alone? She had a son in America. She had divorced a husband, why?

Susie said, "Women have a lot to offer the world besides raising children, I believe in that strongly."

Nguyen drove Susie home on his motor bike and for the next week, he came for her every morning. At first she had dismissed him as a bourgeois colonial puppet because anyone with guts would be with the NLF, but there was a reserve in him, a quiet goodness that made her look more closely. He was studying international law. He spoke half in English, half in French, and he listened carefully, he did not discount her opinions. At the end of the day he would leave her at her door, and it was Susie, finally, who suggested that he stay.

He made love the way she had dreamed a woman would. Gentle and unhurried, he kissed her eyes, her shoulders, her fingertips. He did not seem concerned with getting to "the act." She felt herself easing into his slow, steady rhythm and when he went down on her, she came. Was it a fluke? She had never come, never, making love with a man, and it frightened her.

She stayed in Vietnam far longer than she had planned. Nguyen talked about marrying but he was torn, because taking an American wife would mean rejecting his culture. Susie thought, if I stay, the relationship would be my life. I'd have to learn Vietnamese and we would always have to struggle with racism and intolerance. A child of ours would belong nowhere. Yet Nguyen was a man with whom she felt equal, a man who was in love not with ideas but with her.

When she left Saigon, she had a month left in which to cover as much ground as possible. She took a bus to northern Thailand where in a tea shop she met a group of old men who said they had fought with Ho Chi Minh. Susie stood up and shook their hands. In Hong Kong she rode as close as she could to the border of China and bought twenty buttons of Chairman Mao. In Tokyo she had acupuncture treatments. Her lungs were bothering her and she was still limping from the accident in Taos. The treatments were so powerful that she would limp in and walk out. Maybe, she thought, I should move to Japan, enroll Sam at the International School and study acupuncture.

She hitchhiked alone through Indonesia and Malaysia, her heart pounding every time a car stopped for her. When she reached Penang, she checked into the YWCA. She was exhausted. She couldn't bear meeting more strangers, explaining where she came from and what she felt about the war. She stayed in bed for two days, reading Simone de Beauvoir. She bought a bottle of nail polish and sat on her spring cot painting her fingernails pink. She had to laugh. She hadn't done this since high school and here she was, on an island off the coast of Malaysia where she didn't know a soul, painting her nails.

But it was something familiar. It reminded her of her culture: of Big Macs and Fritos and Bobby Dylan and the Co-op and the Med and People's Park and Sam, oh God she missed Sam so desperately she swore she would never go so far from him again. What was she doing, running around the world? If Sam had needed her it would have taken days for her to reach him. As she sat under the mosquito netting in the Penang Y, she wrote to Nguyen:

> When I think of a life with you, I picture myself always being an outsider. America, as fucked as it is, is where I belong. It's who I am. There are people there who feel the way I do and I can work with them.

It was time to stop tripping, scattering herself. It was time to acquire skills—specifically a knowledge of medicine—so she would have something to offer people instead of merely talking.

"I really respect you for pulling off this trip. It took guts," Jeff said when he saw Susie in Berkeley. Jeff had never said he respected her for anything. He told her he was happy she was settling in Berkeley, they could be more relaxed about sharing Sam.

Home. Answers. Connectedness. Her people. When she walked in the Med she saw a flood of familiar faces. Her hands flew up to her chest. She felt so warm.

It was the fall of '72 and dozens of her friends were coming back to Berkeley. Berkeley was the old country, where everyone has a garden, everyone's into the revolution, everyone knows everyone else and they're connected. "Is that your old lady? Far out. She used to be my buddy's old lady."

There had been a time when they had thought Berkeley wasn't the real world. Many, like Susie, who had left to find the real world when the Movement and their marriages fell apart were returning. They had discovered that Berkeley was as real as anyplace else. They had kids who went to real schools and ate real food. They had roots in Berkeley—a shared history and a culture they had built themselves.

Sam was starting kindergarten and his school celebrated the birthdays of Martin Luther King, Malcolm X and Susan B. Anthony. His classmates had names like Fidel, Circle, Lorca, Ponderosa Pine and Butterfly. The boys learned cooking and the girls took shop.

The first day Susie got up at 6 A.M. to fix Sam's breakfast and watch him clamber up the steps of the yellow school bus, she had to turn aside and cry. My baby's growing up. But mostly she wanted him to be happy. And he was. He came home singing at the top of his lungs, "I Love Trash" from "Sesame Street."

They were living on Channing Way in a four-room cottage scaled like a doll's house and covered with vines. Susie's front window looked out on a ten-foot-high red fist that had once sat in People's Park. Most of her neighbors were women living alone with their kids. They traded baby-sitting and kept a "free box" on the sidewalk for hand-me-downs.

The culture they had built was, it turned out, a matriarchy. Where were all the men? Many of them had not been able to cut themselves loose from ideology and had gone down with the ideas. A few were in mental hospitals. Rennie Davis was following the Guru Maharaj Ji. Jerry Rubin was starting his life over with yoga. Jeff had joined the Communist Party. Marvin Garson had transported himself barefoot and penniless to Israel as an immigrant to be cared for by the state.

The women were doing what they had always done. The very chores they had so rebelled against—cooking and raising kids— had kept them grounded and they had endured.

One day after school Sam opened the front door and bellowed his customary greeting, "Mom? Home!"

"Where's Circle?" she asked. "I thought he was coming with you."

"He had to go to his father's. Mom?"

"Mmmm." She was fixing celery sticks with peanut butter.

"How come all the kids in Berkeley live with their moms?"

"I don't know about the others, but when your Dad and I decided not to live together, I said I really wanted you to live with me and he said okay."

Sam sucked on his thumb. As if working through an arithmetic problem, he said, "That's how you two arranged it, but if it was up to me I would live one year with my father and one year with you and one with my father."

Susie was taken by surprise. Maybe he needed to be with his father. "If that's what you want, talk to your Dad and maybe we can work it out," she said. Sam didn't bring it up the rest of the year but Susie knew he would in time. "I respect him for it, he's taking control of his life."

She changed the sign above her desk from "No Expectations" to "Focus and Follow Through." She went to see the dean of several medical schools, who were polite but warned her she would have difficulty being admitted because of her age. She refused to be discouraged. She enrolled in chemistry and anatomy classes. She joined the Berkeley Women's Health Collective, which was running a self-help clinic.

The clinic was a far-out place, filled with posters of amazons and Wonder Woman brandishing a speculum. There was a phone line manned twenty-four hours a day, and a slide show of clitorises and breasts of all varieties and women curled like pretzels examining themselves.

When it was Susie's turn to climb on the table and examine her cervix, she was astounded. "So that's what it looks like." She wanted to examine everyone—her friends, her mother. And she knew this was how she wanted to practice medicine: in a collective, rather than a classy private office. Every visit to the collective would be a learning experience. The patient would participate in making the diagnosis and choosing treatment, and "the Doctor" would be demystified.

Susie knew, though, that she couldn't disclose her ideas in applications to medical schools. "I have to play by their rules so I can get my license. Then I can do what I want." She sighed. "It's a compromise. I'm mature enough so I can do it, but it kills me."

She and three other women wrote a proposal to the dean of U. C. Medical School, urging him to take affirmative action. The proposal said, "There should be a special program for women who've earned advanced degrees in the liberal arts because they were discouraged by pervasive social pressure from pursuing a deep interest in medicine." They argued that age should not be held against them. They were stable, they had proved themselves excellent scholars, they had already had their children and could fill the need for women doctors.

Susie's life, between school, part-time work, the health collective and Sam, was as hurried as it had ever been, but there was an inner calm about her. She didn't have to make every meeting and party. She stopped hanging out at the Med because what was it accomplishing? She cut her hair to shoulder length. "I wanted to look my age."

She was sitting one evening in January of '73, reading Sam *The Jewish Child's Bible Stories*, editing as she read, changing "God" to "the earth" and having both Adam and Eve bite the apple in the Garden of Eden, when the phone rang. She answered it without moving Sam from her lap.

"Sue Berman?"

"Yeah."

"This is a voice from your past, Sara Davidson."

"Farrrr out!" Susie said.

It had not been easy for me to place the call to Susie, asking if I could interview her. We had not seen each other since 1967, when I was in Berkeley after the firing of Clark Kerr and Susie had accused me of working for a "shitty newspaper." I remembered the switch in her eyes that had flicked off.

Susie, after my call, started to worry that I was coming to judge her. I was a sophisticated New Yorker. I would be hyped-up, fast-talking, name-dropping, chain-smoking. "I thought you'd have a cigarette holder or something."

I arrived in San Francisco in a downpour, rented a car, stopped at Cost Plus Imports to buy an umbrella and a rain hat and headed across the Bay Bridge to Channing Way. Susie was watching from her door. Before I could park, she ran out of the house, stuck her head in the window and kissed me. My rain hat fell off. The car stalled. It was all so confusing. She spotted the Cost Plus bags. "You still buy that shit? Oh Sara. You look exactly the same."

We sat in her kitchen drinking tea. "I expected something really different," she said with a laugh. "I thought you'd show up in some fancy hip outfit—suede pants and turquoise rings." I was wearing wet jeans, moccasins and a purple leotard.

"You know I'll be thirty in a few weeks?" Susie said. "The last ten years I did everything wrong. This time I'm gonna do it right."

When I told her about the book I wanted to write, she was intrigued. "I'd like to be able to pull out the truth and break through the images I was living for so long." I told her the interviews would raise disturbing memories. "It'll be heavy."

She nodded. "The heavier the better."

The screen door banged and in walked Sam, a wiry five-year-old who had a sober gaze that suddenly broke into giggles. Susie fixed him a sandwich and asked about school, not using any different voice than she did with me.

"Hey, I have an idea." Susie went to the closet and pulled out a plastic bag decorated with peace symbols. She turned the bag upside down. Out tumbled photographs, news clippings and marijuana seeds. "Remember this?" She held up a picture that had been taken in the A. E. Phi house the day we moved in. Susie was wearing a Cal sweat shirt and loafers, unpacking her giant wardrobe trunk.

Then there was a picture of Jeff with short hair, speaking to a crowd by Sproul Hall. Sam slithered onto her lap. "What are all those people doing there?" he asked.

"Listening to your daddy make a speech."

"What was he saying?"

"He was very angry because the United States was doing something bad."

"What?"

Susie wrinkled her forehead. "I don't remember."

The next photograph was taken six months after Sam was born. "That's me," he yelped. "Right." She and Jeff were lying in bed nude and Sam was crawling between his mother's legs, reaching for her pubic hair. "Aren't we free?" Susie said sarcastically.

The next picture was a famous one. It was the picture I'd seen in a bookstore in New York that had made me wish I'd stayed in Berkeley. Susie was sitting in the rubble of People's Park. Her hair billowed around her. She had Sam in her lap and her arm was raised, finger pointed at the camera. On her sweater was a button, "In revolution one wins or dies."

"I can't even deal with that picture," Susie said. "People love it, they think it's an image of courage. But pictures lie. I was miserable that day. Jeff was at the park with Leslie and I didn't know where to look or what the fuck to do. I was yelling at the photographer, 'No.'"

We talked until three that morning and slept curled together in her double bed. Susie dreamed she was dancing in an all-girl revue. "It was a corny Hollywood musical," she said sleepily in the morning, "but the chorus was made up of women from all nations. We danced in sparkly costumes and everyone loved us."

Sam interrupted her, "Mom, you know what?" He carefully pronounced each syllable. "I like to hear about dreams but I don't like to have them."

"Why?"

"Because they scare me. Even the good dreams scare me."

"You know how to make them not so scary?" Susie said. "Wake me up. Share your dreams with me."

Sam went off to school singing "I Love Trash," and Susie and I started talking about sex. She clapped her hands. "Okay, kid, get out your notebook. I'm gonna tell you about my first orgasm."

As I listened to her talk about the years with Jeff—how she had felt dead and dry and had never come, and how the vibrator had "changed my life"—I was so shocked I had to pace about the room. My image had been the reverse—that she was lusty, recklessly flirtatious and knowing. During the year she had lived surreptitiously with Jeff, she used to shuffle into the Co-op on Saturday morning and make a show of yawning. Candy and I would whisper, with envy, "We know what *she's* been up to."

Ten years later in her house on Channing Way, Susie said, "I'm still fucked up about orgasms. And I'm feeling defensive with you, like I'm wondering if you talk about sex with these sophisticated New York ladies."

In the week I stayed with her, Susie wore me out, talking and running to meetings and the Med and to see movies on radical therapy. There were moments when the rhetoric made my head ring. Susie would complain that I didn't understand her: "You don't have a political analysis. I feel like I'm shouting at you across a gulf."

The night before I left, as she sat under the quilts on her bed, she told me about her plans to revolutionize medical care.

"When I've become a doctor and started a radical clinic and helped people gain control over their bodies, you know what I really want to do?"

"What?"

She pulled the sheet up to her eyes. "Be a glass blower. And raise more kids. I won't have to help the world anymore."

Suddenly her bed began to jiggle. Lamps rattled on the tables. The walls shook and the ceiling thumped. "What the hell . . . an earthquake?"

Susie winced. "No, it's the guy upstairs fucking. He's a black psychologist and he runs women through by appointment. He has no furniture, just pillows on the floor which is why the whole place shakes."

An ominous whooshing noise was rising. "That's his god-damned record of the ocean," Susie said. "He likes to fuck to environmental sounds." She nodded toward the ceiling. "This thing keeps me constantly aware of sex."

I left the next day and the image of Susie sitting on her mattress with the house vibrating around her is one I carry burned in my mind. She is nestled against pillows. Her face is tiny. Her eyes look ancient. A woman is moaning and screaming and the man is moaning and the ocean waves are crashing. All of Susie's things are rattling: ferns and hanging ivies; a fish tank; shells; all the beautiful old fabrics. The oil lamp flickers. A string of bells jingles. Susie looks so terribly small, and perishable.

28. TASHA

Tasha was sitting in my New York apartment, perched on the edge of the couch with her needlepoint, never sinking back, always balancing at the edge as if she might fly up at any second. It was the fall of 1972 and we had been meeting every Monday at ten. She would arrive at my apartment, make six phone calls, check her answering service, drink two mugs of coffee and alight on the couch. I was usually wearing jeans, while she wore tailored pants and sweaters, gold earrings and a jade ring.

What surprised us in our first interviews was that we had lived together at Berkeley and not known one another. "You were like an ice princess," I told her. "I was glad when Steven Silver dumped on you. I thought you were vain and selfish and looked down on me because I wasn't beautiful enough to be in your league."

"Good God." She gave her tinkling laugh. "I thought Susie, Candy—all three of you—were much better looking than me. And I was intimidated by your brains. I told Mark the other day, Sara could memorize books by flipping through the pages. The night before a final she would be out at some party, then she'd breeze in and get the highest grade in the class."

"Are you crazy? I was so compulsive I overstudied. By the last night, I had nothing left to do."

"Oh no," she said. "You never studied. I know that. You were doing fun things and you thought I was so beautiful and had it made. You were beneath me. But I was going through hell."

Over the next six months I came to love Tasha so dearly that after the hours we spent together I soared through my day. I was entranced by her fairy tale imagery, her eye for the magical, the clue. I watched her progress as she finished her book on myths and sold it to a publisher. The day she signed her contract, she flew into my house creating a wake of sparks. "I don't care what happens with my life just as long as I keep on living!"

Two weeks later she was down. She and Mark had been fighting. Nothing was adding up. "Sure I've written one children's book and I study Tai Chi Ch'uan but it's like being a dilettante. I wonder why you're even talking to me. I'm going to be thirty and what have I done?"

"Don't be silly," I said.

She glanced at me warily. "I think one of the reasons you want to find out about me is that I look like such a wreck, and I used to have long blond hair."

Tasha had, by this time, shaken my confidence in my memory of how she had looked at nineteen. Perhaps it had been my exaggeration. She certainly didn't possess that ethereal beauty now. She looked, as my husband said, "like a normal person."

So I began calling people who had known her at Berkeley. Each time I asked what they remembered of Tasha, their voices went misty. "She's the reason I grew my hair long," one girl said. A man who had been her friend rolled up his eyes. "She was too beautiful to be touched by mortal hands."

If you've tasted a moment of harmony with the universe, how do you handle your usual state of disharmony? How do you go back to your mechanical life after you've tasted being divine?

Baba Ram Dass

When Tasha had returned from Sufi Camp in Chamonix in the summer of '72, she had felt her life was about to change. She was seeing everything through a different lens. It was no longer painful to go to cocktail parties and be asked, "What do you do?" because she knew life was not just about doing.

When she dreamed of breaking free from Mark, it was no longer to live with a doctor in the suburbs and have babies. It was to live by herself in a room with one frying pan. A devotional life. Meditating, serving people from a place deep within her, a different place than the one from which she had sold paintings.

"The pull I'm feeling is toward the eternal," she told me. "Mark's been away for a week, and I know what it's been like to wake up in quiet, meditate, walk the dog and see the world from that pale pink point."

Not knowing quite why, she began to look for a job. There were so many beginnings, she was fearful there would have to be endings. A friend who worked at the Metropolitan Museum told her they were looking for someone to create an after-school program for ghetto kids. Tasha wrote a proposal based on the research she had done for her book on myths. She called it, "The Magic Trip to the Fourth World." She planned to use pieces in the museum as touchstones for exploring legends and dreams. The education committee was enthusiastic, but the job they offered was part-time and the salary would be only $300 a month.

In the same week, she received another job offer: securing artworks for the Chase Manhattan Bank. They would pay $20,000 a year and there would be lavish buying trips around the country. She called me from a pay phone. "I'm out of my mind, I don't know what to do. The bank job would take up all my time and I wouldn't be free to study Tai Chi or mythology. But I know I could do the job and I need the money. I haven't earned a penny in two years."

"Why do you need money . . ."

"I have to run, 'by."

"Wait a minute . . ."

"No. They're cleaning the street, they're spraying water on the phone booth, good-by!"

She hopped in a cab and went back to the studio, where she found Mark in bed, groaning with pain from an infected wisdom tooth. She drove him to the doctor and came home, relieved to be alone. She wanted to sit quietly and hear what to do. She sat on her meditation cushion. She closed her eyes. The telephone rang. She wouldn't answer it. It rang and rang. She picked up the receiver. It was Mark, he had just remembered an errand that had to be done that day. Could Tasha please, it was urgent, run up to the gallery for him?

When she arrived at Hilda Carson's the receptionist told her she had a phone call. Who on earth would be calling her there?

Steven Silver. Good God, she thought. What else could fall on my head to confuse me? Steven said he was in town for a few days and was so anxious to see her.

"Tell me," she said, "I'm dying of curiosity. Did you ever finish your thesis?"

"No." He laughed self-consciously. "I've become a gestalt therapist. I've broken out of all my prisons."

"That's ironic because I'm about to step back into mine."

She suggested they meet for coffee at the Third Avenue El, a hole-in-the-wall coffee shop with Formica tables. She picked it because it was anonymous and dumb, she didn't want to meet him in a romantic setting.

When she hung up she looked at her watch. She had two hours. She could do the errand for Mark or dash home, wash her hair, put on eye make-up and rose essence and change into a pale blue sweater and pants that fit just right.

She did the errand. If she went to all that trouble, Steven would know. She arrived late, but Steven was later and she was seated in the otherwise empty café when he walked in.

Was it a joke? He was wearing loud orange herringbone pants, a suede cap, a suede jacket and clunky turquoise bracelets. His hair was riddled with gray and hung curly and unmanageable to the middle of his neck. He checked it in the mirror. "Do you want to stay here?" he asked.

"Sure, why not?"

"I've got some beer at a friend's apartment. It's just around the corner."

Aha, Tasha thought, he's decided he could still dig me. If I'd weighed 150 pounds he would have had a quick cup of coffee and split. But he looked so weird she wasn't getting any pangs so she said okay.

As they walked out the door she said, "Listen, when we get to this place there'll be no seduction scene."

Steven gave his old, spaniel-eyed smile. "I've changed. If there is a seduction scene it'll come from you."

"Then we're safe," but she noticed as they crossed the street that his hand moved naturally to the right spot on her back. She liked that in a man.

The apartment was on Seventy-second Street and looked the way Madison Avenue looked in autumn—rich and golden. There were Bokhara rugs, cloisonné vases and an antique bed with an ocher velvet spread. Tasha thought it felt like Sunday, not Friday as it was, and the meeting wasn't taking place in New York. It could have been San Francisco, the light. It could have been a dream.

She sat on the floor and Steven sat beside her. He said he loved her hair shorter and darker. She looked younger than she ever had.

Come off it, how could that be, she thought.

"I wish I could spend a week with you and just talk," he said.

Sure, just talk.

He told her he was the best gestalt therapist in Berkeley. He charged forty dollars an hour and his hours were all booked. He was studying bio-energetics. He knew about the Sufis. He liked to work with couples. He and his wife were separating.

"Look," she said, "I want to talk about my work." She described the two job offers and he said, "You can't work for the bank, obviously. It would stunt your creativity and that's a trap you've worked out of once. Your enthusiasm for the mythology program is far more meaningful than the money. If you're good at what you love doing, somehow the money gets there."

He told her that after he had resigned from his teaching job, poems had begun to flow after a dry six years. "Can I read you one?"

He took a manuscript from a brief case and as he read, looking up frequently from the page, Tasha felt her heart opening. When he finished, she said, "That's a sequel to 'Evil is Playing with Possibilities,' isn't it?"

He pretended he was about to fall over. "You're the only human being who would know that." He touched her arm, as if the touching were a casual gesture. "Are you busy later on? There's a poetry reading . . ."

She shook her head no. "Mark's just had surgery and even if he hadn't, I wouldn't go there with you."

He stood up. "Then I want to make a call."

She said jokingly, "As long as it's not Sandra Jason."

He froze. His eyes were insolent and at the same time sheepish. "I really fucked things up, didn't I?"

The awful part, Tasha thought, was that he still might be calling Sandra Jason.

"Isn't there some way I could spirit you off for a week?"

"No, and please don't call or write me. It would only disturb Mark and it's unnecessary. If I ever get to Berkeley I'll call you." She asked him to write down names of new poets he admired. "It feels wonderful talking with you about poetry. I remember what I miss now. You opened that door for me."

He helped her to her feet, kissed her on both cheeks and held her adoringly. She could only remember the good things. From the corner of her eye she saw the ocher velvet bed. She felt loose and beautiful. They could have a quick affair and she could tell him, "Sorry, Steven, it just isn't the same."

He kissed her neck and whispered, "Natasha." Who was she kidding? Any sex with Steven would leave marks. She twisted loose. "Good seeing you," she said and slipped away.

At the studio, Mark was delirious with pain and she had to run around getting him ice packs and prescriptions and making Jell-O, all the while she whistled to herself, "California Dreamin'."

First thing on Monday, she called the Chase Manhattan Bank and refused the job. It was the right decision, she was sure of it, but the following morning as she was awakening, she heard a male voice speaking with a thick German accent: "I am Ludwig Ludwig and I'm going to start without you." Her eyes popped open. She told Mark what she had dreamed. He laughed. "I'm not surprised. Ludwig would love to take that job with the bank. The Ludwig in you who's efficient, organized."

Tears started from her eyes. "Am I shutting a door behind me? I feel like I'll never be able to go back to that world of glamour and high-paying jobs. I'll be walking out on limbs."

Mark said, "You have to close doors so that new ones can open."

"But I don't even know if I can do the museum job. It may be a dead end."

He stroked her hair. "I'll take care of you."

As the time approached for the museum job to start, Tasha was spending ten hours a day at the library. She didn't know enough about myths. She didn't know how to talk to kids. She couldn't even remember being eight years old.

The first day at the museum there were twelve children and by the end of the six-week session, there were thirty. Most of them were boys and all but two were black. They brought their brothers and sisters and cousins and friends until she had to say no more because they were building something and new people would hold them back.

She started by telling them the Hopi creation myth. "The Hopis believed there are four worlds, and the one we live in is the fourth," she said. "The first world was called Endless Space. The second world was called Dark Midnight. The third world was called Kuskurza—we have no English word for it—and the fourth was called World Complete, because it's the world of all choices. When people emerged in the fourth world, they were told to follow a cloud by day and a star by night. In the fourth world, each person has to find his own way."

She told the children they were going to make spirit sticks like the Indians made, to contact the good spirits. They would use all the elements. Wood from the earth. Shells from the ocean. Feathers from the birds of the air and beads from the fire. "Whatever else you see that's magical, bring it here and put it on your spirit stick."

She passed out notebooks, "secret notebooks where you can write down your most private thoughts." At the start of every session she asked them to write down a dream they'd had recently or draw a picture of it. Most of the kids scribbled away but one boy, Charleston, sat by himself shredding an eraser into bits. "Did you have a dream last night, Charleston?" He shook his head no. "Would you like to have a dream?" Umm hmmm. "Okay, close your eyes and when I put my finger on your nose, say the first thing that pops in your head."

He closed his eyes and after a moment she touched his nose. "A dog came in my room," he said. "In the middle of the night. I screamed, but wasn't nobody around and the dog kept comin' but its tail was waggin'. I says to myself, that dog is my friend. I's gonna call my dog Purple Pearls."

Tasha helped Charleston make purple pearls for his spirit stick. The sticks grew more colorful week by week, as they explored different chambers of the museum. One day Tasha showed them a case of African statues. "Everybody stand like one of the statues. When I say go, move like the statue. When I call your name, say what the statue is saying. Okay, go! Charleston, what does your statue say?"

Charleston was stomping in a circle. "Hate."

Tasha: "Let's all be the statue and chant it. Hate! Hate! Now, Genille."

Genille said shyly, "Will you be my friend?" Tasha had them skip about, shaking hands. Afterward, she thought, they'll never forget that case of statues because they've been inside it.

On the last day, they completed their spirit sticks and formed a circle holding them in the air. What a sight: thirty children with sticks three feet long, festooned with red feathers, purple feathers, yellow feathers, shells, jewelry, tin cans, bells, parts of dolls, paper flowers and magic charms. They danced in a circle, twirling and shaking the sticks as they followed Tasha in the center. "We're going to take vows," she said. "Repeat after me. I am earth. I am fire. I am water. I am air. I am all things. All things are in me."

They danced toward the center raising their sticks. "I belong to the fourth world," they chanted after Tasha. "The fourth world is the world complete. In the fourth world, you have to find your own way. In the fourth world, all choices are there."

"And now," she said, "it's time for us to choose a new name. If you were an Indian child, you might take the name of an animal that would be your companion through life."

"I'll be Flying Eagle," one boy said.

"Silent Fawn."

"The Great Bear."

Charleston was the last to be heard from. "I want my name to be Orange Skin," he said dreamily, and Tasha did a double take because orange was the color of insanity.

They held hands, closed their eyes and passed a squeeze around the circle and then the journey to the fourth world was over.

She caught a plane for Paris that night to make the opening of Mark's show. More than a thousand people crowded into the Galerie Lyon to see his Altar Pieces, extensions of wood and metal that seemed to sway and balance in defiance of gravity. Mark said the pieces had been inspired by his meditations. After the opening there was a dinner for thirty at the Tour d'Argent, followed by more parties and dinners so that Tasha had no chance to catch her breath.

After a week, she received a telegram from the Metropolitan, asking her to supervise all their programs for children. Could she return to New York at once?

Mark ripped up the cable. "You just arrived. What about my program on French TV? You promised to help. What about our trip to Brittany? I've been planning it for months."

"Calm down," Tasha said. "I will not be bullied. I promised you I'd help so I will. I'll tell the museum I'm coming back in two weeks but that's it."

They rented a Porsche and drove to Brittany in silence except for irritable exchanges about road directions. They arrived at midnight at Carnac, where Mark wanted to see the megalithic avenues—a mysterious assembly of primitive stones.

The room they found in a country auberge had two narrow beds in which they slept with their backs turned. At dawn they went downstairs. The concierge, a plump woman in a blue and white apron, was making crepes out of buckwheat flour, fresh eggs and newly churned butter. The crepes were so light and the early June sunlight through the window so warming that Tasha and Mark suddenly felt happy. They looked furtively at each other, burst out laughing and in a festive spirit, set out to see the stones.

From a distance the stones were like a prehistoric army petrified in formation. There was a giant stone in the lead, twenty feet tall, behind which there were rows and rows of stones aligned in columns two miles long. Mark parked the car.

"How did they get here?" Tasha asked.

"No one knows. They were erected before the Gauls, probably by the same people who built Stonehenge. It's said that if you stand on the coast opposite the lead stone in Carnac, on a day without fog, you can see Stonehenge."

They walked down the rows, feeling small in the shadows, looking at the forms and examining the surfaces.

"Don't you get the feeling this is a power spot?" Tasha said.

"Unbelievable. Listen." He motioned for her to put her ear to a stone. She heard whistling like a lyre.

"I'm afraid."

"Don't be," he said.

They found that the stones had many sounds—knocking, rumbling, roaring—but you had to be completely still to hear them. At noon, they drove to a hostelry where they ate fresh-caught langoustes and drank local wine. Then they sat in the garden of a monastery listening to renunciants sing Gregorian chants. By evening they felt such exaltation.

For a week they returned to the stones every day. Mark took photographs and sketched, while Tasha meditated and danced along the rows with her arms over her head. "I did so much dancing," she recalls. "And I found one rock that felt like me." She smiled. "It was small and feminine and had a rounded sphere like a woman's belly. It was not one of the great stones, but it had a presence. I had to visit it every day, and one afternoon when I was sitting beside it, I understood: this is why I'm with Mark. I couldn't have this experience, I couldn't share this miracle to the fullest, with another type of man.

The Tai Chi studio was in a loft on the Bowery in the border zone between Chinatown and Skid Row. On the sidewalk outside, derelicts lay in sputum heaps and white-haired Chinamen minced along with canes. There was a black metal door with Chinese letters, then a dim stairwell with walls of mildewed brick, but when you reached the top floor, you came into a long white room that made you feel fresh.

A gong was struck. Thirty people rose and formed two lines. In silence they performed slow, sinking, circling movements, following the lead of a tall young man whose grace was breath-taking and completely nonchalant.

Tasha stood in the middle of the front row, wearing loose black pants and Chinese slippers. She had been coming to classes two and three times a week, but only to classes taught by this tall young man, whose name was Peter. She learned best from Peter. His voice was harmonious and his phrases were so clear. She wondered if he was homosexual. He was slender and had super pale skin. Tasha overheard him say he lived in Bucks County, Pennsylvania. Maybe he was married. He didn't wear a ring but his shirts were always pressed and why else would he commute to Pennsylvania if he weren't married?

As she rode uptown on the subway, Tasha had daydreams in which she and Peter did Tai Chi together and meditated and cooked vegetables which they ate with ivory chopsticks in a white, sunlit room. One day after class he stopped her at the door. "Would you like to have dinner with me?"

Her face turned red. "I can't, tonight . . ."

"Later this week? There's something I'd like to talk to you about."

"You'd better let me call you. I live with somebody."

Peter wrote his number on a pad.

Tasha waited three days before calling him. Confucius said three was an auspicious number. She met him at a café on Mott Street, where they ate tofu with black mushrooms. Peter told her she looked remarkably similar to a woman he had lived with.

"The first time I saw you, I knew you weren't Mary but I was struck by something so familiar, something in the eyes." He laughed, easily. "Then out of the blue, Mary called from San Francisco. She's studying Tai Chi there and tells me the oddest thing, there's a man in her class who looks remarkably like me. Something in the eyes . . ."

Tasha gave her tinkling laugh. So he wasn't homosexual. But why did he live in Pennsylvania?

He told her he was in Reichean therapy with a doctor there. An hour later they were walking by the East River and he was showing her how to look for orgone energy in the sky.

She did not see Peter except at Tai Chi classes, after which she always had to hurry back to the studio to meet Mark. He was having another show in Paris in October but Tasha had an idea. She would stay home and renovate the studio. It hadn't been painted in ten years and all the fixtures were breaking. She could never do the job with him there because it would interfere with his work and drive him crazy.

The day Mark left, she brought in a team of painters, carpenters, electricians, plumbers, plasterers and rug cleaners. She bought new dishes and towels. She had a new kitchen and bathroom installed with Italian tiles. She lived in saw dust for four weeks but it was worth it because the results were spectacular. Half the space was completely empty for Mark to work in, with cabinets along the walls. The other half was divided, by Tibetan screens, into quarters in which they could live and entertain. The day before Mark was due back, she sat in the Eames chair in the center of this spanking clean, renovated, painted and polished space and swiveled about, admiring every detail.

Then she was in tears. "I knew I couldn't live there. I'd gone to all this effort to convince myself to stay and it hadn't worked." She cried and cried. What about Carnac? She and Mark had reached such heights in Carnac, but wasn't that why they could separate now? "We had done whatever work we were supposed to do together, although what that was exactly I'll never know."

Mark landed at the airport with his arms full of presents and a resolution: this year they would break their pattern, take a winter vacation, go to Italy or Scotland. She drove home making small talk but one step inside the studio and she broke. "I can't do it. I've got to split, and it's not temporary, it's not a trial. It's not because there's anyone else because there isn't. It's because it has to happen."

Her face looked wretched. Mark wanted her to sleep in the studio that night.

"But in the morning I have to get up and leave."

She did not realize until she was out on the street with a suitcase and her Shih Tzu dog in his kennel that it was November 7, 1973—ten years, exactly, from the day her father died.

VII. WINTERLUDE

1973–

I imagine that anyone who has lived in the stultifying environment of a suburban tract for twenty years . . . finds the problem of permanence rather dull. But those of us who have lived differently, as I have, find it a matter of crucial importance.

Ingrid Bengis, *Combat in the Erogenous Zone*

29. SARA

The symmetry of it all was unnerving. On January 23, 1973, I had walked in the kitchen to fix supper for myself and flicked on the radio. "Ladies and gentlemen, the President of the United States." I had not known the President would be on the air. I had known, only, that it was 6 P.M. and safe to turn on the radio and not hear Michael.

I stood in the center of the floor. President Nixon was announcing that in sixty days, all American troops would be withdrawn from Vietnam. I looked at the calendar. I marked the date in my journal with this note, "I have seen a historical era begin and end."

For ten years, through all that had happened in the country, the Vietnam War had been the backdrop. The long, skinny maps on the front page, the body count, the names like Khe San, the protests, the shutdowns of campuses—all that was soon to fade and what was to replace it was the Watergate Scandal. In the spell of Watergate, the country was drifting into muzzy times of inflation, depression and a cross-generational obsession with security and money.

The day before Nixon's announcement, Lyndon Johnson had died in Texas. The following day, I met Michael in his office to sign a separation agreement. Michael answered the door wearing a shirt I had embroidered with desert scenes. He hugged me, silently. I took off my coat and placed it by his desk. I noticed that the picture of me had been removed and in its place was a Polaroid shot of a blonde with a red bow in her hair. On his writing pad, I saw a phrase, "My wife is a seeker in another land."

"What was your weight this morning?" he asked.

"I don't know."

"Mine was one seventy-nine."

He introduced me to the lawyer who had drawn up the papers. As Michael and I sat across from each other, leafing through the documents, the lawyer whistled to himself.

From time to time I heard rustling and looked up. Michael did not seem to be concentrating, merely turning pages.

I laughed.

"What is it?"

". . . both parties agree that the dishwasher, presently being used by Michael, belongs to Sara. . . ."

He laughed quietly. Our private conspiracy.

When the lawyer had gone, Michael opened a half-bottle of New York State champagne. "I order it by the case from Columbus Circle Liquors. I have a split every day before lunch, it's more festive than a gin and tonic."

"You mean you're changing your ritual?"

"That's right. I change lots of things."

Silence. My eyes flicked to the Polaroid shot. Michael said, "Nothing serious. There are three or four women I'm seeing, but I'm not in love. How 'bout you?"

I shook my head no.

"I'll tell you." He took a sip of champagne. The sight of his hand, the sorrel-colored skin, the familiar way he held the glass near the base . . . I blinked back tears.

He paused, and said, "I'd rather be talking to you than anyone."

We had decided to separate the night I had returned from New Mexico. We had already been apart six weeks; it would be easier to split right away than readjust. Fast, I found an apartment on West Eightieth Street in the heart of Needle Park, started an affair, packed my clothes, took an acid trip with new friends and negotiated an agreement with Michael. He would give me a sum of cash and I would leave him everything—the apartment, the car, all the books and records, the furniture, except for one item: the dishwasher. I did not want dishwashing in my future.

When people learned I was separating and said they were sorry, I said, "Don't be, it's what I want."

"Well it can't be easy."

"Easier than I thought. I don't feel lonely in the least."

And I didn't. I had taken up with a new crowd of friends who were interested in mysticism. The men had met at Harvard and the women had gone to Eastern schools and all of them were talented, articulate and funny. There were lots of phone calls and spur-of-the-moment dinners and running to movies and to hear R. D. Laing and to see the Whirling Dervishes from Turkey and to visit a Chinese herbalist and then to cook a Szechuan feast in someone's loft. Michael would not have wanted to do any of these things, nor would he have been open to the people.

It was a relief to be out of the battle. No demands, no arguments about what time to eat and who would do the dishes. No fear of setting off Michael's rage. No interruptions when I wanted to work.

I took magazine assignments, again, determined to find a way to write about people without the detachment and flip sarcasm of my early work. At Thanksgiving, I remember that I felt truly graced. I was in Pound Ridge, with eight friends, staying in a country house owned by the parents of a young man named Tony. The parents were in Europe and we had the run of the house, the pond, the orchards. At one point, I stood before a mirror and saw a young woman with life ahead of her: wind-swept vistas, limitless possibilities.

After dinner, as we sat around the living room, smoking Thai grass, someone wondered aloud if we would ever set up homes like this for ourselves. Tony said, "It's not long before our ten-year reunion at Harvard. Lots of our classmates should have made it."

"That's right, we're supposed to be grownups."

They laughed. I looked about the room. We were all near thirty, but not one of us was presently married and none had had children. I told my friend Sally, "When we're forty, I don't think it will be cute anymore." She smiled. "That's what my younger brother says. He thinks we're all narcissistic aesthetes. Fin-du-siècle decadents. The best of our generation and we're not reproducing." But Sally didn't seem very concerned. "I don't think it's possible," she said, "for us to have those kind of permanent relationships. Too many forces are pulling us in different directions."

As winter set in, I noticed I was catching more colds than usual, gaining weight and having difficulty making ends meet. In January, when I met Michael to sign the separation papers, I left his office in tears. I felt miserable. I kept thinking, I'm not that different, I haven't done any of the things I thought being married to Michael was preventing me from doing. I'm not traveling in India or taking Arica or living on the land. I'm in Manhattan hustling articles.

That night at two in the morning, Michael called. "I'm resigning from the station," he said. "They've hired a new program director, an ignorant fool whom I despise. You know what flashed in my head? Go to California with Sara and have a baby."

I sighed. "Don't resign." I knew that in the morning he would probably not remember this conversation.

The following week, I was having lunch with a friend who was about to become managing editor of *Ramparts*. We had finished a bottle of wine and were starting on a second when he asked, "What have you been working on lately?"

"Well, I spent five months writing an article no one will publish."

"Give it to me, I'll print it."

"No you won't." I laughed. "It's not for *Ramparts*. It's about God."

He took the article and called the next morning. "I want it," he said. "It's the first piece I've read that makes Ram Dass and mysticism comprehensible."

"You're kidding!" I cut the piece in half and toned down my gushing exuberance which had become, by now, a source of embarrassment. When the issue hit the stands, the article drew more response than anything I had written. I received hundreds of letters from people who said I had changed the course of their lives, which, although gratifying, was ironic because I was at a point where I could not bear going to Hilda's meditations.

I was not in the mood to hug people and stare in their eyes. At first I forced myself to continue going, hoping that if I went through the motions, the feeling would return: that high, that certainty I was on the right path, that sense that it was all enough. But seeing other people sigh with bliss only made me more depressed. Why had I lost it? I had a terrible suspicion that I had been on the brink of crossing over and had chosen to step back. Why? Lack of courage? Or was it, rather, that the process was long, there was no single crossing and there were to be many more turns of the wheel? My friend Tony, who was having a similar experience, called it "the fall from grace." What made it so painful was the realization that we were not, as each of us had had occasion to announce, "a different person now." No decision, we had found, was more than a predilection of the moment, and no perception was absolute except that all would change.

I began to favor words like "seems" and "appears" in my writing. I was wary of the declarative sentence. I would hedge: "This seems to be the dawning," instead of, "This is the dawning."

My depression deepened as spring came on. I called Michael for solace and we began to meet, after his show, for dinner at Maxwell's Plum. As we laughed and talked in the flickering room with gaslights, a copper ceiling and large ceramic animals dangling in air—leopards, lions, roosters—I was seeing once again what I had not seen in years: the qualities in Michael that had led me to fall in love with him. He was deeply understanding, a loyal fan and childlike in his exuberance, and he was also demanding and enraged and impossible and yet he could be so buoyant, so nourishing.

"You *can* do it."

"Woe is *not* you."

The differences between us were seeming less important.

"I'm going to Palm Springs for three weeks," he said suddenly. "Why don't you come with me?"

As we sat by the pool at the Palm Springs Tennis Club, he read *Open Marriage* and I read *Combat in the Erogenous Zone*. What am I doing here, I thought. Michael and I were out of sync. He would blurt, "I think I'm one of the best radio men in the world, and you don't think that." How could I respond? We tried to make love, to work on our "problem," but it was mechanical, our hipbones grating. At night we soaked in the jacuzzi pool. Michael said, "What causes me so much anguish is that I see now that I want the same thing you've always wanted—a relationship where everything is out in the open. 'Come into the garden, there's nothing to fear.' But I'm blocked with you, Sara. I'm afraid to go to the depths with you. And yet I've come so far with you."

"Why is it so hard for us to let go?" I asked. "Other people do."

"I know," he said. "But we're not other people. What makes it so hard for us is that the five years we were married coincide with the time when there was a flowering of our talents, when both of us blossomed and we built the foundations that will last us all our lives. Also, it was the time, historically, when so much happened. All our ideas were completely overturned. We lived through that and somehow we managed to build a basement that will endure, rain or shine. So whoever comes to live in the house in the future will live on top of what we built together. That's why it's hard."

So we embarked on what was to be a three-year course of reunions and separations. Michael would open toward me and I would feel hope, then abruptly he would withdraw and I would flutter with rage. Hope-rage, hope-rage, until we washed ashore, divorced, I in California and he in New York.

When I returned from Palm Springs to my small apartment filled with discarded furniture and the smell of transience, I felt dazed. I missed my purple couches. I wept before the television when Archie and Edith Bunker celebrated their twenty-fifth anniversary. I could not attend baby showers, it was too painful, and I cried at movies like *The Quiet Man*, cried when I saw ordinary women living in harmony with traditional patterns. Yet even as I cried I knew the harmony of those patterns was illusory, and that the strength and optimism I had felt before were going to return.

In June I finished interviewing Tasha and arranged to go to California in the fall to be with Susie. I wanted to track down others I had been close with at Berkeley. I suppose I imagined that in the process, I might sort through some of the wreckage of the decade and get a fix on myself.

Everyone was eager to see me, all of them were curious about the others and I was the link.

"Is Tasha still beautiful? Does she still have long blond hair?"

"I heard Susie Berman was underground, making bombs."

"I heard Rob Kagan was living in Oakland with a black welfare mother and five kids."

They were not always happy to have their memories disturbed. When I flew to London to spend a month with Candy, her first child, Rebecca, was five months old. "Sare," Candy called out in her mellifluous, sighing voice. She hooked an arm through mine and showed me through the house that she and Bobby had purchased near Hampstead. Rebecca was asleep in a bright yellow room, and in the study were bookcases stuffed with copies of *Foreign Affairs* and *American Scholar*. But alongside a pile of psychoanalytic journals was a touch of the old Candy, a porno tabloid with the headline, "Office Fuck."

I pointed to it. Candy laughed. "I love to read the personals."

While Rebecca napped we sat in the garden among lilacs and rows of tulips. "As you can see, I don't get much sun," Candy said. Her skin was chalk white but she looked rounded and lovely in a long brown skirt and Victorian yellow blouse.

"Will you be going back to work soon?" I asked.

She shook her head no. "I took a year's leave. It will be hard on my patients but I figure, I'm the only mother this baby will have. Why leave her with an au pair to go help other people who didn't get what they needed from their own mothers?"

"What about your analysis?"

"That'll continue."

"But it's been . . ."

"Eight years. No end in sight." She made a crinkly-eyed, coyote smile.

"Aren't you curious to try living without analysis?"

"Not at this point. I love the process and there seems no end to what I can learn."

For several hours we reminisced, and I asked if she would recount her memory of the night Tasha's father had died.

She squinted into the sun. "What I remember most strongly is Mrs. Taylor calling and my having to say Tasha wasn't home. I remember feeling so awful for Tasha. How could she ever forgive herself?"

"For what?" I asked.

"For leaving her father. Going to bed with another man at the moment he died."

Another man? I debated whether to interrupt Candy or let her go on.

"What is it?" she said.

I hesitated. "Tasha didn't sleep with anyone that night."

"Yes she did. I'm positive! I . . ." She tilted her head. "What does Tasha say?"

I told her that Tasha, Susie and I concurred on this detail: Tasha was on her way home from the city when it happened. She walked in shortly after her mother's call.

Candy said slowly, "That's very freaky. All these years I've had a terrible memory. But would I swear to it?" She paused. "No. I don't remember running around looking for the guy's phone number. I don't remember seeing her that night. It's all blank."

Rebecca started to cry, Candy rushed from the garden and a few moments later, Bobby came home from the university where he was teaching American history.

"Hi Sare."

Six years in London had not made a dent in his California accent or boyish looks. He put his arms around Candy as she nursed the baby and they cuddled as they had done in Cambridge. "This baby has ruined our lives," Bobby joked. "Candy never leaves her except to go to her analyst where she talks about the baby."

Candy retired to her bedroom after dinner and Bobby and I sat up drinking cognac.

"Do you really like living here?" I asked. "Can you see spending your life an expatriate?"

"Yeah," Bobby said. "We have a lot of friends now, and I don't feel like I've missed anything. I don't feel deprived because I haven't lived on a commune or had a bisexual experience."

I laughed.

"If that means I'm closed or afraid to take risks and stuff, then I accept your contempt."

"Bobby. How can I have contempt for anyone, when I don't know that all the people who took risks, or what we called risks, are better off than you?"

"I don't know," Bobby said. "Guys like me are afraid . . ."

"Of what?"

He smiled impudently. "Of the Germaine Greers of this world."

The next morning, Candy said she had not been able to sleep because of what I had told her about Tasha. "What's so horrible is to realize what you do to people in your mind. You assign them a role and they live on that way, and sometimes you think about them and sometimes you don't, and then you find out they have a real life someplace that's nothing like what's in your head." She poured coffee for herself and sat at the blond wood table, watching the coffee grow cold.

"I don't think I can be in this book," she said. I had a sinking feeling. "I think one of the reasons Bobby and I have been able to make it through the hard periods is that we've been so isolated. We were really thrown back on ourselves. We couldn't diffuse our energy running around, and we weren't influenced by crazes. We've led a very ordinary life and I want to keep it that way."

"I understand, but I plan to change names and take measures to protect your privacy." I pleaded, "At least think it over."

"I can't." She stiffened her arms against the table. "I'm sorry, because I wanted to spend the time with you, but the process is so emotional and it raises things I don't want raised. I don't want to think about anything for the moment except the baby."

"It *is* interesting," I said, "that you're the only one of us who's still living with the same man."

Candy looked at me, finally, with her brown eyes set so closely together. "The marriages I know of that work seem to be where both people can accept the fact that it isn't going to be great all the time. There will be problems and you can't fix them overnight, maybe you can't fix them for years, but it's all right, they'll be resolved over time. Things will get better and bad again and better and bad again and that's your marriage.

"Does that sound middle-aged?"

I was silent a moment.

"No," I said. "It sounds wise."

If Candy had represented the conventional path, it was Rob Kagan who, in all these years, had represented the other direction. Rob was the boy with the twinkly blue eyes who had once put my alarm clock in the freezer to see if we could stop time. He had gone further out on drugs and fantasy than anyone I had known, and so, in 1973, I delayed calling him, fearful he would surely judge me dull.

When I drove to his house in the Oakland Hills, I found Rob reserved. The house was almost empty, Oriental in feeling. Rob's hair, which had been shoulder length when I last saw him, was short and speckled with silver. He was sitting on a rug with his wife, whom he called Sun Bee, and his partner, Joe.

"Did you bring a bag with you?" Rob asked.

"My purse."

Sun Bee gave a shy smile. "Is there anything interesting in your purse?"

"No. Just notebooks and glasses."

"Glasses," Sun Bee said. "Let's see."

I took out the glasses and she tried them on, as did Rob and Joe. I did not know what to make of Sun Bee. She was dressed like Baby Doll in a short, white lace dress, rhinestone barrettes in her gold hair and a pair of dainty cowboy boots "that once belonged to a French madame." Rob and Joe were wearing jeans and paint-stained shirts. They had been restoring an old house which they had bought cheaply and planned to sell for a profit. After that, Rob said, they would buy a better house, fix it up and sell it for a larger profit.

"You must be stunned to hear me talking about money," he said. "I'm stunned myself. It's heresy. But when I moved to the country I found I needed money to build things." He opened a picture book of vintage sports cars. "Money gives you access to perfect things, like this car." He pointed to a Lamborghini. Rob said that as soon as he acquires enough money, he wants to buy premium land in a beautiful setting, "like Hawaii, hopefully near a community of talented people. There are special places all over the world, but I want to find one that has good weather."

"If you do, let me know," I said.

"I will. But I'm not as optimistic as I once was."

Joe laughed. "Forget it, man, you're looking for utopia and it doesn't exist."

"It *does* exist," Rob said. "I lived in one for five years. Berkeley from 1964 to '69 was utopia for me."

Sun Bee said, "For me it was '66 to '67."

Rob: "It was the perfect life. Everything you ever wanted to do, you could do. It was exciting and there was love between the people and we were creating new things every day."

I asked him what I had been asking everyone. "Why did it end?"

Joe whistled. "Man, if I could tell you, I would."

Rob said, "Things got jaded and we lost heart, I guess. In my own work, I put on the most brilliant extravaganza that could ever be, as my master's thesis. I spent six months preparing the event and after it, anything else would have been a step down.

"Also, around that time, I took an acid trip and saw my life as total madness. My room looked like the habitat of an insane person. All the items were on display—shoes and tools—things were hanging from hooks at different elevations and spread in patterns on the floor." Rob said he had started toward a cannon ball because he had to get rid of it, but then he spotted a collage of broken doll heads and as he was moving for them his eyes hit on a little stuffed grandmother standing by two stuffed peacocks. Clutter! He sat on his bed, paralyzed, and when the drug wore off, he gathered everything in his truck and took it all to the Berkeley dump.

Kris, his girl friend, had already decided that "this glorious experimentation was not for her anymore. We had done a lot of trading around, sexually, and it was thrilling and I wanted to keep that going forever, but what I didn't realize was that Kris was moving farther and farther away until one day she just wasn't there. When that happened, when I realized she was gone, oh God, I went down. Sun Bee had to take me in and nurse me."

Rob organized sixteen of his friends to buy land five hours north of Berkeley. He had a vision that they needed to build again from scratch, but when they drove to the land, most of the people changed their minds. The land had no water or electricity, and the climate was freezing in winter and 110° in summer. Rob and Sun Bee were the only ones to move there. Rob started to build. He pushed his body to its limits, building four houses, one for every season; a barn; a garden; an outdoor bath and sauna; a root cellar; a dance hall; a pool with swings and slides. Sun Bee painted pictures and wrote poems and baked shortcakes. As soon as I get the water pipes in, people will come, Rob thought. When I get the pool finished . . . when the dance hall is built . . . For almost four years he dug, plowed and hammered by himself, and many visitors came but no one stayed. At the end of the fourth year, Rob and Sun Bee planned a wedding. All the buildings were completed and everyone could see what a paradise he had created. Hundreds of friends came in vans and on horses. They barbecued six turkeys and eight whole salmon and for a week, they feasted, danced and swam. People marveled at the houses and the pool and the waterfalls and the view from the outdoor bath, but after the wedding ceremony, they left. Everyone. A week later, Rob put the land up for sale and returned to Berkeley to make money.

"What a story," I said. Rob looked exhausted from the telling. "In a way, I was like a king who got deposed. I hate to use the word, but I had been very 'powerful.' I enjoyed whatever I wanted. Maybe I had to work in exile all those years as penance, to atone or something."

Joe lit a joint and passed it to Rob. "It's not just you, man. Everyone I know has this feeling that somehow, we made a mistake. And as school kids, the worst thing you can do is make a mistake."

"What went wrong?" I asked. "All these bright, idealistic, committed people—how could they have miscalculated so badly? Was it mass hallucination? Were our perceptions wrong?"

Rob said he didn't think so. He smiled, and I saw, for the first time that evening, the twinkles in his eyes. "That's the lesson of revolutions—they never turn out the way you expect. That doesn't mean your perceptions were wrong. It just means . . ." He raised his eyebrows like two peaks. "It means things didn't turn out that way."

30. SUSIE

Susie was one of the few people in Berkeley who did not have a sense of failure. In the spring of '73, she and Roxanne were sitting in the Med and Roxanne was saying that everyone she knew was depressed. "Do you realize how many of our friends who dropped out are now scrounging to get *any* kind of job? Do you know how many Ph.D.'s are working as carpenters? Some of them have been out of the economy so long they've forgotten how to talk."

Susie said, "I'm not depressed. I'm proud of our generation. We got a President out of office, we turned the country upside down. Fuck, America was a political wasteland in the fifties and we got it politicized to the point where even housewives were out marching."

"Well they ain't marching anymore," Roxanne said. "And all the problems are still around. It makes me so frustrated."

"You've got to fight that," Susie said. "You can't get sunk in despair. We've got lives to lead here, work to do. It's not all acid trips and taking over the government."

In May, Susie received notice that she was accepted to U. C. Medical School. Joyous relief! The work question was settled. She sent Sam off to spend the summer with Jeff and from May to

August, she studied chemistry and biology. She barely spoke to a man. She was tired of affairs—she had fucked more than a hundred men by now and she figured it was probably her historical destiny to live alone.

In August she started hearing about a philosophy instructor, Glen Lucas, who was organizing men's liberation groups. Roxanne thought Glen and Susie might get along. He was struggling with the same issues as she was, from the men's side. Susie was skeptical.

She met him at a picnic.

She'd expected him to be fat with kinky hair. He wasn't. When she saw him walking across the grass, saw the blue eyes, the smile, she thought, uh-oh.

They played baseball together.

He took her out for coffee.

He went home.

He called her. She was packing to move. He came over and helped her. She let him. She remembered back to Russ, how she wouldn't let him put a mop handle on a mop for her. Things had changed.

Glen and Susie talked more than they packed. He went home.

They drove to Inverness for the day. They ate clam chowder and talked. They had sixteen conversations going at once. He went home.

They went swimming. He kissed her for the first time. It felt easy.

On Sunday he took her to the Alameda Flea Market. They were roaming through the stalls holding hands when Susie realized they had been together four days and she couldn't remember whether they had slept together. That night they did.

At one point they talked about their marriages. Glen said he had needed to marry a child. His child-wife had worshiped and depended on him. Then he grew up. They were divorced. For the past several years he had been nurturing a fantasy: he wanted to find a scarred woman. Someone who wasn't perfect, who had suffered and lived.

Susie undid her blouse and showed him the scar where her tattoo had been.

Many months later, Susie was talking to Glen on the phone when she became aware that Sam was listening. She hung up, went over and took him in her arms. "That was Glen," she said.

"I know," Sam said.

"I guess I love him a lot."

Sam twisted away from her. "Yeah, but . . . but who do you love more?"

Susie thought, this is one of those moments. What I do now is really important. She rocked him in her arms. "Oh, Sam, you're my boy. I'll never love anyone the way I love you. You don't ever have to worry that if I love other people, I won't love you as much." She told him to cry if he wanted. He did, and twenty minutes later he was puttering with his toy train set.

"Hey," Susie said. "Isn't life funny?"

"Ummm hmmm." He sucked on his thumb.

"What do you think is the funniest thing?"

He giggled as if he were embarrassed. He put his finger to his temple. "Me."

On a still, cold November night, Sam came home from having dinner at a friend's. "Hey, Mom, somebody's been shot!" Susie switched on the news. Marcus Foster, the Oakland superintendent of schools, had been ambushed and killed in a parking lot. A terrorist group called the Symbionese Liberation Army claimed responsibility for the murder and issued a platform for revolution. Who the fuck were the SLA? None of Susie's friends, no one in Berkeley seemed to know. Then the SLA kidnaped Patricia Hearst and demanded as ransom $4 million to feed the poor.

I stopped by Susie's cottage the night Mrs. Hearst made a weeping appeal for Patty's return. Susie was in tears, "I think of Sam and how I'd feel if he were taken," she said. "But it's complicated. I sympathize with the SLA. Their platform is beautiful. They've dramatized how many people are starving in this rich country. It's freaking me out, making me wonder, oh my God, am I gonna have to go join them?"

She added, "I bet Patty's getting a fantastic political education." Hadn't Susie herself been given a private crash course in radical politics by Jeff and his friends? She remembered how important she had felt. She was right and everyone in her past life was wrong.

It wasn't days, though, before Susie decided the SLA was "a band of crazies. Their idea of revolution seems to be murdering black educators, kidnaping nineteen-year-olds and gunning down people on the street. That's what happens when you push the rhetoric of violence to its conclusion. That's not my politics. Nobody I know takes that line seriously anymore. I'm committed to making my struggle with medicine."

The last time I saw Susie was in Los Angeles. She had brought Sam from Berkeley to visit her parents, and the whole family had gathered for a picnic: her brother; two stepbrothers; their wives and children. They barbecued hamburgers and played baseball and afterward, Susie said, "When I see them all with their nuclear families, it looks good to me. Why don't I have one? Half of me wants to live with Glen in a rose-covered cottage. I don't want any more trips. I want substance and depth."

Her voice dropped to a whisper. "The other half of me knows monogamy won't work for people who've been through the wars that we have. I need time to myself, and Glen wants his own space."

I gave her a draft of this book to read and when she returned it, she broke down. "I'll be okay." She wiped her eyes. "It's just that . . . when I see it all in print, I see those years as a kind of madness. We were like children throwing tantrums. The times were exciting but boy were they scary." She sighed. "It doesn't feel so scary to me now. I'm still committed to change, but it will be quieter. I don't think we're gonna have to kill people."

"Don't you feel the wonder has gone out of the world?" I asked. "Everyone seems calmer, nobody is being attacked for the way they speak or wear their hair. Nobody feels so threatened, these days, except financially. But there's a jaded quality."

"Not for me," Susie said. "I can't wait to see what's ahead. I want to set up a clinic with people who have skills and can be models. In five years we'll have something real to look back on, instead of some newspaper clippings."

A horn honked. It was Susie's mother. They were going to Saks to shop for clothes and then to UCLA so Susie could register for a workshop on "Being Hopeful About Social Change." Before she left, she showed me her first stethoscope. Her white coat. She could hardly wait to listen to the beating of hearts.

31. TASHA

"Hello, this is Natasha Taylor Fine Arts. I can't come to the phone now, and I know it's annoying to get a machine, but I *do* want to speak to you. So please leave a message and I'll call you as soon as I can."

It was the fall of '74, a year since Tasha had left Mark. Two years since I had left Michael. Five years since Susie had left Jeff. Tasha was curled on a nutmeg-colored leather couch, recording the message for her answering machine. She wore a long white bathrobe and held her dog, Gin, in her lap.

"You look younger," I said, surprised. It was 3 A.M. and she had not been sleeping much, but her eyes were clear. Gone were the pained, sad shadows of defeat that had made me start when I had come upon her in the elevator of the Prince George Hotel.

She nodded. "Mark was heavy on me. But I miss him, you know? The last year has been so bizarre. I left a spectacular home with a distinguished sculptor and started sleeping on the floor at Rachel and Greg's. I got involved with a Tai Chi instructor. Then I apprenticed myself to a Hassidic rabbi, so I'm studying Talmud and Torah and keeping Shabbos and dancing Friday nights with the women until my feet bleed."

She held up a bruised sole and Gin licked it.

She burst out laughing. "I always said I'd never have a dog with a pushed-in face. I'd never live in a building with a doorman, and I'd never work in the art world again. I thought there was going to be no road back." But she had found, once she set off on her own, that she wasn't ready to "walk out on limbs." The image of a room with one frying pan faded, and she bought a co-op apartment in the East Seventies, where she set herself up as a private dealer.

She filled the apartment with art. Three of Mark's pieces stood before a wall of windows. All through the rooms were mammoth canvases illuminated by track lighting. The carpets and furniture were in tones of beige and white. The place had a formal feeling, except for small touches: a portable stereo, beside which were spread several albums by Paul Simon and one by Shlomo Carlebach, the singing rabbi.

I asked about Peter, the Tai Chi instructor.

Tasha smoothed back her hair. "I love Peter, but lately he's been mentioning that word that scares me, you know, the one that begins with 'm'?"

"I thought you said Peter was your karmic mate."

"I did think that at first. We taught Tai Chi together and it felt wonderful being with a man my own age. There was something clean and pure about our love-making, where with Mark, there was always something dark and forbidden. Peter gives the best massages in the world. When he touches me, I know he's *listening*."

She sighed. "We're very well mated when you match him with one of me—the spiritual, Villagey person who likes to do Tai Chi and cook soups and dance with Hassids in Brooklyn. But it's not so hot when you match him with the other me—the one who likes art and good restaurants and sophisticated talk and trips to Europe—and that's real. I never thought it was me. That's been the biggest shock. All the parts of my life that I characterized as Mark and not me turn out to be me as well.

"The other shock," she said, "is that I miss Mark so intensely, even after a year. There's nothing I can do about it because it still wouldn't work, but I love that man."

She shook her head. "Peter is the opposite of Mark. No glamour. No money. We never go out socially. I love being with him but I don't know what's around the corner. I'm afraid that Peter's too young and won't offer me the life that in my heart of hearts, I would want."

Tasha said she was thinking of seeing a psychiatrist again. "I have a real sense of my not being able to pay prices. That may be the tragedy of my life. I can live with a man for seven years and be faithful, but the idea of marrying—forget it! I can't make the leap. I can't go through the ceremony if there's any ambivalence and there always is. I want a feeling of clarity."

I had planned to end Tasha's story here, but the following year, when I returned to New York with a draft of this book, Tasha was living with someone new. She had told me his name was Bob Goodson, that he had a gallery across the street from Hilda Carson's and that he was like "a big honey bear."

She sent me a photograph of the two of them at the Basle Art Fair. "I know this man!" I told her. He lived in the same building in which Dr. Collins had his office, the building to which I had trudged faithfully for five years, four times a week. I had often seen Goodson in the elevator and had wondered who he was. I imagined he was a painter, a sensual, romantic figure.

"I used to wonder too," Tasha said. "He'd come into Hilda Carson's or I'd see him in Central Park with his wife and two little children. I thought he was super attractive and very married."

Tasha was in the Hamptons with Bob Goodson the night I arrived in New York. They had left keys for me with the doorman. I let myself into the aparment where Bob had lived with two successive wives and now was living with Tasha and his fourteen-year-old son.

"Help yourself to anything you want," said a note. The kitchen was stocked with Pepperidge Farm cookies, frozen steaks, family-sized bottles of catsup and a full year's supply of dog food. There were Hoffritz knives on a magnetic holder; a washer/dryer and dishwasher; wire baskets loaded with potatoes; catalogs from gourmet stores and *House and Gardens* cookbooks on a shelf by the butcher block table. In the hallway was a basketball hoop. In the master bedroom was a collection of pipes. In the closets were neat piles of freshly ironed linens.

It was not the kind of home that Tasha, or Susie, or I had ever set out to create. It was a home like those we had grown up in.

At midnight, Tasha and Bob returned from the country. They

spilled into the apartment with bags and boxes, two dogs and a cat and the fourteen-year-old son. They called each other "love."

"What, love?"

"Sure, love."

They settled on the couch, both of them wearing jeans and sweaters tied about their shoulders, and then Tasha told me: "Sara, this is the man I want to spend my life with. This is the only man I've ever loved completely. I have no doubts—this is my mate."

My eyes flicked to Bob. He was smiling. He told me that when he met Tasha, "I'd just gone through my second divorce. The last thing in the world I wanted was another tie-up, but I thought, wow, this is a terrific girl. I'd be crazy not to open myself to such a girl. Every morning I pinch myself, I can't believe I could be so lucky."

"No, I'm lucky," Tasha said.

"We both got lucky." They sighed and held each other.

I was in shock, not only because of what I knew of Tasha but because of a belief—a veritable edifice I had been constructing —that it was not possible in 1975 for two strong, complex people to feel no ambivalence about marrying.

Yet Tasha and Bob did not seem to be speaking from a haze of double madness. They lived together a year before they married, and Tasha never wavered from what she told me that night: "This is the greatest high of my life. It breaks me up, tears come to my eyes when I see that everything was a preparation for this."

Maybe, I thought, it is possible. Maybe there is hope. So many of my other friends had given up. I listened as Tasha described the moment she had known she would marry Bob. They were in the South of France, staying at the Grand Hôtel du Cap Ferrat. "We had been sitting by the water since eight in the morning, talking, and suddenly it was five at night. We went back to the room and were sitting there, talking, and suddenly we weren't talking, just looking. I looked right in him, right to his soul, and I saw this great person." She lifted her arms and let them fall. "That was it. I knew why I hadn't been able to make a commitment before—it had never been right. This was my man."

I nodded. It seemed too pat, like a fairy tale, the fitting of the glass slipper, yet I was wishing for Tasha that what she was saying would hold true.

"I'm so healthy," Tasha said, "it must be right. I feel inwardly glowy, attractive and very sexy. You know all those years that I worried about my breasts, all that stuff you wrote about? I can't even get a charge off it now. For the first time in my life, I feel beautiful."

It is the summer of '76 and I am living by the ocean in Southern California. I have fixed up my house as if I intend to stay. I've planted a cactus garden and furnished the rooms with wicker and Mexican tile. People tell me I speak like the natives. They say I look "laid back."

I don't know.

During the four years it took me to write this book, I felt I was living out of time. I pulled a net around me to screen out the world. I stopped reading the papers and watching television. I was indifferent to the news. I ignored new albums by the Rolling Stones and I missed the coming of Daylight Savings, wandering through the day, baffled that no one was in the right place. The retreating was in part a way of protesting the seventies: they were not worth keeping up with.

For months I sat in the Bancroft Library at Berkeley, fishing through archives of leaflets handed out on campus. I listened to tapes of speeches made on the steps of Sproul Hall. I spent my days with people who felt like refugees. We had predicted that the center could not hold but it had, and now we were in pieces. "Loose change," I told a friend.

For four years I felt I had blown it, my generation had blown it, the sixties had blown it, and we would never again see the heights. And then, one day this summer, I heard myself reciting that line and became aware that I don't feel that way anymore. Not at all. I looked around me. Well.

It was as if I had been doomed to relive the decade, year by year, draft after draft, until I could put it to rest, and suddenly found it had been done. Without my noticing how or when.

I suppose I could give reasons why I no longer feel despairing or disillusioned. I could talk about the concrete, lasting effects of the decade: the end of the draft; the profound revolution in sexual relationships; the granting of the right to vote to eighteen-year-olds and the right to abortion to women. And so on. But reasons are not what it's about.

I'm afraid I will be criticized for copping out. ("We want to know what you *make* of it all, what this period meant in terms of a society, a culture.") But the truth is, I have not found answers and I'm not sure I remember the questions.

What I know is that the world seems interesting this summer. In June I voted in the presidential primary in a lifeguard station, with surfboards and oars stacked on the walls. The lady registrars were neighbors and called, "Hi Sara." Last week, I learned how to juggle, bought a backpacking tent, read a new novel, wrote twenty pages in my journal and had intense encounters with old and new friends. I could feel a stirring in the air, a quickening pulse, and I thought about moving out again, and on.

July 1976
Venice, California